The Environments of the Poor in South Asia

The Environments of the Poor in South Asia

Simultaneously Reducing Poverty, Protecting the Environment, and Adapting to Climate Change

Edited by

ANUSHREE SINHA

ARMIN BAUER

PAUL BULLEN

Co-publication of the Asian Development Bank
and Oxford University Press India

OXFORD
UNIVERSITY PRESS

Oxford University Press is a department of the University of Oxford.
It furthers the University's objective of excellence in research, scholarship,
and education by publishing worldwide. Oxford is a registered trademark of
Oxford University Press in the UK and in certain other countries

Published in India by
Oxford University Press
YMCA Library Building, 1 Jai Singh Road, New Delhi 110 001, India

© Asian Development Bank 2015
6 ADB Avenue, Mandaluyong City
1550 Metro Manila, Philippines
Tel +63 2 632 4444
Fax +63 2 636 2444
www.adb.org

The moral rights of the authors have been asserted

First Edition published in 2015

ISBN-13: 978-0-19-945363-4
ISBN-10: 0-19-945363-2

Typeset in Dante MT Std 10.5/13
by The Graphics Solution, New Delhi 110 092
Printed and bound in India at Repro India Ltd., Mumbai

The views expressed in this publication are those of the authors and do not necessarily
reflect the views and policies of the Asian Development Bank (ADB) or its Board of
Governors or the governments they represent. ADB does not guarantee the accuracy of
the data included in this publication and accepts no responsibility for any consequence
of their use. ADB recognizes 'China', as used in this publication, as the 'People's
Republic of China'. By making any designation of or reference to a particular territory
or geographic area, or by using the term 'country' in this document, ADB does not
intend to make any judgments as to the legal or other status of any territory or area.

Note: In this publication, '$' refers to US dollar, unless stated otherwise.

The contribution of the Asian Development Bank Institute (ADBI) and the National
Council of Applied Economic Research (NCAER) is acknowledged.

Contents

Section VI Slumland Poverty

Tables, Figures, and Boxes

Tables

Figures

Boxes

Foreword

Making Sustainable Development Inclusive*

In the context of global climate change, debates on environmental sustainability and on poverty reduction got a new dimension. In India, for example, there is an intense political debate about the nature of environmentalism. On the one side, there are those who believe that environmentalism is really a middle-class, elitist pastime, and has no relation to the development challenges that the country faces. On the other, there are many who would argue that the growing environmental movement or environmental consciousness that we are seeing today is actually the environmentalism of the poor and that it is because of the threat to livelihoods that environmental issues are coming to the forefront today.

In the process of mainstreaming environmental issues as part of the poverty reduction agenda, it seems to me that there are two very important aspects that we have to keep in mind: (a) climate change impacts on people through public health and (b) natural resources are important factors for both climate change adaptation and mitigation as well as for improving poor people's income in the rural areas of Asia. Despite massive global discussions on climate change, at the national and local levels, poverty reduction remains the major political challenge. As climate change and the poverty agenda come closer through public health issues, these need to be put more into the centre of political discussions.

* The 'Foreword' is a revision of the keynote address given at the Asian Development Bank Conference on the Environments of the Poor, New Delhi, 24 November 2010. The address was delivered by the then Honourable Minister Jairam Ramesh, Ministry of Environment and Forests, Government of India.

It is a pleasure for me to introduce this book titled *The Environments of the Poor in South Asia*. It is part of a wider three-volume publication by the Asian Development Bank (ADB), in cooperation with Institute of Southeast Asian Studies (ISEAS) and National Council of Applied Economic Research (NCAER), also covering country studies on Southeast and East Asia, as well as thematic chapters on the subject. This volume brings together different points of view and analytical work that is being carried out in various parts of the South Asia region. The book in its effort to link climate change and environmental issues to mainstream development and especially poverty reduction efforts in South Asia is opportune and very relevant.

India is the biggest country—by size and people—in the South Asia region. The Indian development experience shows a lot of success and also some failure. They may or may not be relevant for our neighbouring countries. While this views focus on the experiences of India, I think that strengthening the poverty–climate–environment nexus through the public health agenda is crucial for many countries in the region.

The Interrelations between Climate Change, Natural Resources Development, and Public Health

Climate Change—More than an International Agenda

Let us take the climate change aspect first and analyse the relationship between environmental and poverty reduction issues in the context of climate change. It is believed in many quarters in India that we have not caused the problem of global warming; so why should we take actions to address it? We have not had an aggressive domestic agenda on climate change. Our domestic actions have been dictated by our international negotiating positions.

Now, why do we need a domestic agenda? The obvious reason, which should be clear to us all, is that there is no country in the world that is going to be as profoundly affected by climate change as India. Many countries have points of vulnerability to climate change, but I cannot think of any other country in the world that is more vulnerable than India. Let us look at some of these points of vulnerability.

First, of course, is our dependence on the monsoon. Even though less than 18% of our GDP now depends on agriculture, there is no running away from the fact that variations in GDP growth are driven by variations in the performance of the monsoon. In spite of all the impressive gains that we have made in terms of diversification of our economy, the fact is that two out of three Indians still depend on agriculture or agriculture-related occupations for employment. Therefore, there is extraordinary dependence on the monsoons, not just by the agricultural sector, but also by the other sectors of the economy due to its spillover and multiplier effects. An analysis of data from the last 50 years shows that 40%–45% of our fluctuations in GDP are on account of variations of monsoon alone. So the monsoons are critical. What happens to the monsoon is, to my mind, perhaps the single-largest determinant of prosperity in India.

The second point of vulnerability arises from the fact that we have a large population living in our coastal areas. We have a large peninsula with millions of people living on the coast who can only be classified as highly vulnerable to rising mean sea levels. Now, if there is one aspect of the Intergovernmental Panel on Climate Change (IPCC) that cannot be scientifically challenged, that has the strength of robust evidence behind it, it is the fact that climate change is going to affect mean sea levels. This is almost an incontrovertible conclusion that has been arrived at. Therefore, while we are rightly concerned about Maldives, Bangladesh, and all other countries vulnerable to a rise in mean sea levels, the fact is that there is no other country as vulnerable to this threat as India, just in terms of the sheer number of lives affected—we have 250–300 million people living on our coast starting from the Sunderbans in West Bengal, extending all the way up to Gujarat. I am talking of almost 13 states and union territories and a large portion of the population of India.

The third point of vulnerability arises from what is predicted to happen to the Himalayan glaciers as a result of global warming. Evidence on this, of course, is somewhat mixed. I, myself, do not share in its entirety the gloom and doom that is painted by many climate evangelists for the future of the Himalayan glaciers. But the fact of the matter is that the health of the Himalayan glaciers is a cause for great concern. If the majority of Himalayan glaciers continues to retreat in the manner that they have been, they are going to seriously affect the amount of water availability in the North Indian rivers that are the lifeline for almost a billion people living in India, Nepal, Bhutan, and Bangladesh.

And finally, the fourth major point of vulnerability arises from our dependence on the extraction of natural resources. The fact is that

India has embarked on an 8%–9% GDP growth drive in the last five years, which we hope to sustain over the next 15–20 years at the very minimum, and to do so will require increased extraction of our mineral resources. More and more we are discovering that coal reserves (which are essential for power generation) and other minerals are located in our forest areas. So the more coal we produce, the more forests we destroy, and the more forests we destroy, the more we add to our greenhouse gas emissions, besides all the concomitant ecological losses.

I do not think that there is any country in the world that is as clearly and categorically vulnerable to climate change on so many dimensions: monsoons, the rising mean sea levels, the retreat of the Himalayan glaciers, and the anticipated deforestation in response to the extraction of natural resources. We therefore need to recognize that India is profoundly affected by climate change and that the response to this impact must be a mix of adaptation and mitigation. Though the 'M' word (mitigation) was a taboo in India until recently, it is very important to our future. Although we are a very small emitter in per capita terms, we are today the world's fourth largest emitter in absolute terms. China is at number 1, with 23% of world greenhouse gas emissions, the United States giving the Chinese a run for their money at 22%, the EU would be about 13%, and India and the Russian Federation are roughly almost on par at about 5%.

Modelling studies conducted by the NCAER bring to light certain grave facts. They show that the great advantage of having a denominator (that is, population) that is 1 billion plus, growing by 10 million every year, is that on a per capita basis, we will always have low emission levels, but in absolute terms, if we continue our greenhouse gas emission profile, we could end up accounting for anywhere between 8.5% and 9% of world's greenhouse gas emissions by the year 2030. As responsible global citizens, we should be concerned and we need to act now. An expansion in our international role comes with certain responsibilities. This does not mean we abdicate our negotiating position. It means that we are responsible for two agendas— not only must we negotiate internationally from a position of strength, we must also work on the domestic front, taking substantive policy actions.

It seems to be very clear that India and other countries in the South Asia region are vulnerable to climate change and this immediately connects environmentalism and poverty reduction. It is the poorer regions and communities of our subcontinent that will bear the burden of this vulnerability. While this will call for adaptation—and adaptation would mean largely a major investment in agriculture—this will also call for a very significant investment in mitigation.

Public Health Changes the Terms of the Environmental Debate

The second dimension of this link between environment and poverty reduction is related to public health. I believe that the public health dimensions of environmental issues have been grossly neglected in this country. And this is one reason why environmental issues do not get the strong response they deserve. When I tell my 'growth-walla' friends (that is, those in the government who think that economic growth will solve all problems of India), 'you know environment is an important issue', they say, 'but you know 9%–10% GDP growth is more important'. If I could tell them that by not dealing with environmental issues directly, we are really debilitating the Indian population and eroding the long-term sustainability of this growth, I would probably get a better response from them.

I think that we need to change the terms of the debate on environment in this country. We need to present it as a public health issue. This is not a marketing gimmick. One of the weaknesses of our country is that we do not have a strong base of epidemiological data. But from whatever anecdotal evidence we have been able to gather from the various institutions and experts, I can confidently say that there is a very close connection between conventional environmental and public health issues. For example, about 25 years ago, the proportion of children with respiratory diseases in Bangalore, the IT capital of India, was less than 10%. But today, data seems to suggest that almost 30% of people in Bangalore suffer from asthma or some other respiratory diseases. Bhatinda, a prosperous agricultural region of Punjab, has today emerged as one of the major epicentres of cancer. This has been directly attributed to land degradation and more importantly to water contamination and water pollution.

So when one really looks at the environmental effects of many economic activities, whether it is in agriculture or industry, one will find that there are many negative health impacts that are significantly related to these activities, which, in my view, will act as a severe drag on our ability to sustain our high rate of growth for a long period of time. There is an excellent report on Indian poverty carried out by Anirudh Krishna from Duke University that has been recently released. Anirudh, a former Indian Administrative Service officer, has been a professor at Duke for a long time. He has done one of the most comprehensive analysis of Indian poverty. The one powerful conclusion that he has confirmed in his analysis (spread over more than a decade) is that rural expenditure on health is the primary reason families decline into poverty. Health expenditure, the inability to spend on health or the debt that you incur, all lead a family to poverty.

There is today a very solid body of evidence to suggest that rural indebtedness in India is driven by expenditure on health. Today, a very significant part of the expenditure on health would come from environment-related factors. So I am convinced that if we can persuade people to see the environmental issue as a public health issue, we would get somewhere in our attempt at integrating and mainstreaming the environment into the developmental process.

Natural Resources

The environment is a determining factor of climate change and public health; the environment is also a determining factor of natural resources which are so crucial for both poverty reduction and for economic growth. It is absolutely clear that sustaining 8%–9% GDP growth over the next two decades or more will have a significant effect on our natural resources. It is going to have a significant effect on coal, as I mentioned, on forestry, on water, and on land. A primary determinant of this growth is going to be our ability to use these natural resources in a sustainable manner.

Most of the natural resources that are required to fuel economic growth in India are located in our forest areas, and most of these forest areas happen to be in the poorer regions of our country. Out of the 600 districts of our country, the 188 districts in which the tribal population is a very substantial proportion account for approximately 60% of our forest area. Therefore, there seems to be close connection between poverty, forests, tribal population, availability of natural resources, and, might I add, social violence as well. It is a strong correlation. So we have to look at and address this dimension.

Poverty—An Ecological Phenomenon

The role of environmental factors in poverty and for poverty reduction is a new dimension of development thinking. We have looked at educational poverty and health poverty, and we also measure poverty as consumption poverty. But ecological poverty, or the notion that poverty can arise from ecological factors, is a very important and new idea that we need to look at more.

From my experience, I can say that in many parts of India, the single most important cause of poverty is land degradation. Land degradation is caused by a variety of environmental factors—some natural, some man-made. When land degradation is arrested, we will see a dramatic reduction in poverty. A very good example of this is one of the most successful World Bank projects on the reclamation of sodic soils in Uttar Pradesh. In the central part of Uttar Pradesh, small farmers mainly belong to the weaker and discriminated sections of society. This area is really the poverty bowl of India and farmers are suffering immensely because of low yields from the land that they are cultivating, as these lands are mostly wastelands and have sodic soils. A World Bank project was designed in the 1990s to reclaim the sodic soils. I can tell you that large parts of Uttar Pradesh, the most populated Indian state, have been transformed solely by this critical intervention, which was to restore the productivity of the land, especially for the small farms cultivated by farmers belonging to the weaker sections of our society.

Ecological poverty is extremely important and must be given adequate attention. We need to make a very systematic effort to design interventions that will ensure that ecological factors do not exacerbate poverty levels. In fact, many civil society organizations in India have worked very successfully on watershed development projects, water conservation, rainwater harvesting, and the intelligent use of water for agricultural purposes, all of which have had dramatic effects on poverty levels.

Environmentalism Is Meaningful Only as Environmentalism of the Poor

In conclusion, I would like to reiterate that to me, environmentalism is meaningful only as environmentalism of the poor. There are, of course, lifestyle environmental issues, but for the most part, livelihood environmental issues are what we are concerned with. And I think if we look at the environment in the context of climate change, public health, and natural resources, we will be able to appreciate better the connection between environmentalism and poverty. We really need to redefine the terms of environmental debate in our country because today environment protection is considered by many to be a drag on development. The whole debate has been 'conservation versus growth', or 'environment versus development'. I think this is a meaningless debate and if it is formulated in this fashion, the environment cannot win this debate. Who can argue against 9% economic growth? Therefore, we have to redefine the terms of the debate on the environment and look at it in terms of poverty reduction. This is certainly a giant step forward.

This book titled *The Environments of the Poor in South Asia: Simultaneously Reducing Poverty, Protecting the Environment, and Adapting to Climate Change* is a joint publication of the NCAER in India, Asian Development Bank (ADB), and Oxford University Press. Interesting case studies and analyses contributed to this book. They were studied by practitioners implementing government programmes on the environment, as well as by researchers from premier South Asian think tank institutions and development partners, such as Bangladesh Institute for Development Studies (BIDS), Centre for Poverty Analysis in Sri Lanka (CEPA), Cities Development Initiative for Asia (CDIA), German Agency for International Cooperation (GIZ), Department for International Development of the Government of the United Kingdoms (DFID), Gujarat Institute for Development Studies (GIDR), Institute for Integrated Development Studies in Nepal (IIDS), Pakistan Institute for Development Economics (PIDE), South Asian Network for Development and Environmental Economics (SANDEE), as well as from the universities of Calcutta, Rajasthan, and Tamil Nadu. Their studies makes a valuable contribution to the international and regional debate—also in the context of the reforms of the Millennium Development Goals on how climate change and the poverty agenda can be better brought together.

Jairam Ramesh
Member of Parliament, Rajya Sabha and former Minister of State (Independent Charge), Ministry of Environment and Forests, Government of India

Acknowledgements

Poverty of opportunities, bad living conditions, and insecurity are often related to environmental degradation. The poor—both urban and rural—are mostly the biggest victims of environmental degradation. At the same time, poverty exacerbates ecological problems. Environment-related poverty is often also closely related to regional and cross-border (particularly water) issues. A major portion of Asia's poor can be found:

- living in remote forest areas (the upland poor, often also indigenous people);
- among the fisherfolk communities (the coastal poor);
- on marginal land areas (the dryland poor);
- among flood-prone locations (the wetland poor); and
- in congested cities and towns with bad shelter conditions (the slum poor).

In addition, natural hazards, such as earthquakes, tsunami, and major storms make the poor particularly vulnerable to external shocks.

The linkages between the environment and poverty reduction were highlighted in a conference that Asian Development Bank (ADB) and 17 development partners organized on 24–26 November 2010 in Delhi. Poverty, climate, and environment linkages are mostly emphasized in the context of sustainable livelihoods, impact of pollution on people's health, and climate change and disaster vulnerability. The Asia-wide regional conference added to these four dimensions and discussed the spatial dimensions of poverty, what makes green growth pro-poor, and climate change adaptation for poverty reduction.

We would like to thank Suman Bery (former Director General of the National Council of Applied Economic Research [NCAER] and

Member of the Prime Minister's Economic Advisory Council) for making the conference and the book a success.

In addition, we would like to thank our various partners who helped make the conference and this book a success: development partners from donor organizations (AFD, DFID, GIZ, ILO, JICA, and UNDP/UNEP), research networks (ADBI, EEPSEA, NCAER, SANDEE, TEEB, and TERI), and funding facilities and other initiatives (CDIA, GMS-EOC, and APCF).

This book is a condensed version of the Delhi conference discussions focusing on South Asia. There are two other volumes, one on Southeast Asia, East Asia and the Pacific (published in 2013 by ADB and ISEAS) and the other on general considerations of poverty and the environment in Asia and the Pacific as a whole (yet to be published by ADB). We would like to thank Oxford University Press for joining with ADB in publishing this second volume of *The Environments of the Poor* series.

The South Asia volume highlights contributions from distinguished scholars and government partners in Bangladesh, India, Nepal, and Sri Lanka. In particular, we would like to thank former Minister Jairam Ramesh for his inspiring Foreword, and for championing our conference. Further acknowledgement goes to the authors of this book: B. Agastin, G.M. Arif, Anvita Arora, Shanila Athulathmudali, Amila Balasuriya, Banashree Banerjee, Dilruba Banu, S. Farooq, Karin Fernando, Santadas Ghosh, N. Iqbal, Rajesh Jaiswal, Mats Jarnhammar, K.R. Kakumanu, Mohd. Shahadt Hossain Mahmud, K. Palanisami, Sunil Ray, C.R. Ranganathan, G. Bhaskar Reddy, Binayak Sen, Amita Shah, Faizan Jawed Siddiqi, Min Bikram Malla Thakuri, Shyam Upadhyaya, and Mohammad Yunus.

THE ENVIRONMENTS OF THE POOR—USING A SPATIAL APPROACH

ANUSHREE SINHA
ARMIN BAUER

Reducing Poverty by Protecting the Environment and Adapting to Climate Change

Introduction

This is the second volume of *The Environments of the Poor* series. It focuses on the poverty of the dryland, upland, coastland, wetland, and slumland environments of South Asia, a poverty that is being aggravated by so-called climate change. As a result of broad-based economic growth in the past decade, the region has seen a rapid decline in income-based poverty. But this successful development will be difficult to maintain because of changes in the environment. The book finds an increase in the incidence of poverty that can be attributed to environment factors and to climate change. Floods, landslides, declining natural resource productivity, droughts, and urban pollution exert disproportionate effects on the lives and livelihoods of the region's poor and vulnerable. They suffer more losses, illnesses, injuries, and death as a result of resource degradation, natural disasters, and pollution than the non-poor because they are more dependent on natural systems for their livelihood. They usually live in unsafe housing or in areas prone to disasters and pollution. While the Asia-Pacific region will continue to reduce poverty in both the income and the social dimensions, environmental poverty is likely to increase—becoming the main form of poverty in the near future. It is estimated that by 2020, more than two-thirds of the vulnerable and poor in the region will suffer from environmental poverty—up from less than one-half today. In South Asia, dryland and slum poverty will then constitute the major areas of deprivation for low-income households, followed by coastal and flood-related poverty.

The book argues that the poverty agenda and the environment agenda are coming together through a spatial approach in which the surroundings in which the poor live are the determining factor in their poverty and vulnerability. The method used in the book for achieving an inclusive green economy and an inclusive climate change response involves a certain approach to poverty. This approach leads to a focus on a certain kind of poor person and a certain cause of poverty in which the environments in which the poor live are the main determinants for their low living standard. The book, therefore, follows a spatial (area-based) approach and links that to the natural and man-made environment in which the poor live (that is, 'the environments of the poor').

The concept of environment here goes beyond the ecosystem approach as it identifies not only natural conditions as the major cause of poverty but also dynamics that are caused by development, growth, environmental pollution, and climate change. Environmental poverty is different from the ecosystem approach for pro-poor growth in that it analyses the needs of the poor before coming up with programmes for poverty reduction in the area where the poor live. Such answers to the problems of the poor who live in specific environments may not be programmes related to natural resources as followed in the ecosystem approach. However, there may be many overlaps. The environmental poverty perspective categorizes poor people in a manner that demon- strates how environmental conditions affect their well-being. From the perspective of the poor and their needs, the environments in which they live have potential for pro-poor growth. The spatial environments, in which the poor live, can be divided into dryland, floodland, coastal, upland, and slum areas.

Climate change aggravates environmental poverty, and adaption is therefore also a poverty reduction strategy that can help the climate as well. The book highlights four important areas where climate change adaptation can help the poor, namely (a) building resilient communal infrastructure, (b) rebalancing agricultural production and food security towards new technologies that need less water and towards new food production systems (such as aquaculture), (c) urban planning for safer living, and (d) addressing environmental health through such things as urban non-motorized transport or through a stronger focus on cooking energy (rather than electricity generation and distribution).

As a response to climate change as well as to the global economic crisis, countries in the region are promoting green growth. However, green growth strategies have not been integrated into their inclusive growth discussions. Often, green technologies in developing countries are not very labour-based. Modern technologies for promoting green growth often do not sufficiently address the concerns of the poor, while traditional technologies are not much discussed in the context of green growth. Similarly, the potential benefits for the climate, the poor, and the environment can also change the traditional approaches to agricultural and rural development.

The book argues that environmental problems do not necessarily require environmental solutions. Applying a spatial approach to the poverty and environment interface has major implications for development policy and assistance. It will require some realignment of conceptual approaches and investments to serve a poor people–first perspective rather than global or national environmental goals with little direct impact on the poor and vulnerable. From the perspective of the poor, poverty reduction and not green growth remains in the centre of development objectives.

The foreword to the book is written by the former minister of rural development (and former minister of state of environment and forests) Jairam Ramesh. Minister Ramesh makes the case for seeing the climate change agenda more under a people's health perspective. He argues that environmental policy will at the end only be effective if it is dealing with the 'environmentalism of the poor', meaning that climate change policies are only sustainable if they are offered in a way to also include the poor. He argues that climate change needs to be more a domestic rather than only an international agenda. As it makes people, and especially the poor, vulnerable especially to dryland and flood-affected and coastal dimensions of poverty, the linkages between climate change and poverty reduction are increasingly becoming a political factor for governments to help people adapting to climate change. The minister argues that the major interface between climate change and poverty reduction goes through public health policies. He makes the point that this triangle relation will not only change the environmental debate but also political realities in India and other parts of South Asia. In that context he raises some sceptical views about the growth orientation of many development plans which often neglect the implications for the environment and on poor people's health. He reiterates that climate change policies are only meaningful if they are pursued in context of the environmentalism of the poor. He foresees that the provision of sustainable livelihood and the improvement of the poor's health will become the core determinants of the future development debate.

C.R. Ranganathan, K. Palanisami, K.R. Kakumanu, and B. Agastin argue that climate change adaptation strategies are particularly needed for the rural and agricultural areas. While structural interventions (such as, building flood embankments, dikes, or seawalls or enhancing the natural setting or landscape), market-based instruments such as credits and crop insurance, and policies are wide-ranging and have helped to reduce the impact of climate change on poor people's livelihoods, South Asia is far away from mainstreaming adaptation and addressing future climate scenarios in an effective manner. The authors argue that in the South Asian context it is particularly important to address water-related issues in order to mitigate the risks of flood-related and dryland poverty. They caution against simplistic infrastructure-focused measures that do not adequately consider the economy of the poor and their food intake behaviour.

Dryland Poverty

Section 2 of the book deals with dryland poverty. Amita Shah from the Gujarat Institute of Development Studies (GIDS) gives an overview on the dryland scenario in South Asia. She claims that the poor in 40% of the region's landmass is threatened by drought. With climate change, the desertification and degradation of dryland continues, and poverty in the areas worsens. She argues that the recent discourse in the wake of climate change, which focuses on stimulating growth rates, tends to overlook the potential of those areas to provide for the poor. The central argument of the chapter is that the dryland regions in South Asia would develop better by means of traditional water-saving agricultural technologies, economic diversification, and a reorientation towards nutrition agriculture and labour mobility. The chapter also draws policy implications for India's preparedness for and adaptation to climate change.

Chapter 4 is by Sunil Ray, a senior researcher at the Institute of Development Studies (Rajasthan) in India. He shows that adaptation by the poor to climate change in dryland agriculture is only possible if the shrinking space for livelihood generation in agriculture is arrested through the restoration of dryland agricultural areas. The chapter gives examples of how farmers in the arid Indian state of Rajasthan who gradually became vulnerable to food insecurity as a result of climate change restored agroecology and improved the production conditions of their agriculture. He argues that investments in dryland agriculture need to be complemented by wage employment schemes for the poor that are designed to add value to the ecology of the land. He calls this process of creating double value the agroecological rift. Both these routes have contributed a great deal towards new livelihood security for the poor.

Coastal Poverty

Section 3 of the book deals with coastal poverty in Bangladesh, India, and Sri Lanka. In Chapter 5, Mohammad Yunus and Binayak Sen show that adaptation strategies in coastal regions of Bangladesh are strongly related to migration to the bigger cities, because the nearby areas do not provide sufficient economic opportunities for the poor. The coastal poor have greater food insecurity, ill-health, natural resource–dependent livelihoods, and homelessness than the inland poor. The coastal poor, especially those residing closest to sea, have to rely more on wage labour, the sales of assets, and distress migration, as they also get less assistance from the government and NGOs for coping with natural disaster–related crises. The non-poor who live in this environment are also vulnerable, but they have better access to formal credit and other forms of support. These facts have implications for climate change policies in those areas as the poor tend to migrate to the urban centres, especially Dhaka.

In Chapter 6, Mohd. Shahadt Hossain Mahmud shows how the poor adapt to flood-related poverty in Bangladesh. About one-third of the country's total area is considered a coastal zone. Global warming increases the vulnerability of the coastal poor day by day and aggravates their poverty. The Government of Bangladesh has initiated some measures to address climate change mainly through large-scale adaptation infrastructure, but those are insufficient to address the core problems of coastal poverty. Bangladesh needs to scale up those measures, while exploring other options.

Shanila Athulathmudali, Amila Balasuriya, and Karin Fernando are research fellows at the Centre for Poverty Analysis (CEPA) in Sri Lanka. The authors summarize climate change adaptation behaviour of the poor in coastal Sri Lanka. In Sri Lanka, efforts to address climate change are still in their early stages and interventions are not yet scaled up. The chapter uses an actor-based approach to analyse elements that aid and impede adaptation. It highlights types of popular participation and NGO involvement that can make climate change adaptation more effective. It finds in tourism one way to adapt to climate change and provide employment in poor coastal communities.

Floodland Poverty

Section 4 of the book provides examples of floodland poverty in India, Bangladesh, and Pakistan. Santadas Ghosh, senior researcher at the Visva-Bharati University near Kolkata, discusses adaptation behaviour of the poor in coastal areas of West Bengal. The Sundarbans, which is spread across Bangladesh and India, is the world's largest mangrove delta and a world heritage site. The Indian part contains 48 forested and 54 densely populated islands. People on these islands have very few livelihood choices, and the region is highly vulnerable to negative effects of global warming. This chapter discusses the coping behaviour of the households in the Sundarbans after a cyclonic disaster devastated the single crop in the region. The study finds that households adapted by engaging in multiple earning activities, such as fishing, prawn-fry collection, and migrant labour. This adaptation by the people of the Sundarban islands and the mainland resulted in similar socioeconomic conditions for both groups. The diversification of income opportunities, especially through public work programmes, reduced pressure on the forests and rivers. This suggests that adaptation and poverty reduction increases resilience to climate change.

Rajesh Jaiswal from the National Council of Applied Economic Research (NCAER) in Delhi discusses watershed development as a way to create sustainable livelihoods and at the same time address climate change adaptation in rural India. Watershed development programmes, such as the building of contour trenches on upper slopes, the fencing of common land to allow regeneration, the checking of dams, the plugging of gullies, and the promotion of soil and water conservation on agricultural land have been implemented in India since 1986. Between 1994 and 1999, about 10,000 watershed projects were launched in India. As a result, poor people have had greater access to irrigated land and safe and reliable drinking water. This change allowed them to diversify their cropping patterns and find wage employment in rural areas. While most watershed projects were implemented with the objective of soil and water conservation and livelihood enhancement of the rural poor in rainfed areas, more recent programmes also address climate change–related problems, such as flooding in high rainfall areas and storm protection in coastal areas. The author argues that watershed development policies need to be redesigned to more effectively address climate change risks—and not be limited to water resources management.

G.M. Arif, N. Iqbal, and S. Farooq provide a district-level analysis of the 2010 floods in Pakistan. Environment degradation is one of the major recent challenges faced by Pakistan. This chapter contains a preliminary analysis at the district level of the impact of the 2010 flood on poverty. The analysis shows that the flood disproportionately affected the regions of the country characterized by high deprivation, poor infrastructure, and unfavourable demography. Flooding damaged crops, infrastructure, and public and private property. The damage to crops and infrastructure has probably pushed 6–7 million people into poverty.

G. Bhaskar Reddy, director of the Odisha Watershed Development Mission in India, shows that the agrarian economy of Western Odisha, where in some districts up to 70% of the population live below the poverty line, is particularly vulnerable to climate change. The Western Odisha Rural Livelihood Project (WORLP) was designed to address both poverty reduction and climate change vulnerability. While the project has increased the resilience of the region, future global warming–induced challenges should not be addressed any more through livelihood programmes such as WORLP alone. There is a need to institutionalize the climate change adaptation capacities of the rural poor.

Upland Poverty

Shyam K. Upadhyaya from the Institute for Integrated Development Studies (IIDS) in Kathmandu, Nepal, shows that upland poverty is increased by climate change. The upland hills and mountains of Nepal make up 77% of country and are home to 52% of population. All poverty indicators for the area are higher than those for the plains. Climate change has worsened the conditions of upland poor, especially as they are becoming more exposed to flooding and landslides caused by the melting Himalayan snow and river rises. Nepal has been a pioneer in adopting alternate energy technologies such as micro-hydro, biogas, solar energy, and improved cooking stoves, and in innovative forest management practices such as leasehold and community forestry. While these programmes are beginning to reduce poverty and conserve the environment, they are not sufficient to address the effects of climate change on the upland areas. The capacity of the upland poor to cope with the adverse effects of climate change needs to be increased. Traditional growth-oriented development programmes often do not do that.

Min Bikram Malla Thakuri argues that a modernization of the cooking energy would address gender and environment dimensions of upland poverty in Nepal. He shows that indoor air pollution (IAP) from burning solid fuels for cooking is a major environmental health problem in Nepal, predominantly affecting children and women. The problem is more severe in upland areas as the households there need more energy for cooking and heating. High transportation costs, poor reliability of supply, and poor purchasing power are the main factors hindering the adoption of clean fuel and clean technologies in those areas. There is a need to introduce locally acceptable technologies (increasing access to credit) and social marketing to encourage use of clean fuels and technologies to mitigate IAP problem in those areas. Such interventions contribute to improvement of health, female empowerment, and environmental protection. They also contribute to climate change mitigation by protecting the forests from being cut.

Slumland Poverty

The last section of the book looks at determinants of slum poverty in South Asia. Banashree Banerjee, an international consultant on urban planning, summarizes the characteristics and policy responses of slum poverty in Asia and assesses the new challenges of climate change. Urban development and climate change increase environmental risks in the slums of Asian cities, but they also provide opportunities for improving living conditions of the slum poor. Climate change is felt in slums in the form of greater, more widespread flooding, landslides, and heat waves. Innovative approaches are needed to improve the housing and mobility conditions of congested areas and increase the adaptation capacity of the slum poor. Adaptation through market forces seems to be more effective than government interventions, but the current legal and institutional environments and government incentive structures in most Asian cities still poses a major challenge to the poor living in slumland areas. Climate change adaptation in the cities could also create new employment opportunities, especially in housing and shelter (using green building technologies), non-motorized transport, urban agriculture, and waste management and city cleaning. The chapter provides examples from Asian cities which are using such policies to adapt to climate change and thereby reduce urban poverty.

Dilruba Banu from the German technical assistance agency GIZ in Bangladesh discusses the implications of climate change for slum poverty in Bangladesh. He argues that the environment and climate change intensify urbanization in Bangladesh and increase the number of slum poor. High temperatures, heavy rainfall and flooding along the river and swamps where the poor live, cyclones, and other extreme weather events—all related to climate change—are new phenomena in the life of city poor in Bangladesh. Women and children are affected more than male adults. The chapter argues that effective adaptation requires bottom-up designed public programmes based on the slum poor's priorities, needs, knowledge, and capacities. However, most city infrastructure programmes are give priority to protecting the rich against climate-induced hazards.

Anushree Sinha of the National Council of Applied Economic Research (NCAER) in Delhi connects slum poverty to women's migration and the weak health provisions in informal settlements. Her chapter examines the link between the climate- and environment-related migration of the poor and the increasing female population in urban slums. It shows that the migration rate of women is much higher than that of men mainly due to family reasons, but once in the city, women from the slums are more successful at finding paid employment. The chapter states that the overall living conditions in Indian slums deteriorated from 2002 to 2008, and that this is mainly due to the expansion of informal slum areas due to migration. As a result, women's living and health conditions in the cities are also getting worse. Women attribute this more to a lack of basic public facilities than to climate change.

Anvita Arora, Mats Jarnhammar, and Faizan Jawed Siddiqi discuss opportunities of climate change adaptation through urban transport offered by the poor. The authors argue that non-motorized traffic offered by the poor could be a major solution to the problems of traffic jams and chronic congestion which affects everybody in the city. However, while cities are struggling to keep up with the ever-increasing need for public transport through investments in public mass transport systems such as buses and light rail, such investments often do not sufficiently benefit the poor. Instead, informal public transport (IPT) could play a more vital role in urban mobility. It needs a special place in urban transport planning and policy. Such transport schemes could play a much more important role in short-distance (up to 5 km) transport needs, while being environment and climate friendly and creating massive employment opportunities for the poor. IPT has the potential to perform a critical function in a pro-poor and green urban transport system. But for this to happen, policies and investment patterns would have to change.

C.R. RANGANATHAN
K. PALANISAMI
K.R. KAKUMANU
B. AGASTIN

Reducing the Vulnerability of the Poor to Climate Change by Mainstreaming Their Adaptations to It

Most rural poor in developing countries depend on agriculture and are highly influenced by climatic change. Hence, sustainable livelihood approaches are used at both policy and project levels to initiate new poverty reduction activities and modify existing activities. Practices relevant to climate change adaptation around the world are wide-ranging and include development of technology, management, infrastructure, livestock, groundwater, and knowledge. Both structural interventions (such as building flood embankments, dikes, or seawalls or enhancing the natural setting or landscape) and non-structural interventions (policies; and knowledge development, awareness, methods, and operating practices, including participatory mechanisms) have helped to reduce the impact of climate change. Further, market-based instruments such as credit and crop insurance were developed to help poor households in many developing countries cope with uncertainties. The uptake of such adaptation practices is lagging, but informal institutions are playing a key role as they rely on enforcement methods and are not supported by the government. Mainstreaming adaptation and enhancing adaptive capacity could be increased by encouraging partnerships between informal processes and formal interventions. The cost of adaptation is higher in developing countries. Nonetheless, more attention is needed in addressing future climate scenarios through agricultural research and development, irrigation development, infrastructure, and improved irrigation efficiency.

The main concern raised by global warming is that climatic variations will alter the water cycle. Indeed, in many cases the hydrological cycle is already being affected (Dragoni 1998; Intergovernmental Panel on Climate Change [IPCC] 2007). The hydrological cycle involves processes of evaporation and precipitation which are predicted to shift with climate change. A decrease in monsoon rainfall reduces surface flows and net recharge of groundwater. The variation in rainfall for the Indian subcontinent is statistically significant (Srivastava et al. 1992) and there is an increasing trend in surface temperature, with decreasing trends in rainfall (Singh and Sontakke 2002). Monsoon rainfall is considered to be the main climatic phenomenon in the Indian subcontinent and the adjoining Asian and African regions. A high degree of correlation also exists between rainfall and agricultural production (Gadgil 2003).

There are also potentially huge implications for groundwater management as a result of global warming. An average drop in groundwater levels of 1 metre would increase India's total carbon emissions by more than 1% because of the additional fuel needed to extract the same amount of water (Mall et al. 2006).

The adaptation activities that require climate risk information are new infrastructure, resource management, retrofit, behavioural, institutional, sectoral, communication, and financial (Wilby et al. 2009). In addition, the elements of effectiveness, efficiency, equity, and legitimacy are important for the success of sustainable development in an uncertain future. The degree of success depends on the capacity to adapt and the distribution of that capacity.

In this chapter, we review some of the adaptation strategies for reducing the vulnerability of the poor to climate change by explaining

- the effects of climate change on agricultural production,
- adaptation experiences in the context of sustainable livelihoods,

- the integration of structural and non-structural measures,
- the amelioration effects and their costs, and
- the role of informal institutions in implementation.

Impact of Climate Change on Agricultural Production

Since many of the rural poor in developing countries depend on agriculture, it is one of the central arenas in which the threat is posed by climate change. Impact of such climate change on agriculture will be one of the major factors influencing the future food security. Researchers have taken up the studies to find the impacts of climate change on wheat, maize, and various other crops and have found that production will reduce over time with the increase in temperature by 1°C. Several other approaches are also being used to measure the sensitivity of agricultural production to climate change, viz. cross-sectional models, agronomic–economic models, and an agroecological zone (AEZ) models. The agronomic and AEZ models essentially seek to quantify the impact of these anticipated changes on agricultural production systems mostly by simulating these changes under controlled conditions. Economic components are added subsequently to amplify these effects to larger areas and in terms of economic impact. Cross-sectional models differ in essence from these models by recognizing that during the process of climate change the systems subjected to such changes do tend to evolve to minimize the risks involved and stakeholders in these systems do tend to adapt through technological and various other options. The cross-sectional studies suggest that adaptation could reduce crop losses in developing countries. The cross-sectional approaches examine farm performance across different districts or regions using Ricardian type of models.

Adaptation

Climate change has a multidimensional effect on humanity in terms of several socioeconomic parameters. Identifying the parameters that have the ability to adjust to or recover from the negative impacts and take advantage of positive impacts of the current climate variability is essential. Hence, research has taken advantage of climate variability across large geographical areas to study different adaptation strategies.

Till et al. (2010) reviewed 17 studies covering data from more than 16 countries in Africa, America, Europe, and Asia and found 104 different practices relevant to climate change adaptation (Table 2.1). The number of practices mentioned per study varied from 1 to 29. The adaptation practices address a wide range of adjustments in the behaviour of individuals, groups, and institutions and in the use and development of technologies. The changes in adaptation practices range from construction of reservoirs for irrigation to adjustment to ancient farming practices. As adaptation takes place on more than one level and involves more than one actor, introducing or adjusting crops by making simple changes to the mix of traditional crops can help smallholder farmers adjust to climate change.

Most of the adaptive practices were adjustments in farm management and technology (53%); followed by knowledge management, networks, and governance (15%); diversification (14%); government interventions (13%); and farm financial management (5%) (Till et al. 2010).

Water storage plays a major role in adaptation to climate change. By providing a buffer, water storage reduces risks and offsets some of the potential negative effects of climate change. Water storage can increase both water security and agricultural productivity.

Sluice management increased rice production by 14%. The options of canal lining providing additional wells and sluice rotation increased rice production by 30%–36%. The maximum production increase

TABLE 2.1 Adaptation Practices per Category

Category of Adaptation	No. of Different Practices	No. of Practices Mentioned, Including Multiple Answers
Farm management and technology	51	117
Diversification on and beyond farm	7	33
Farm financial management	5	10
Government interventions in infrastructure, health, and risk reduction	22	29
Knowledge management, networks, and governance	19	31
Total	104	220

Source: Till et al. (2010).

occurred when both management and physical investment strategies were used. The cost–benefit ratio (CBR) is higher for rotational water management than for sluice modification, which has the lower CBR and negligible internal rate of return (IRR). The IRR is higher for sluice management and rotational management than for other management strategies.

The other options are food storage and management strategies for sustainable livelihood. In Ethiopia farmers are heavily reliant on rain-fed subsistence agriculture. The Ethiopian case is a good illustration of the urgent need for appropriate investments in water storage. Such storage would increase agricultural productivity and ensure that farmers have options for adjusting to the coming up climate changes (International Water Management Institute [IWMI] 2009).

In the Cauvery basin, Indian farmers adopted several strategies additional to changing the cropping pattern. This included drilling new bore wells, deepening existing wells, introducing water-saving irrigation methods, and reducing the number of irrigations (Table 2.2).

Marginal, small, and large farmers gave the response that due to the change in rainfall patterns, temperature, and groundwater levels, most of them are delaying and/or changing the cropping pattern and reducing the number of irrigations. For instance, the number of irrigations for a rice crop reduced from 19 to 10, and it varies based on farm canal network and soil water-holding capacity. In some cases, farmers are changing to livestock rearing as the secondary source of income.

It can be seen that cultivation of a major stable crop (paddy) has decreased more than have commercial crops such as sugarcane and cotton. About 20% of farmers who raised paddy five years ago shifted to other commercial crops. The percentage of commercial crop growers increased from 11% to 14% for cotton and from 2.2% to 7.2% for sugarcane. Other farmers switched to maize and sorghum crops, which require less water. The percentage of groundnut cultivation increased from 0.6% to 1.1%. Coconut cultivation remained the same (1.1%). The shift has implications for food security and the overall economy.

Institutional set-up for managing resources also plays a key role in the adaptation. The institutions are formal and informal. The former ones are legally introduced and enforced by state institutions, which are embedded in the state operations based on laws that are enforced and monitored by the government. The latter ones rely on enforcement

TABLE 2.2 Adaptation Response of Marginal, Small, and Large Farmers to Climate Change Impact (Frequency)

Item	Change in Rainfall Pattern			Change in Temperature			Change in Groundwater		
	Marginal	Small	Large	Marginal	Small	Large	Marginal	Small	Large
Number of farmers who adapted	14	15	14	10	13	14	7	13	14
Drill new bore wells	3	1	1	1	0	0	0	0	0
Deepen existing wells	1	0	1	1	0	0	1	0	1
Adopt drip irrigation methods	0	3	2	0	4	1	0	4	1
Change cropping pattern	5	8	9	4	8	8	1	6	8
Conventional water-saving irrigation methods	3	5	5	2	5	5	4	6	4
Grow rain-fed crops	5	3	5	3	3	8	2	6	3
Change to livestock rearing	8	5	5	6	5	5	6	4	5
Cultivate annual crop to perennial crops	2	11	5	4	11	8	3	8	9
Delay cropping season	9	11	10	10	11	10	7	9	10
Reduce the number of irrigations	8	8	8	7	8	4	8	7	6

Source: Palanisami and Ranganathan (2008).

TABLE 2.3 Institutional Adaptation Case Studies

Author	Region/Country	Institution	Activity	Adaptation Strategy
Luna (2001)	Philippines	Informal	Disaster Management	Integrated Relief and Disaster Management
UNFCCC (2002)	Northern Tanzania	Formal and Informal	Working Closely with Traditional Institutions	Engaging in agroforestry using Degraded Crop Lands and Range Land
Lasco et al. (2006)	Philippines	Informal		20 Different Practices Such As Tree Planting, Conservation, Community-Based Organizations
Kakumanu (2009)	India	Informal	Water Resource Management	Creating Awareness and Training on Water Management Activities
Fleming and Smit (2010)	Canada Subarctic Region	Formal	Facilitating Capacity to Adapt to Changing Conditions	Decreasing Snowfall, Changing Wildlife Abundance and Migration Patterns

Source: Authors' compilation.

methods not supported by the government. The informal institutions have roots in local communities and are embedded within existing customs, traditions, rules of conduct, and beliefs. At the lowest levels, informal institutions prevail over formal ones (Sokile and van Koppen 2005). In fact, informal institutions are extensions and local-level translations of formal institutions and formal institutions are derived from and depend on the informal ones for their stability and strength. Although formal institutions play a bigger role in modern societies, the importance of informal institutions should not be disregarded (World Bank 2002). Formal institutions offer rigid enforcement, while informal institutions use locally rooted compliance based on tradition. Case studies from various countries also show the role and success of formal and informal institutions in disaster and water resource management in adapting to the changing conditions (Table 2.3).

Hence, adaptation could be mainstreamed and adaptive capacity increased by encouraging partnerships between informal processes and formal interventions.

Integrating Structural and Non-structural Adaptation into National Economies

While non-structural measures for climate change are policies, knowledge development, awareness, and methods and operating practices, structural responses involve building physical structures using engineering and hazard-resistant and protective structures that reduce or avoid negative effects of hazards (International Strategy for Disaster Reduction 2010). Structural interventions can involve building artificial physical structures in the landscape (e.g., dykes and seawalls), modifying the natural setting or landscape to provide protection from climate-related coastal hazards, planting mangroves, beach nourishment, constructing reservoirs, etc. Under a disaster risk reduction (as opposed to a climate change adaptation) initiative, there is a greater likelihood that design limits for structural measures, such as flood embankments, will not be adequate in the face of climate change. Initiatives focused on climate change adaptation are more likely to design structural measures with consideration for new predicted effects. For water resources, water storage can be viewed as a continuum of surface and subsurface options.

Not all storage and moisture control options serve all purposes. For example, increasing soil moisture can benefit agriculture, but it will not contribute to hydropower production or industrial and domestic water supply.

As mentioned, non-structural measures for climate change (disaster risk reduction) are policies, knowledge development, awareness, and methods and operating practices. Methods and operating practices include participatory mechanisms that can reduce risk and related effects. These non-structural measures are to be planned in such a way that they can serve the poor and small farmers in both disaster risk reduction and climate change adaptation. The measures associated with training and awareness help people and institutions apply skills and knowledge in different circumstances as they emerge.

There is an ongoing debate about how credit and crop insurance market failures affect the extent to which, and the speed with which, farmers in developing countries adapt to climate change, and what the policy implications are. Adger (2003) finds that social and institutional capital are crucial for the adaptation capacity of farming communities. Eakin and Appendini (2008) argue that traditional autonomous adaptation to climate variability is more flexible than planned adaptation activities are likely to be. Shewmake (2008), studying South African farmers, argues that many farmers are already highly vulnerable to climate fluctuations, and hence risk is being substantially affected by additional climate change. Eakin (2005) studies climate vulnerability in Mexican farming and finds that market integration per se makes little difference to coping capacity. Even farmers who sell most of their produce may remain highly vulnerable to climate fluctuations because they have limited access to credit or insurance markets.

Further, climate change poses a great challenge to the insurance market, but at the same time offers large-scale business opportunities. Significant progress has been made by insurers in developing new products and services to compensate for the negative effects of climate change. Mills identifies 422 real-world examples from 190 insurers, reinsurers, brokers, and insurance organizations in 26 countries. Many of these products (nearly half of them from the US) have the potential to dramatically reduce greenhouse gas emissions in some of the most energy-intensive parts of the economy.

Rainfall-based crop insurance is useful for compensating farmers for crop failure in the most vulnerable agroclimatic zones of India. The Government of India has introduced weather-based crop insurance in most states. However, the Food and Agriculture Organization (FAO) suggests that emphasis should be put on other management activities, such as plant and animal breeding development, crop and animal husbandry practices, and that the diversification of farm enterprises and insurance is not only the option.

Farmers' willingness to pay for weather-based crop insurance depends on their economic interests, social and ecological values and norms, awareness of the problem, and self-perception. Farmers think of rainfall in terms of a process rather than in terms of a quantity (Ingram, Roncoli, and Kirshen 2002). They will not accept forecasts unless they are adjusted to their understandings.[1] Farmers' acceptance of seasonal climate forecasts increased when the forecasts were provided as part of local climate forecasts.[2] Table 2.4 lists adaptation activities that require climate risk information.

TABLE 2.4 Adaptation Activities that Require Climate Risk Information

Adaptation	Examples of Activity Using Climate Information
New infrastructure	Cost–benefit analysis (CBA), infrastructure performance and design
Resource management	Assessment of natural resource availability, status, and allocation
Retrofit	Scoping assessments to identify risks and reduce exposure to extreme events
Behavioural	Measures that optimize scheduling or performance of existing infrastructure
Institutional	Regulation, monitoring, and reporting
Sectoral	Economic planning, sector restructuring, guidance, and standards
Communication	Communicating risks to stakeholders, high-level advocacy, and planning
Financial	Services to transfer risk, incentives, and insurance

Source: Wilby et al. (2009).

[1] Patt and Gwata (2002) confirm these findings.
[2] A study in Zimbabwe by Grothmann and Patt (2005) revealed this.

Benefits and Costs of Structural and Non-structural Measures

Adaptation is the adjustment of a system to moderate effects of climate change as a means of taking advantage of new opportunities or of coping with the consequences (Adger et al. 2003). Building resilience will be a key way to reduce vulnerability to climate change (Stern 2006). Adaptation is not limited to discrete projects (Leary 1999), such as dams and sea walls. It includes a wide range of adjustments by entities such as households, firms, and other institutions in response to the effects of climate change and variability. These include managing natural resources, inputting mixes in production, and changing laws, programmes, policies, and investments. In general, adaptation to climate change presents itself as an economic problem because it addresses the bigger problem of allocating scarce resources to attain sustainable development. Ignoring climate change by not building adaptive measures will eventually damage economic growth and other aspects of human and natural well-being. It threatens to reverse the gains in these areas over the past several decades. The risks posed to development by climate change will be managed more efficiently if they are put in the mainstream of development.

Adaptation measures as a response to climate change can be short-run or long-run (Table 2.5). Adaptation categories will not consist of explicit adaptation decisions (Stern 2006). The climate and planned adaptation will affect the choices firms and households can make, and hence also their behaviour, but they will not affect their overall objectives. In practice, this means that CBA is likely to be the only framework within which it is meaningful to assess climate change policies (Agrawala and Fankhauser 2008).

In agriculture, the adaptation to climate change focus on implementing measures that help build rural livelihoods most resilient to climate variability and disaster. Even though a large number of studies of central estimates of adaptation costs have not emerged, a relatively narrow range of global estimates has emerged from various studies following a variety of methodologies (Nelson et al. 2009). Based on the information provided in the national adaptation programmes of action of five least-developed countries, immediate necessary adaptation activities will require $133 million, which is about $25 million on average

TABLE 2.5   Examples of Adaptation Types

Type of Response to Adaptation	Autonomous	Planned or Policy Driven
Short run	Making short-run adjustments (e.g., changing crop planting dates), spreading the losses (e.g., pooling risk through insurance)	Developing greater understanding of climate risks (e.g., researching risks and carrying out a vulnerability assessment), improving emergency response (e.g., early warning systems)
Long run	Investing in climate resilience if future effects are relatively well understood and benefits easy to capture fully (e.g., localized irrigation on farms)	Investing to create or modify major infrastructure (e.g., larger reservoir storage, increased drainage capacity, higher sea walls), avoiding the impacts (e.g., land use planning to restrict development in floodplains or in areas of increasing aridity)

Source: Stern (2006).

for each of these countries (Stern 2006). Extrapolation to all 50 least-developed countries results in a need for investments of around $1.3 billion. According to Stern (2006), the overall multinational commitment needed to assist developing countries to adapt to climate change is $234 million–$634 million. Nelson et al. (2009) examine welfare in future scenarios with and without climate change, estimate the costs of adapting to climate change, and examine the benefits in terms of reduced vulnerability to climate change. Aggressive agricultural productivity investments are needed to raise calorie consumption, which means it is important to increase investments in adaptation (Table 2.6).

The additional annual investment needed to return the child malnutrition numbers to the no climate change results is $7.1 billion under the wetter National Center for Atmospheric Research (NCAR) model scenario and $7.3 billion under the drier Commonwealth Scientific and Industrial Research Organisation (CSIRO) model scenario. These results

TABLE 2.6 Developing Country Agricultural Productivity
Investments to Respond to Climate Change

Investment Area	Increase (%)
Growth in Crop Yield Over Baseline	60
Growth in Animal Numbers	30
Production Growth of Oils and Meals	40
Growth in Irrigated Area	25
Growth in Rain-Fed Area	−15
Growth in Basin Water Efficiency by 2050	15

Source: Nelson et al. (2009).

point to the importance of improving the productivity of agriculture as a means of meeting the future challenges of climate change (Nelson et al. 2009).

Key Insights

Adaptation is increasingly seen as an inevitable answer to the challenges posed by climate change. It is an essential component in the development of disaster and risk management policies. It is clear that an important first step in the economic analysis of adaptation to climate change is the assessment of the effects of various climate change scenarios at disaggregated levels. National- and state-level assessments of each country are needed for designing effective adaptation strategies. A useful way forward may be constructing cost curves that demonstrate the costs of various adaptation strategies. In addition to the analysis of costs and benefits of adaptation strategies, careful economic analysis of the instruments that could facilitate adaptation is essential. Researchers should aim to understand water resources and storage under different social and ecological conditions. There is a need to design short-term training programmes for different stakeholders, and for careful long-term learning through collaborative research.

Crop insurance is a risk-management mechanism for covering crop failure. Most farmers are not aware of the insurance premium calculations in several parts of developing countries. Hence, training and awareness programmes could help farmers learn about the procedure.

State or national governments should carry out studies of the river basins or regions to identify vulnerable areas by calculating the vulnerability index. This would help policymakers concentrate on the most vulnerable areas by developing adaptation strategies.

It is important to examine both short-term and long-term interventions. The adaptation practices being used in extreme situations should be documented, and the documented interventions should be grouped under short-term and long-term categories. Short-term interventions normally include the adoption of new crop varieties and new water management practices suitable to the changes in climate.

Policy Recommendations

In light of the above discussions, we recommend the following:

- Quantify climate change effects on various regions and countries using updated information.
- Determine the adaptation strategies needed for various country situations. Determine how much investment is needed in research, irrigation, infrastructure, technology transfer, etc. In the case of agriculture, research and development aspects that boost crop productivity should be targeted.
- Design and implement interventions through regional stakeholder participation.
- Make agriculture adaptation a major agenda point within the international climate negotiation processes, with food security as the main goal.
- Integrate ongoing and proposed development programmes with climate change adaptation with the active participation of community and government agencies. Technology transfer and upscaling should be given priority during implementation.
- Validate the adaptation strategies and the cost of adaptation periodically through national and international consultations.

References

Adger, W.N. 2003. 'Social Capital, Collective Action, and Adaptation to Climate Change.' *Economic Geography* 79: 387–404.

Adger, N., S. Huq, K. Brown, D. Conway, and M. Hulme. 2003. 'Adaptation to Climate Change in the Developing World.' *Progress in Development Studies* 3(3): 179–95.

Agrawala, S. and S. Fankhauser. 2008. *Economic Aspects of Adaptation to Climate Change: Costs, Benefits and Policy Instruments.* Paris: Organisation for Economic Co-operation and Development (OECD).

Dragoni, W. 1998. 'Some Considerations on Climatic Changes, Water Resources and Water Needs in the Italian Region South of the 438N.' In *Water, Environment and Society in Times of Climatic Change*, edited by A.S. Issar and N. Brown, 241–71. Dordrecht, The Netherlands: Kluwer.

Eakin, H. 2005. 'Institutional Change, Climate Risk, and Rural Vulnerability: Cases from Central Mexico.' *World Development* 33(1): 923–38.

Eakin, H. and K. Appendini. 2008. 'Livelihood Change, Farming, and Managing Flood Risk in the Lerma Valley, Mexico.' *Agriculture and Human Values* 25: 555–66.

Fleming, L. and B. Smit. 2010. 'Responding to Climate Change in the Canadian Subarctic: The Role of Formal and Informal Institutions.' *Poster at the State of the Arctic Conference*, Miami, USA, 16–19 March.

Gadgil, S. 2003. 'The Indian Monsoon and its Variability.' *Annual Review of Earth and Planetary Sciences* 31: 429–67.

Grothmann, T. and A. Patt. 2005. 'Adaptive Capacity and Human Cognition: The Process of Individual Adaptation to Climate Change.' *Global Environmental Change* 15: 199–213.

Ingram, K.T., M.C. Roncoli, and P.H. Kirshen. 2002. 'Opportunities and Constraints for Farmers of West Africa to Use Seasonal Precipitation Forecasts with Burkina Faso as a case study.' *Agricultural Systems* 74(3) December: 331–349.

Intergovernment Panel on Climate Change (IPCC). 2007. *The Physical Science Basis: Summary for Policy Makers.* Contribution of Working Group 1 to the fourth assessment report of the Intergovernmental Panel on Climate Change. Available at www.ipcc.ch/ipccreports/ar4-wg1.htm.

International Strategy for Disaster Reduction. 2010. 'Terminology on Disaster Risk Management.' Available at http://www.unisdr.org/we/inform/terminology.

International Water Management Institute (IWMI). 2009. 'Flexible Water Storage Options and Adaptations to Climate Change.' *Water Policy Brief* 31.

Kakumanu, K.R. 2009. 'Economic Analysis and Management of Irrigation Systems Under Subsidized Electricity Regime in the Semi-arid Region of Andhra Pradesh, India.' *Farming and Rural Systems Economics* 99.

Lasco, R.B., R.V.O. Cruz, J.M. Pulhin, and F.B. Pulhin. 2006. 'Tradeoff Analysis of Adaptation Strategies for Natural Resources, Water Resources, and Institutions in the Philippines.' *AIACC Working Paper No. 32.* Washington, D.C.

Leary, N. 1999. 'A Framework for Benefit-cost Analysis of Adaptation to Climate Change and Climate Variability.' *Mitigation and Adaptation Strategies for Global Change* 4: 307–18.

Luna, E. 2001. 'Disaster Mitigation and Preparedness: The Case of NGOs in the Philippines.' *Disasters 2001* 25(3): 216–26.

Mall, R.K., A. Gupta, R. Singh, R.S. Singh, and L.S. Rathore. 2006. 'Water Resources and Climate Change: An Indian Perspective.' *Current Science* 90 (12, 25 June).

Nelson, G.C., Mark W. Rosegrant, Jawoo Koo, Richard Robertson, Timothy Sulser, Tingju Zhu, Claudia Ringler, et al. 2009. *Climate Change: Impact on Agriculture and Costs of Adaptation*. Food policy report. Washington, D.C.: International Food Policy Research Institute (IFPRI).

Palanisami, K. and C.R. Ranganathan. 2008. *Assessment of Vulnerability and Quantifying the Impact of Climate Change on Agriculture in Cauvery Basin, Tamil Nadu*. Report submitted to UNESCO, New Delhi.

Patt, A.G., R.J.T. Klein, and A.C. de la Vega-Leinert. 2005. 'Taking the Uncertainty in Climate Change Vulnerability Assessment Seriously.' *Comptes Rendus Geosciences* 337(4): 411–24.

Shewmake, S. 2008. 'Vulnerability and the Impact of Climate Change in South Africa's Limpopo River Basin.' *IFPRI Discussion Paper* 804, IFPRI.

Singh, N. and N.A. Sontakke. 2002. 'On Climate Fluctuations and Environmental Changes of the Indo-Gangetic Plains, India.' *Climatic Change* 52: 287–313.

Sokile, C.S. and B. van Koppen. 2005. 'Integrated Water Management in Tanzania: Interface between Formal and Informal Institutions.' *International Workshops on African Water Laws: Plural Legislative Frameworks for Rural Water Management in Africa*. Johannesburg, 26–28 January.

Srivastava, H.N., B.N. Dewan, S.K. Dikshit, G.S.P. Rao, S.S. Singh, and K.R. Rao. 1992. 'Decadal Trends in Climate over India.' *Mausam* 43: 7–20.

Stern, N. 2006. *The Economics of Climate Change: The Stern Review*. Cambridge: Cambridge University Press.

Till, B., A. Artner, R. Siebert, and S. Sieber. 2010. 'Micro-level Practices to Adapt to Climate Change for African Small-Scale Farmers.' *IFPRI discussion paper* 00953.

United Nations Framework Convention on Climate Change (UNFCCC). 2002. 'Conserving Grazing and Fodder Lands through Reforestation. Database on local Coping Strategies.' Available at maindb.unfccc.int/public/adaptation/adaptation_casestudy.pl?id_project=117.

Wilby R.L., J. Troni, Y. Biot, L. Tedd, B.C. Hewitson, D.M. Smithe, and R.T. Sutton. 2009. 'A Review of Climate Risk Information for Adaptation and Development Planning.' *International Journal of Climatology* 29: 1193–1215.

World Bank. 2002. *World Development Report 2002: Building Institutions for Markets*. Oxford: Oxford University Press.

DRYLAND POVERTY

3

AMITA SHAH

Dryland Poverty and Climate Change in South Asia

Forty per cent of the world's landmass is dryland. Almost the same proportion of the landmass in Asia is dryland. Dryland poses a threat and challenge to the poor of Asia. According to dryland scenarios, desertification and the degradation of dryland will continue and become stronger. Drylands are an important source of food production and economic resilience for millions of people. Recent discourse has overlooked the potential for growth, so solutions are sought outside the arena of productive spheres. The central argument of this chapter is that the dryland regions have potential for growth. Productive capacities need to be increased by investment. The potential for dryland consists in economic diversification, scope for high-valued and nutrition agriculture including livestock, labour mobility, and the ability to cope under harsh conditions. Given this backdrop, the chapter presents a profile of Asian dryland areas and poverty. It discusses the likely effects of climatic changes in India's drylands. Policy implications are drawn.

The Context

Interaction between the Environment and Poverty

The discourse on the interaction between the environment and poverty has received increasing attention in the wake of multiple crises, such as climate change, food insecurity, and the global economic slowdown of the past few years (Scott 2006; Shah 2009). The contemporary discourse has highlighted two aspects of the interaction: (a) the multi-patterned reality where the poor are seen as victims, rather than merely the cause, of degradation (Dasgupta and Maler 2004; Markandya 2001); and (b) an increasing emphasis on dryland as a source of agricultural growth and livelihood support for large segments of the rural population (ADB 2008; Shiferaw 2002). Both aspects assume special significance with the increasing challenges posed by the climate change scenarios—globally and for the large agrarian economies in Asia.

According to available estimates, as much as 40% of the region's rural population lives on drylands, half of which lives on $2 or less per day (ADB 2008, 14). The situation is likely to worsen if desertification and the degradation of dryland continues and accelerates (Stern 2007). This may have serious implications for loss of land productivity and food security (UNCCD 1998, 15).

Development Deficiency

Due to the low productive potential of their natural resources, dryland regions have historically been accorded low priority in investments in agriculture, infrastructure, and human resources development. The underinvested regions have lagged behind, not only in farm production, but also in access to basic amenities (Mearns and Norton 2010). With low and uncertain rainfall, dryland communities have been coping in various ways, including by economic diversification, risk-taking entrepreneurialism, growing high-valued crops, livestock rearing, precautionary migration, and strong social networks. The entrepreneurial behaviour and flow of remittances that bring private investment have worked where (a) drylands (comprising multiple sources of livelihood such as crops, livestock, crafts, and seasonal migration) were one of a number of ecological systems within a country; (b) national policies have protected the development of various sectors of the economy; and (c) primary sector is free from the adverse effects of aid and trade from developing economies.

Development discourse on dryland economy has recognized dynamic characteristics of the region, as against viewing the region merely as agriculturally low potential and poverty ridden. This has strengthened the case for increasing public investment in dryland areas as a means of promoting economic growth and poverty reduction. Recent research on India and China has indicated that investments have had positive outcomes in terms of production and income (Fan and Hazell 2001, 2).[1] Apparently, the new perspective is also being reflected in policy responses to climate change, which have focused on combating the desertification and land degradation (UNCCD 1998). The focus of what people write about dryland region has started to shift away from mitigation to adaptation in dryland areas (Dobie 2001). This change has come in the wake of growing concerns over food security. Dryland agriculture is an important contributor to food security, as well as a source economic resilience for millions of people (Hassan, Scholes, and Ash 2005; Mortimore 2009).

Dryland Agriculture and Food Crisis

The available estimates suggest that dryland crops account for about 60% of the global farm production. Cereals other than rice and wheat are mainly produced under unirrigated conditions. This gives cereals a special significance for food security as they could be produced across wide-ranging agronomic conditions and also by the poor not having access to irrigation. This has then implications especially for the food producing poor farmers (FAO 2008). Notwithstanding this contribution, dryland agriculture is facing a serious threat from the growing dependence on groundwater. This has implications for poverty in the region.[2]

The above scenarios for poverty in dryland regions call for increasing productive capacities by increased investment (ADB 2008; Dobie 2001; Mortimore, M. et al. 2008). The challenges presented by climate

[1] According the study by Fan and Hazell (2001), agricultural growth in many low-potential areas, including such areas could, at margin, be comparable to that in many high-potential areas, and have a greater impact on poverty and environmental problems in the areas in which they are targeted.

[2] The poverty discourse, in the recent period, has highlighted the fact that while the highest concentration of poverty (World Bank 2006a), especially chronic poverty, is found in the forest regions, dryland areas are increasingly heading towards a deep spiral of poverty (UNDP 2006), owing to the rapidly depleting groundwater resources combined with increasing degradation of land in these regions.

change could be met by public investment. An important element in this approach is to create productive assets that can help households cope with climate change. Enhancing the productive base needs to be probed under the varying socioeconomic and climatic scenarios prevailing in drylands across the region (Morris, Kelly, Kopicki, et al. 2007).

Against this backdrop, the chapter focuses on three objectives:

- To assess the dynamics between dryland areas and poverty across Asia.
- To assess (a) the likely effects of climate changes on poverty and (b) the implications of the effects of climatic changes for poor.
- To map major policy responses to the situation of the drylands in general, and draw recommendations for India in particular.

The chapter is based on desk review of data and existing literature in Asia followed by a detailed analysis of India.

Dryland Areas and Poverty in Asia and the Pacific

Drylands have little water, which constrains two major linked activities, namely primary production and nutrient cycling.[3] As per United Nations Environment Programme (UNEP) categorization, dryland accounts for 60.9 million sq. km of land, 41.3% of earth's surface.[4] About 35% of the world's population is located in drylands, and about half of them are poor (Dobie 2001). Fifty-eight per cent of dryland is semi-arid and dry sub-humid. Such dryland accounts for 85% of the people living on dryland as hyper arid and arid areas of the dry land is very sparsely populated. While only 25% of dryland is under cultivation overall (65%

[3] Over a long period of time, natural moisture inputs (that is, precipitation) are counter balanced by moisture losses (evapotranspiration). The water deficit thus affects both natural and managed ecosystems (Hassan, Scholes, and Ash 2005). Drawing from these two concepts, aridity index is worked out as a ratio of mean precipitation and evapotranspiration, by using the modified Thornwaite formula. Drylands constitute those areas where the aridity index ranges between 0.05–0.65 (UNCCD). United Nations Environment Programme (UNEP), based on the aridity index, has grouped the landmass into six categories. Of these, drylands cover four. These are hyper arid, arid, semi-arid, and dry sub-humid.

[4] The UNCCD, however, excludes hyper arid area from the ambit of the Convention (Hassan, Scholes, and Ash 2005).

of it being rangeland), 47% of sub-humid land is cultivated, and 35% of semi-arid land (Safriel and Adeel 2005). The area under dryland is more or less same in Asia and Africa, but a larger part of dryland in Africa (than in Asia) is hyper arid with very low human habitation.

Excluding the Middle East, Asia consists of 29 countries with a population of about 3.6 billion and a land area of 24.1 million sq. km. That accounts for 54.2% of the world's population and 18.1% of its land (see Table 3.1). Dryland in Asia is concentrated in Central Asia, West Asia, India, and Mongolia. Fourteen countries in Asia have more than (and equal to) a third of the area under dryland. These include six countries in Central and West Asia, one in South Asia, and two in East Asia. The extent of dryland in Southeast Asia is almost nil, except in Indonesia and Thailand, which have 3% and 7% dryland, respectively.

Together, the countries with at least 33% dryland house 80.9% of total population of Asia. They are also include areas of high population density, such as India, Pakistan, Sri Lanka, Nepal, China, and Armenia. Bangladesh, the Philippines, Viet Nam, Indonesia, and Thailand are the other major countries with a population density of more than 100. Population density is lowest in Mongolia and low in 6 out of 10 countries in Central and West Asia, as well as in the Lao People's Democratic Republic in Southeast Asia.

Dryland and Poverty

It is difficult to assess poverty in drylands as the poverty estimates are based on the state and country levels whereas drylands are identified at more disaggregated level, that is, below the state level. However, it can at least be said that large parts of drylands are inhabited by large proportion of the poor as about 90% of drylands are located in the developing economies parts of Asia, besides Africa (Mearns and Norton 2010). According to the Millennium Ecosystem Assessment, people living on drylands are more deprived than people living in ecosystems covered under assessment (Safriel and Adeel 2005). A comparison of the two important indicators of human well-being, viz. gross domestic product (GDP) and infant mortality rate (IMR) across all the seven ecosystems assessed suggests that the dryland ecosystem has lowest GDP and highest IMR (ibid., 7). Much is contributed by poverty in Africa and South Asia.

TABLE 3.1 Indicators of Population and Dryland in Subregions in Asia and the Pacific

Country	Total Population 2007 (Millions)	$1.25 (% of Population)	$2.0 (% of Population)	Total Land Area (in Million sq. km) (2002)	Total Dryland (in Million sq. km)	Dryland (% of Total Area)	Population Density (People per sq. km)
Central and West Asia (11)	272.1	21.50	48.54	5.58	5.08	92	49.30
South Asia (6)	1,383.95	42.47	75.55	3.35	1.81	54	412.10
Southeast Asia (9)	568.6	18.80	40.49	4.33	0.09	02	131.02
East Asia (4)	1,364	15.93	36.34	10.89	1.02	09	125.20
Total Asia (30)	3,588.65			24.15	8.0	33.12	148.59
World	6,615.9			130.66			

Source: Author's compilation.

Of the 23 countries in Asia for which poverty estimates are available, 15 have more than their 20% of population under the poverty line ($1.25 a day). The remaining three countries, namely Afghanistan, Myanmar, and Maldives, also have fairly large proportion of people in poverty. This suggests that 18 countries in Asia have at least a fairly large poor proportion. Of these the five countries, namely Afghanistan, Pakistan, India, Mongolia, and China, have higher proportions of dryland than the rest of Asia. With the exception of China, they also have higher proportions of poverty.

The Asian Development Bank (2008) has estimated the amount of poverty in areas with various types of environmental degradation. The estimates are worked out mainly by using the proportions of poor and the dryland in different countries. The estimates are based on two sets of areas—one with (pro-poor) growth potential and the other with environmental constraints in poverty reduction. Table 3.2 presents a summary of the poverty estimates in the subregions within Asia and the Pacific.

According to the ADB estimates, the incidence of poverty ($1/day) in Asia and the Pacific is 20%. This ranges from 30% in South Asia to 10% in Southeast Asia. About 74% of all poor people live in rural areas, and the rest in urban areas. As much as 41% of all the poor in the region belong to the category of rural poverty caused by environmental constraints, with 23.5% of the total poor being rural dryland poor. There are about 162.5 million people in the region who live in poverty due to environmental constraints posed specifically by dryland conditions. Of these, 46.6% are located in South Asia and another 40.5% in East Asia. Within these two subregions, India, parts of Nepal, China, and Mongolia have largest numbers of dryland poor.

There are two important features of dryland poverty: (a) pockets of high concentration; and (b) transient nature of dryland poverty. Together, these features may have implications for designing appropriate growth strategies, and agriculture-led growth.

Climate Change and Dryland

As per the Global Assessment of Human-induced Soil Degradation (GLASOD), the loss of productivity due to soil degradation is highest in Asia as compared to the other regions. According to this assessment, more than 1,341 million hectare of productive land has been affected

TABLE 3.2 Poverty and Dryland Poverty ($1/day) in Asia and the Pacific

Categories	Asia-pacific		West and Central Asia	South Asia	Southeast Asia	People's Republic of China and Mongolia	The Pacific
	No.	% of Poor					
1. Population (in million)	3,470.0		322.7	1,284.4	546.7	1,307.1	9.2
2. Total Poor	692.6	100.0	51.8	386.0	56.2	196.2	2.4
	[19.9]*		[16.0]	[30.0]	[10.3]	[15.0]	[26.1]
3. Rural Poor	515.0	74.3**	38.2	263.0	47.5	164.4	2.0
R-poor in Areas with Growth Potential	232.3	33.5	14.7	113.9	20.8	82.1	0.8
R-Poor with Environmental Constraints	282.8	40.8	23.5	149.1	26.7	82.3	1.2
Dryland Poor	162.5	23.5	15.5	75.7	5.4	65.9	0.0
4. Urban Poor	177.6	25.6	13.6	123.0	8.7	31.8	0.5
Urban-slum poor	82.3	11.9	5.0	68.7	3.1	5.4	0.2
Urban-other poor	95.3	13.7	8.6	54.3	5.6	26.4	0.3
Vulnerable ($2/day)							
Total No.	1,987.8		170.4	1009.4	258.9	544.3	4.9
Rural	1,626.9		142.9	804.7	220.4	452.6	6.3
Urban	360.9		27.5	204.6	38.5	91.7	−1.5
Rural-Dryland	820.2		84.1	358.5	20.7	356.7	0.0
Urban-Slums	223.1		19.6	148.4	51.2	3.6	0.3

Source: ADB (2008).

Note: * Indicate poor as % to total population;

** Indicate % to total poor.

by desertification. The rate of desertification has increased in a number of countries, for example, India, China, Mongolia, and some of the countries in Central Asia. Asia has half of the world's total irrigated area affected by water logging and soil salinity. According to the fourth assessment of IPCC, the global temperature has increased by 0.74°C over the period of 1906–2005. It is further noted that the increase in temperature has increased in the recent years and likely to increase by two to seven times in future. Annual rainfall has fallen in various parts of Asia and the Pacific, such as northeast and north China, the coastal and arid plains of Pakistan, all of Indonesia and the Philippines, parts of northeast India, and parts of Japan. At the same time, rainfall has increased in other parts of China, in the Arabian Peninsula, in Bangladesh and along the west coast of the Philippines (ESCAP 2009, 68).

Cropland, Irrigation, and Food Security

With its erratic and low rainfall combined with high temperatures, Asia has worldwide the highest dependence on irrigation as compared to other groups of continents (Table 3.3).[5] The projected variability in

TABLE 3.3 Extent of Irrigation across Continents (% to Arable Land)

Continents	1980	1990	2002
Africa	6.0	6.7	7.0
Asia	31.3	33.8	37.9
Caribbean	22.0	23.3	26.5
Latin America	10.4	12.0	12.1
North America	9.1	9.3	10.5
Oceania	3.6	4.2	5.6
Europe	11.5	14.0	8.8
World	15.7	17.6	19.7

Source: FAO (2008).

[5] This, of course, is a reflection of two somewhat contradictory scenarios. First, the relatively larger concentration of drylands in the region necessitates dependence of irrigation through external sources as large parts of the cropland remain devoid of the required soil moisture for most of the time, unlike that in the northern countries (IPCC 2001). Second, several of the Asian countries have fairly moderate rate of precipitation, unlike that in a number of countries in Africa and the Middle East, thus making it possible to develop diverse irrigation systems including in the drylands.

precipitation may have significant effect on crop production. Wheat, rice, and maize account for 85% of total cereal production in the world. Asia has a fairly large share in the production of these cereals that have special significance for food security especially among the poor.

Dryland crops, especially low water–intensive crops, such as oil seeds, coarse cereals, pulses, spices, horticulture, medicinal plants, fodder, and fuel crops, are some of the important crops for food security. At present these crops are relatively neglected by research and by the development programmes in India including the pricing and public distribution systems.

Global food production needs to be increased by 40% in 2025 from the level of 2,000 (Cosgrove and Rijsberman 2000). But this has to be achieved with only a 9% increase in irrigation. The future growth in food production, therefore, rests heavily on drylands. Dryland does not imply no irrigation; it implies limited irrigation, to supplement soil moisture.

Under this scenario, an emphasis on low water–intensive crops, such as dryland horticulture, medicinal plants, and fodder and fuel crops, assume importance. The challenge is to improve efficiency of water use in a sustainable manner. This can be done through four major ways:

- Crops and Yield: Stress on water availability in Asia is likely to be increased by climate change (IPCC 1998; Sivakumar, Das, and Brunini 2005). As a result of climate change, the crop yield in middle- and high-latitude areas in Asia will increase, while it will decrease in areas of lower altitude (Luo and Lin 1999). The scheduling of the cropping season and the duration of the crop-growing period will also be affected. Agricultural productivity in tropical Asia is sensitive not only to temperature increase, but also to changes in the monsoon.[6] Similar studies in Indonesia and Philippines also confirmed these results.[7]

---

[6] Experiments in India reported by Sinha (1994) found that higher temperatures and reduced radiation, associated with increased cloudiness, caused reduced yields to such an extent that any increase in dry-matter production, as a result of CO_2 fertilization, proved to be of no advantage in grain productivity.

[7] Amien et al. (1996) found that rice yields in east Java could decline by 1% annually as a result of increases in temperature. Since rice is one of the main staple foods, the adverse impacts on crop production would have a significant effect on trade in agricultural commodities, hence on economic growth and stability (Matthews et al. 1995).

- Tropical Forests: In the semi-arid parts of tropical Asia, tropical forests are generally sensitive to changes in temperature, rainfall, and seasonality. Arid and semi-arid lands often carry a sizable representation of trees and shrubs as vegetative cover. Deforestation and climate change will undermine sustainable nutrition security in South Asia (Sinha and Swaminathan 1991). Climate change will have a profound effect on future distribution of food.[8]
- Soil Erosion: The effect of climate change on soil erosion and sedimentation in the mountain regions of tropical Asia may be indirect but significant. An erosion rate in the range of 1–43 tons ha^{-1}, with an average of 18 tons ha^{-1}, was calculated in three small experimental plots in central Nepal. Many desert organisms are near their limits of temperature tolerance. Because of the current marginality of soil water and nutrient reserves, some ecosystems in semi-arid regions may be among the first to show the effects of climate change. Climate change has the potential to cause a loss in biodiversity.
- Water and Livestock: Surface water and groundwater resources in arid and semi-arid Asian countries play vital roles in forestry, agriculture, fisheries, livestock production, and industrial activity. Almost two-thirds of domestic livestock are on rangelands, though in some countries a significant share of animal fodder also comes from crop residue (IPCC 2001).

How Does It Affect Poverty? A Case Study of India

Higher temperatures, reduced rainfall and yield, increased frequency of drought and crop failure, reduced forest cover and diversity, and increased health burden—together, these make a perfect recipe for loss of employment and income on the one hand and increased indebtedness and poverty on the other. Besides these, there are non-climatic triggers and stresses that also accentuate conditions of poverty. These include demographic factors, lifestyle issues, market forces, international conventions, and global trade agreements. They have a significant influence on poverty, given the nature of the state. The multiple forces make assessment of poverty a complex activity. The complexity is reflected in the diverse pattern of links that one finds between dryland and poverty

[8] For details, see ESCAP (2009).

within and across countries. An attempt has been made by ADB (2008) to assess future trends in poverty, including environmental poverty.

The ADB (2008) projections for 2020 indicated that the absolute number of poor people will decline. The number of extremely poor ($1.25/ day) declined from 692 to 414 million during 2005–10. Those living below $2 a day declined from 1,996 to 1,633 million during the same period. The number of dryland poor will decline from 162.5 to 113.8 million over 15 years during 2005–20. It is, therefore, important to understand the anatomy of poverty in general and dryland poverty in particular.

Anatomy of Poverty in India

Drylands account for 69.6% of the geographical area in the country; this consists of arid, semi-arid and dry sub-humid regions (NBSS&LUP 2011). If one excludes arid land, the proportion of dryland comes to 55.6%. Semi-arid tropics (SAT)[9] account for 37% of both area and population, 46% of net cultivated area, 32% of the gross irrigated area, and 37% of the value of production. Importantly, SAT accounts for nearly 60% of the areas that grow coarse cereals, pulses, oilseeds, and commercial crops. The arid zone accounts for 10% of area of India and 4.3% of its population (Rao et al. 2005). By 2005, about 55.3 million hectares were wasteland (NRSA 2000). There are 64 million hectares of degraded land (NRSA 2000).

Dryland Poverty in India

Dryland is home for a large proportion of the poor in India (Shah 2007). However, the incidence of poverty is not significantly higher in drylands than in the humid region (see Table 3.4). The poverty geography of in India coincides to a large extent with the hilly and sub-humid or humid regions of the central and eastern states, rather than in with the western and southern states, where large tracts of dryland are located (Shah 2009). By 2004–05, 79% of India's poor lived in seven states in a central–eastern belt characterized by moderate-to-high rainfall and an above-average proportion of forested areas (Shah 2010). Much of

---

[9] Using the definition of the International Crops Research Institute for the Semi-Arid Tropics (ICRISAT) as a growing period of from 70 to 140 days and mean monthly temperature of greater than 18°C (Rao et al. 2005).

TABLE 3.4 Poverty across Agroecological Zones in India

Agroecological Zone	Squared		Poor on Headcount Basis	
	Head Count	Poverty Gap	Number (millions)	Percentage to Total Poor
Humid	23.7	4.4	59.374	40.3
Semi-arid Temperate	14.6	2.2	21.387	14.5
Semi-arid Tropic	24.3	4.4	60.180	40.8
Arid	12.6	2.0	2.182	1.5
All India	21.3	3.8	147.478	100.0

Source: ICRISAT Database 1998 and National Sample Survey 1999–2000.

where the poor live is also identified as high-potential rain-fed areas (Fan and Hazell 2001). At a macro level, the poverty geography presents a somewhat unusual picture, which has been described as:

> drier states (in [the] west) harbor lesser poverty proportions than wetter ones. In general the states…which were under the Zamindari regime[10] of yesteryears and have experienced ineffective agrarian and land reforms and [the] [G]reen [R]evolution, have been the losers, while those in the west…have been [the] gainers. Within these contours[,] if the monsoon fails, all suffer and vice versa. (NIRD 2000, 9)

Relatively lower poverty in several parts of the dryland region is also attained by unsustainable exploitation of the groundwater. Hence, if that exploitation is not stopped, the trend may lead to a deep spiral of poverty among this sub-set of dryland regions that, so far, has performed well.

Response to Climate Change: Growth and Investments in Lagging Regions

The above spatial patterns of poverty in India highlight the multi-patterned, complex, and structurally rooted nature of poverty in India.

[10] Zamindari regime refers to absentee landlords who have statutory rights for collecting land revenue during the British rule in India and is similar to feudal system that existed prior to the colonial rule. The system was abolished in the post-colonial era, though the actual implementation of the Zamindari abolition act has been rather weak.

The threats posed by climate change, therefore, become part of complex scenario. The initial policy response to climate change, however, appears to be somewhat disjointed and devoid of a long-term strategy that would promote agricultural and allied sectors that strengthen food security and generate employment among a large mass of poor communities. The Eleventh Five Year Plan (XI Plan) document refers to a long list of commitments in terms of both adaptation and mitigation under climate change scenarios. It is, however, noteworthy that the central thrust of the policy response for adaptation is speeding the process of development: 'The most important adaption measure is development itself. A stronger economy is more able to adapt both in terms of cost of adaptation and technological capability' (Planning Commission 2007, 205). Policy initiatives and adaptation measures in the National Plan that affect the primary sector include varietal research in agriculture, coping with water scarcity, and institutional mechanisms for disaster management. There are a number of policy initiatives, such as watershed development, afforestation, development of irrigation and other infrastructure, and skill formation. These adaptation measures are not organically linked to the growth strategy of promoting dryland framing. The thrust is to boost input-intensive and irrigation-centric crop farming in the lagging regions where return to investment is high. This would still leave out the revival of ecologically suitable dryland farming systems in areas that are designated 'low potential'. To revive such systems an altogether different policy approach is necessary. Such an approach would not only alter technologies and prices, but also institutional mechanisms (Mortimore 2009, 61–72).

Dryland Coping Mechanisms

In India the incidence of poverty is not high in dryland areas. The poverty geography coincides with high-potential rain-fed areas in the central–eastern states. A number of mechanisms have been developed over time for people in dryland areas to cope with dryland conditions.

While outmigration is a strategy adopted by a large number of people to check further deterioration in their economic status, there are other factors that have helped people in dryland regions to cope with adverse agroclimatic conditions. These include sectoral diversification of the economy at the state level, which resulted in the development of a non-farm economy on the one hand and infrastructure on the other. Gujarat, Karnataka, Andhra Pradesh, and Maharashtra are some of the places where overall poverty is lower than other states in spite of a large proportion of area being dryland. The other important coping mechanism has to do with commercialization of agriculture, in particular with high valued crops such as oilseeds, cotton, spices, dryland horticulture, and pulses. Better access to quality infrastructure and economic services is important for supporting commercial agriculture. Also diversification in terms of development of allied activities, such as livestock and dairy farming, running fisheries, and agroprocessing is an important coping mechanism in dryland areas.

Yet another feature of traditional coping mechanisms pertains to the sociocultural aspect of people who have survived under harsh environmental conditions over a long period of time. These features are the hard working and enterprising characteristics of self-employed farmers. These features are reflected in their responses to new technology. Examples of how people have coped with dryland conditions over time are the massive expansion of small water harvesting structures in Gujarat, the rapid adoption of water-saving devices for the irrigation in Rajasthan and Maharashtra, the rapid spread of BT-cotton and organic farming for exports in some of dryland areas in the western and southern states.

Despite the various coping mechanisms, frequent droughts have been accompanied by increased malnutrition, especially among the poor. The recent food inflation has aggravated the situation (Dev 2010). Food insecurity is already a grave issue. It is likely to become graver as droughts become more frequent with climate change. Similarly, the Micro Watershed Development Programme—a flagship initiative in place for increasing resource regeneration, farm productivity, and livelihood security in dryland areas—has made major strides in coverage of area and activities and has rejuvenated a large number of small water-harvesting structures. According to the available information, 55 million hectares of land has been treated by major watershed projects in by the mid-2000s. These projects undertake various activities such as soil water conservation and drainage line treatment, promotion of suitable crops and farm practices, development of micro-irrigation, formation of saving-credit groups, and market support. Thus, the initial steps are already taken. What is missing is the appropriate management of harvested water, which is by far the scarcest resource. Harvested water has yet to be made equitably accessible or used in a sustainable manner. Access to drinking and domestic water, the development of pastures and livestock, and afforestation are found to be typically missing in a large proportion of these initiatives (Shah 2010).

An adaptation strategy, therefore, needs to supply these missing links. This cannot be achieved if dryland agriculture remains on the margins of agriculture polices. The National Plan for the United Nations Convention to Combat Desertification talks about these questions. How far these commitments will be taken in a holistic and comprehensive manner has yet to be seen.

Adaptation and Future Opportunities: Going for Dryland Development and Beyond Non-farm Strategies

Drylands and droughts have long existed, and people have found out ways of living under the harsh conditions. At the same time, state policies and the global economic orders have played a role in mitigating adverse effects and promoting livelihood options primarily dependent on dryland systems. The dryland ecosystems have many functions, which may attract investments for provisioning of better infrastructure, especially on the marginal rangeland (Seré et al. 2008). Thus, the solutions may have to come from an optimum use of available natural resources. Such an optimum use would involve bringing environmental management, rather than merely production and consumptions, to the centre of the strategy.

Table 3.5 presents adaptation opportunities identified in the context of Asia and the Pacific, which suggest that thrust, notwithstanding the differential strategies adopted by various countries, is on (a) sustainable agriculture, (b) food grain production along with livelihood promotion, (c) exploration of carbon markets, promotion of intra-regional trade, and cooperation, and (d) environmental regeneration with special emphasis on groundwater resources (ESCAP 2009, 10).

Whereas crop insurance, water use efficiency, and increased international trade are important options, livestock-linked agriculture has yet to move to the centre stage of strategy. Also, particular adaptation

TABLE 3.5   Adaptation Strategies and Polices

I. Adaptation Options (Short term)
    Crops Insurance
    Crops/Livestock Diversification
    Calibrating the Timings of Various Farm Operations
    Adaptive Livestock Management
    Temporary Migration
    Food Reserve
II. Adaptation Options (Long term)
    Cropped Linked Livestock Development
    International Trade
    Efficient Water Use
    Forecasting Management
    Strengthening Livelihood

Source: Author's compilation.

strategies and polices do not necessarily work under all circumstances. Crop insurance, a much-talked-about policy prescription, points to this reality.

Similarly, studies for Asia have shown that price incentives, experienced during the recent inflationary trends, do not necessarily culminate in a significant supply response. Dependence on trade alone may not ensure increased production or supply of food grains under the climate change. Also, there is no specific mention of the institutional or pricing support that was behind the Green Revolution. Such support is at least as necessary for the revival of dryland farming.

The central challenge is the requisite financial commitment. A million dollar question therefore is: what is preventing a shift to sustainable farming despite the loud and repeated policy commitments to adapt to the climate change? Prima facie, there are 10 main impediments to making a shift: (a) working in a systematic way rather than on the basis of crop/input-specific interventions; (b) an area-based approach; (c) a trade-off between growth in agriculture per se and employment generation, or livelihood support; (d) takes longer to realize its full potential; (e) focusing more on local economies than on global trade; (f) basic changes in the property-rights regime, especially with respect to groundwater; (g) favourable pricing and other support; (h) context-specific research and development and extension rather than top-down and generic technological prescriptions; (i) the decentralized stocking and distribution of food grain and the regulation of food inflation; and (j) not just markets, but institutional support to carry out changes over a longer period of time. So the gear of agricultural growth must be changed with careful hand holding, and someone other than the dryland poor must bear the cost of this transition.

Besides moving towards dryland farming systems, the other routes of adaptation also need to be addressed appropriately. These include sectoral diversification towards industry and services in the regional economy; outmigration facilitated by adequate support for those who succeed in migration; employment through infrastructure development; the creation of savings and credit instruments that help as insurance; selective commercialization of crops; and activated markets for inputs, including land for agriculture. The next round of the agenda, therefore, is to move from policy commitments to actual actions. There are constraints and risks involved in doing this, but the risks involved in allowing the already depleted natural resources (soil, water, forests) to deplete further is likely to be much higher.

Summary of Major Findings

The foregoing analysis of climate change and poverty in Asia and the Pacific brought home some observations, as summarized below:

About 40% of Asia and the Pacific is dryland. The region has nearly a third of all dryland worldwide.

1. More than 2.1 billion people live in dryland areas, most of them in Asia and the Pacific. They are suffering from the development deficit. Besides Central and North-West Asia, South Asia is the major hotspot of dryland poverty.
2. There are 515 million rural poor in Asia and the Pacific; of them 162.5 million are dryland poor. By 2010, the number of poor in dryland region is likely to be as high as 113.8 million.
3. Climate change is likely to have significant negative effects on agricultural potential as the region has high proportion of cropped land receiving irrigation. Much of this is likely to be trough groundwater resources that have already been depleted.

4. A number of strategies and supporting polices have been identified for adapting to the climate change. Most of these strategies and policies still continue to operate in isolation and at the margin of farming system.
5. The future growth of agriculture will have to be linked to environmental conservation and employment generation among the poor.
6. There is an increasing recognition of the importance of investing in marginal areas. The approach, however, continues to remain focused on financial returns. Shifting to a new way would require a change in the mindset that governs resource allocation.

The development deficiency in dryland regions highlights the importance of public policy and investment for increasing and fully realizing the potential of such regions. There are, however, risks involved in shifting to a sustainable dryland system. There is also a risk in depending on non-farm strategies for poverty reduction. At the same time, there are large opportunities. The global communities have to share the burden of an adaptation process that is already burdened with a large proportion of the world's poor, including the dryland poor.

References

ADB. 2008. 'The Environments of Poverty: A Geographical Approach to Environmental Factors of Poverty in Asia and the Pacific', Asian Development Bank, Manila.

Adeel, Z., Uriel Safriel, David Niemeijer, and Robin White. 2005. *Ecosystems and Human Well-Being: Desertification Synthesis*. A Report of the Millennium Ecosystem Assessment. Washington, D.C., World Resource Institute.

Amien, L., p. Rejekiningrum, A. Pramudia, and E. Susanti. 1996. 'Effect of interannual climate variability and climate change on rice yield in Java, Indonesia', in L. Erda, W. Bolhofer, S. Huq, S. Lenhart, S.K. Mukherjee, J.B. Smith, and J. Wisniewski. (Eds.) 1996. *Climate Change Variability and Adaptation in Asia and the Pacific*. Dordrecht, Netherlands: Kluwer Academic Publishers, pp. 22–39.

Cosgrove, W.J. and F.R. Rijsberman. 2000. *World Water Vision: Making Water Everybody's Business*. London: Earthscan Publications.

Dasgupta, P. and K.-G. Maler. 2004. 'Environmental and resource economics: Some recent developments', South Asian Network for Development and Environmental Economics (SANDEE) Working Paper No. 7–04, Kathmandu, Nepal.

Dobie, P. 2001. 'Poverty and the Drylands', Global Drylands Partnership, Nairobi, Kenya, p. 1–15.

Fan, Shenggen and Peter Hazell. 2001. 'Returns to public investments in the less-favoured areas of India and China', *American Journal of Agricultural Economics*, 83(5): 1217–22.

FAO. 2008. 'Climate Change, Water and Food Security'. Technical Background Document from the Expert Consultation held on 26–28 February 2008, Rome.

Hassan, R., R. Scholes, and N. Ash. 2005. *Ecosystem and Human Well Being, Current State and Trends*, Vol. 1, Chapter 22. Washington D.C.: Island Press.

IIED. 2008. *Climate Change and Drylands*. Available at: www.ccdcommission.org.

IPCC. 2001. *Climate Change, 2001: Impacts, Adaptation and Vulnerability*. Contribution of Working Group II to the Third Assessment Report of the Intergovernmental Panel on Climate Change in MacCarthy et al. (eds.). Cambridge: Cambridge University Press.

Koohafkan, P. and B.A. Stewart. 2008. *Water and Cereals in Drylands*, Chapter 2. London: Earthscan Publishing.

Markandya, A. 2001. *Poverty Alleviation and Sustainable Development: Implications for the Management of Natural Capital*. United Kingdom: University of Bath.

Matthews, R.B., T. Horie, M.J. Kropff, D. Bachelet, H.G. Centeno, J.C. Shin, et al. 'A regional evaluation of the effect of future climate change on rice production in Asia', in Matthews, R.B., M.J. Kropff, D. Bachelet, and H.H. Van Laar (eds), *Modeling the Impact of Climate Change on Rice Production in Asia*, 95–139. International Rice Research Institute (Philippines) and CAB International, United Kingdom.

Mearns, R. and A. Norton. 2010. *Social Dimensions of Climate Change: Equity and Vulnerability in a Warming World, New Frontiers of Social Policy*. Washington, D.C.: World Bank.

Morris, Michael, Valerie A. Kelly, Ron J. Kopicki, and Derek Byerlee. 2007. *Fertilizer Use in African Agriculture: Lessons Learned and Good Practice Guidelines*. Washington, D.C.: World Bank.

Mortimore, M. 2009. *Dryland Opportunities: A New Paradigm for People, Ecosystems, and Development*. Switzerland: IUCN.

Mortimore, M. et al. 2008. Dryland—An Economic Assets for Rural Livelihood and Economic Growth, IIED, UNDP, IUCN.

NBSS&LUP. 2001. *Land Use in India*. Nagpur: National Bureau of Soil Survey and Land Use Planning.

NRSA. 2000. *Mapping of Wastelands in India from Satellite Imagery*. New Delhi: National Remote Sensing Agency (NRSA), Hyderabad and Ministry of Rural Development, Government of India.

NIRD. 2000. *India: Rural Development Report*, National Institute of Rural Development, Hyderabad.

Planning Commission. 2007. *Eleventh Five Year Plan, 2007-12, Inclusive Growth*, Vol. 1. New Delhi: Government of India, Oxford University Press.

Rao et al. 2005. *Overcoming Poverty in Rural India: Focus on Rainfed Semi-Arid Tropics*. India: International Crops Research Institute for the Semi-Arid Tropics (ICRISAT).

Safriel, U. and Z. Adeel. 2005. 'Dryland Systems', in *Ecosystems and human well-being: Current state and trends: Findings of the Condition and Trends Working Group*, edited by Rashid Hassan, Robert Scholes, and Neville Ash. (pp. 623–62). Washington: Island Press.

Scott, L. 2006. 'Chronic Poverty and the Environment: A Vulnerability Perspective'. Working Paper 62, CPRC/University of Manchester, Manchester.

Seré, C., A. Ayantunde, A. Duncan, A. Freeman, M. Herrero, S. Tarawali, and I. Wright. 2009. *Livestock Production and Poverty Alleviation-Challenges and Opportunities in Arid and Semi-arid Tropical Rangeland based Systems*. International Livestock Research Institute, Nairobi. Available at: www.slideshare.net/ilri/china-grassland-congress-june-16-v3.

Shah, A. 2009. 'Natural Resources and Chronic Poverty in India: A Review of Evidence and Issues'. CPRC-IIPA Working Paper No. 47, Indian Institute of Public Administration, New Delhi.

Shiferaw, B. 2002. 'Poverty and Natural Resource Management in the Semi-arid Tropics: Revisiting Challenges and Conceptual Issues'. Working Paper 14, International Crops Research Institute for the Semi-Arid Tropics (ICRISAT), Patancheru.

Sivakumar, M.V.K., H.P. Das, and O. Brunini. 2005. 'Impacts of Present and Future Climate Variability and Change on Agriculture and Forestry in Arid and Semi-arid Tropics', *Climate Change* 70: 31–72.

Stern, N. 2007. *Stern Review of the Economics of Climate Change*, Executive Summary. London: HM Treasury.

Suzuki, K. 2003. 'Sustainable and Environmentally Sound Land Use in Rural Areas with Special Attention to Land Degradation: An Issue Paper', Asia Pacific Forum for Environment and Development, Expert Meeting Held on 23 January 2003, China.

UNCCD. 1998. *The Social and Economic Impact of Desertification in Several Asian Countries*. Geneva: CCD Interim Secretariat.

UNDP. 2006. *Human Development Report, 2006- Beyond Scarcity: Power, Poverty and Global Water Crisis*. New York: United Nations Development Programme.

World Bank. 2006a. *Unlocking the Opportunities for Forest-Dependent People, Agriculture and Rural Development Sector Unit*. Oxford University Press: South Asia Region.

———. 2006b. *Inclusive Growth and Service Delivery: Building on India's Success. Development Policy Review*. Washington, D.C.: World Bank.

4

SUNIL RAY

Promoting Livelihood Security for the Poor in the Fragile Drylands of Rural Rajasthan

It is possible for the poor involved in dryland agriculture to adapt to climate change only if the shrinkage of space available for livelihood generation is arrested by eliminating of the rift between agriculture and ecology.[1] In this chapter, I show how farmers in the arid Indian state of Rajasthan, who had been made vulnerable to food insecurity by climate change, improved their production conditions and restored the harmony between agriculture and ecology. I explain how dryland poverty has been aggravated by climate change and which steps could be taken to ameliorate the situation. In the first section, I provide an overview of how the dryland poor became increasingly harmed by climate change

[1] If farming method is followed against ecological principles, it may lead to result in rift in the agroecology in terms of loss in soil nutrient, loss of soil moisture, decline in soil fertility, etc. Agroecology refers to farming methods that are based on the applications of ecological principles including (a) recycling of biomass and achieving a balance in nutrition flows, (b) assuring favourable soil conditions, (c) low nutrient loss, (d) promoting the functional biodiversity, (e) promoting biological interactions that regenerate soil fertility, etc. (Altieri 1995; 2002).

and examine the response of the government. In the second section, I examine how the villagers resisted the rift between agriculture and ecology induced by the climate change.

Livelihood Insecurity in Rajasthan

The poor who participate in the dryland agriculture of Rajasthan were pushed to deep livelihood insecurity. The means of living that must endure over time—meaning, thereby, not clinging to one particular mode of earning for survival—dried up to a considerable extent for the dryland poor of the state due to lack of availability of choice (Ray 2008b). It was not only the steep decline in agricultural performance that posed formidable challenge to subsistence living, but also the stagnation of the non-farm sector that reduced the scope for employment and income generation of the poor to a sizable extent (Ray 2008a). The contribution of agriculture to Net State Domestic Product (NSDP) was 55% in 1978–79, declined to 45% in 1990–91, and then became 26% in 2004–05 (Ray 2008a). The poor were left with the choice of devising alternative strategies to ensure their survival. These strategies included mixed cropping, animal husbandry, multiple occupations, and short-term outmigration (Acharya and Vidya Sagar 2007). There are several instances that show how farmers—irrespective of whether they were poor or rich—treated livestock reproduction as a major adaptive strategy for livelihood generation in the event of consistent failure of agriculture (Ray 2007).

However, agriculture seems to have turned out to be an unreliable source for livelihood generation for the poor, largely due to the ecological rift that has occurred as a result of complete change of the rainfall pattern that the state witnessed during the last few decades. For example, until the end of 1970, rainfall pattern was, by and large, not different from what it was so during the decades earlier. However, after early 1980s, its variability and irregularity across regions within the state increased to such an extent that agriculture became unsustainable (Khan 1998). Climate change was the primary factor. This can be gauged from Table 4.1.

Agroecological Rift

The result was that the state was left with a sort of perpetual drought with some variations across different agroecological zones. The

TABLE 4.1   Average Rainfall Received by the State

Years	Number of Surplus Years	Number of Deficit Years	Total Number of Years
1981–90	2	8	10
1991–2000	5	5	10
2001–10	4	6	10
Total	11	19	30

Source: Irrigation Department, Government of Rajasthan, Jaipur.

noticeable aspect was that it was more frequent and pronounced during the last two decades and was much different from the trend set earlier in the past. To be precise, the frequency of drought proneness increased from late 1980s, deviating from its five-year cycle. Every fifth or sixth year had a deficit rainfall year.[2] Excess rainfall (20% to 50% of normal rainfall) repeated after fifth year (Khan 1998). However, Table 4.1 shows that the frequency of deficit rainfall in last two decades was very high which is why the rainfall pattern may be said to have stopped short of fitting into the same cycle. Consequently, the groundwater level declined steeply, leading to an expansion of the dark zone,[3] soil erosion, salinization of soil and groundwater, poor maintenance of agricultural biodiversity, loss of soil moisture, loss of soil nutrient, degradation of village pastures, etc. In other words, a rift is created in the agroecology of the state and has made the poor more insecure in their livelihood. The effect of such an extremely unfavourable rainfall pattern was a large contraction of cultivable land, of which 65% was rain-fed, while nearly 60% of the total land area of the state is covered by desert environment. (Swaminathan 2010). This is associated with a declining average agricultural yield and a growing population. As a consequence of it, per capita production declined in all zones, although the severity was greater in the humid and sub-humid zones.

[2] Khan shows this in his extensive study on rainfall pattern (Khan 1998).
[3] A dark zone refers to an area where groundwater table has fallen beyond a prescribed limit due to over exploitation. The area is identified as critical (grey) before it is dubbed as a dark zone.

Dimensions of Livelihoods Crisis

Besides this, the rising competing claims on an already-fragile resource base of the state resulted in an uncertainty that began to pervade livelihood generation that the poor had never witnessed before (Jodha 2010). It was the smallholdings in agriculture that became the primary victim of the low precipitation that resulted from climate change (Acharya and Vidya Sagar 2007). The biggest threat came from the overexploitation of groundwater, with water tables falling at the rate of 1–3 metres per year. The conditions of availability of groundwater became too critical, especially for the poor farmers who were not financially capable of investing in digging well for drawing it. Of the 237 groundwater blocks in the state in 1984, there were 162 safe blocks. However, these declined to 32 in 2004. Much more serious was the fact that the number of dark zones increased from 22 to 140 in the same period. If the zones that were declared critical were added, almost 81% of groundwater was in the dark zone (Rathore 2007).

The overexploitation of groundwater adversely affected the circumstances affecting the health of the farmers in several ways. For instance, there had been a steep deterioration of the quality of the water over the years. In 1996, only 25% of villages and habitations were affected by chemical contamination. It increased to 61.30% of villages and habitations by 2001. The rise in the fluoride content of the groundwater had been a threat in many areas in the state. The deteriorating water quality caused 60% of the diverse and routine human ailments (Rathore 2007). The groundwater of 27 districts is partly contaminated by salinity (electrical conductivity [EC] > 3000 μS/cm at 25°C), 30 districts are partly contaminated by fluoride (<1.5 mg/1), 16 by chloride (>1000 mg/1), 28 by iron (>1.0 mg/1), and all 33 districts by nitrate (>45 mg/1) (Central Groundwater Board, cited in Government of India [2010]). So the agroecology of the state is being damaged in a way that threatens the nutritional security of the poor. A decline in health should result.

One might have hoped that the livestock sector would provide an alternative livelihood to the poor under such circumstances. But it failed to do so; for it was riddled with a host of problems, the most important of which were the poor performance of agriculture (which feeds cattle with its byproducts) and the deteriorating carrying capacity of the grasslands (Ray 2007). The density of the livestock population increased steeply in all agroclimatic zones over the years due to an increased dependence on it as a source of livelihood. But the regeneration of the grasslands failed to keep pace with the increasing number of livestock. Livelihood generation from this source was not adequate for ensuring its security at the household level.

The adverse effect of climate change on the non-priced goods, such as fuelwood and other forest produce, was no less significant for the poor. Besides, a lack of proper integration of poor farmers into the market has always damaged their prospects of gain from agricultural trade. All these factors aggravated the marginalization of the poor. The result was a deepening of poverty (Institute of Development Studies 2008).

Steps Taken

Although the government and civil society organizations made several interventions that aimed at ensuring livelihood security for the poor, the most successful was the Mahatma Gandhi National Rural Employment Guarantee Act (MGNREGA). It constitutionally guarantees 100 days per year of employment at a stipulated wage rate to all rural households. The state of Rajasthan has been implementing this act since 2006. However, only an average of 16% of total man-days of employment were created as of 2010–11. The state has a long way to go to achieve its goal. How innovative has the government been in its attempts to improve the poor's livelihood security? In the following section we examine this question based on a case study of two villages.

Agroecological Rift and Livelihood Insecurity: A Field-Level Assessment

The agricultural transformation sought by poor farming communities was noticeably different in the semi-arid villages of Rajasthan. Bad Bagpura and Bapu are two villages located in Chaksu tehsil in Jaipur district. Bad Bagpura has a population of 1,189, with 204 households. Bapu has a population of 2,011 who live in 294 households. Poor households in both villages have been struggling for alternative source of livelihood in ways they never had to in the past. This is because over the last two decades or so agriculture gradually stopped generating livelihoods. The pattern of rainfall was exceptionally poor. This contributed to the poor performance of agriculture and the inadequate livelihood generation for the poor. However, what was equally or more important, as I observed in the field, was the faulty agricultural practices that were followed when there is such a low level of rainfall. This led to an agroecological rift that reduced the space for agriculture to ensure food security for the poor. It was not only the traditional poor, including landless, small, and marginal farmers, but also the landed farmers (medium and large) who were victims of the degeneration. An attempt is made in this section to investigate the declining process that had set in our two villages and show how the villagers were able to restore agroecology and revive their agriculture even in low rainfall conditions. Steps taken by the government to meet the livelihood crisis are also examined.

An Unstable Village Economy

Until the early 1990s, the villages under study received reasonably good rainfall. Making a living was never a problem. In tandem, agriculture and livestock were capable of generating income and employment for both women and men. Traditionally, farming occupied both males and females. Seed was traditionally used to produce chickpea (gram), barley, wheat, bajra, maize, guar, jowar, groundnut, etc., during both kharif and rabi seasons respectively. Cow dung was used to make soil more fertile. However, the village economy started witnessing a drift towards instability in late 1980s. The water table started to fall due to a shortage of rainfall. And there were no structures for harvesting water (storing rain water in order to recharge underground aquifers). However, it was not all that bad, villagers reported, until the 1990s, when agriculture began to pay less than average. The economic situation of the poor farmers in particular and the farming community in general was pushed into great uncertainty.

New Agricultural Practices

It was at this stage that the department of agriculture (extension) of the Government of Rajasthan played a key role in reversing the downward trend of agriculture. The farmers did not realize the extent of the challenge awaiting them after the introduction of new agricultural practices. Hybrid seed replaced the traditional seed. This was associated with the application of Diammonium Phosphate (DAP) and urea for increasing soil fertility. Farmers were told that High-Yielding Variety (HYV) of seed was preferable to the traditional one in variety of ways. For example, crops grown on HYV require less water mainly because the time taken for them to be ready for harvest is shorter. The result was the rise of crop productivity.

A new era in agriculture in the village was ushered in. The use of cow dung to increase soil fertility took the backseat. Initially, the new practice was remunerative to the farmer. This is why more and more areas were brought under cultivation. The practice of keeping land fallow gradually disappeared. Of course, the fragmentation of land holdings due to division among household members also contributed to this. The effect of the disappearance of the practice was visible in the decline of livestock. Fallow land that used to produce grass and helped sustain the livestock was increasingly brought under cultivation. Now that the source dried up, livestock gradually ceased to be the alternate source of livelihood generation. Livelihood problems increased when new market-dependent agricultural practices were not complemented by the availability of groundwater.

New Practice: A Mismatch?

It is naive to argue that it was the unpredictably low precipitation for a long period that was responsible for such an untenable agricultural performance. Examining the problems of livelihood insecurity only through the lens of climate change is tantamount to ignoring the adverse effect of other factors. For example, the rise in population never posed a formidable challenge to food security until sufficient food was produced and made available to the household. The new agricultural practices of the early 1990s were perhaps a welcome response to the growing deficit of rainwater and agricultural production that failed to meet the increasing demand for food security in an increased population size. It is true that productivity improved due to the replacement of traditional seed by HYV and organic by inorganic fertilizer. And, of course, there was an immediate gain that accrued to the poor farmers too.

However, after a few years, new practices ceased to bring dividends to the farmers who were caught up in perpetual indebtedness. The reason was simple. Higher input costs far outweighed the productivity gains. Now even the poor that were engaged in agricultural activities were completely dependent on market for both seed and fertilizer. Every year they had to purchase new seed because crop productivity declines if the same seed is used in a following year. The scale of application of fertilizer increased in every subsequent year in order to arrest decline of crop productivity. It means that in each new year, farmers were required to use more fertilizer to obtain same output. Hence, even if the price per unit of fertilizer stayed same, expenditures shot up due to the increased doses. Needless to say, new agricultural practices gained momentum despite the poor rainfall of each successive year.

This had an adverse effect on the agroecology, which the farmers realized much later. For example, many farmers observed that the already-low water-holding capacity of the soil declined as the doses of fertilizer increased. Soil became harder, which was why rainwater never stayed in the field to improve moisture condition of the soil, which, in turn, declined. Farmers had never witnessed this before the new agricultural practices were followed. Added to that, the cost of the extraction of groundwater increased steeply because farmers had to deepen their wells in each year to draw groundwater that continuously depleted. Furthermore, agricultural yield saw a steady decline.

This case illustrates how an agroecological rift had taken place and could manifest itself by upsetting the economics of crop production. Farmers ended up in a terrain that was even more uncertain than before the new practices were followed. They did not know how to keep going with such a market-led cost-intensive agriculture. Livestock that had the potential to provide an alternative source of livelihood dried up. The only remaining solution was migration.

Fighting Agroecological Rift

The rise in population aggravated the problem of livelihood generation for the poor. The available area per person in Bad Bagpura village declined steadily from 0.83 hectares in 1981 to 0.38 hectares in 2010. In Bapu village, the decline was from 0.88 hectares to 0.49 hectares during the same period. The cultivable area declined steadily (Table 4.2).

TABLE 4.2 Availability of Cultivable Area per Person of the Sample Villages

	Bad Bagpura				Bapu			
	1981	1991	2001	2010	1981	1991	2001	2010
1. Total Population (No.)	541	748	924	1189	1120	1414	1933	2011
2. Total Area (Ha)	448	448	448	448	981	981	981	981
3. Area per person (Ha)	0.83	0.60	0.48	0.38	0.88	0.69	0.51	0.49
4. Cultivable area (Ha)	361	389	268	NA	619	638	638	NA
5. Cultivable area per Household (Ha)	4.40	3.38	1.89	NA	3.50	3.08	2.11	NA
6. Cultivable area per person (Ha)	0.67	0.52	0.29	NA	0.55	0.45	0.33	NA

Source: Field Survey.

The poor (landless, small, and marginal farmers together) constituted the majority in both villages (71% in Bad Bagpura and 83% in Bapu). It means that the options for this segment of population for livelihood generation in agriculture shrank with the low rainfall regime brought on by climate change. However, steps taken by the villagers around 1995 to counter the negative effect of climate change on agroecology proved useful for the poor. At the initiative of some local NGOs, including Center for Community Economics and Development Consultant Society (CECOEDECON) and Gramodya Samajik Sansthan, farmers strove to restore resilience to the agroecology mainly through the revival of some traditional practices, including (a) rainwater harvesting and (b) the construction of small 'bunds' (*medbandis* in the local terminology—an earthen, man-made embankment with low height) in the agricultural land to arrest rainwater so that the moisture content of the soil would increase. Moisture conservation through this process brought some relief to the farmers, especially the poor ones. They could now produce crops in rabi season again. This was supplemented by increased recharge of groundwater aquifer as a result of digging farm ponds, desilting village ponds, etc.

Another step was the increased use of compost as a substitute for inorganic fertilizer. This was done to bring back the resilience of the soil that was lost with the new agricultural practices. All these measures, including rainwater conservation, were followed more extensively in Bapu than in Bad Bagpura. For example, for rainwater conservation, a huge tank with a radius of half a kilometre was constructed by the villagers. They also constructed farm ponds, medbandis, etc. As a result, the decline in irrigated area as a percentage of the cultivable area was less in Bapu than in Bad Bagpura, which had experienced a greater decline. This is shown in Table 4.3.

Table 4.3 shows that irrigated area as a percentage of the cultivable area declined in both villages, but the decline was less in Bapu than in Bad Bagpura. It declined by 20.31 bighas of land in Bad Bagpura and 5.15 bighas in Bapu. It was possible for Bapu to achieve more because more groundwater was now available for the cultivation of crops in the rabi session. Table 4.4 shows that area for all crops except mustard and groundnut declined more sharply in Bad Bagpura during rabi season than what it did in Bapu. In both villages, during the same season, there was a steady rise in commercial crops, such as mustard and groundnut.

While the number of wells for drafting groundwater for irrigation did not change in our two villages, higher availability of groundwater

TABLE 4.3   Irrigated Areas as Percentage of the Cultivable Area in the Sample Villages before and after Intervention

Land	Bad Bagpura		Bapu	
	Before	After	Before	After
Irrigated	37.73	17.42	78.87	73.72
Rain-fed	62.27	82.58	21.13	26.28
Total cultivable	100.00	100.00	100.00	100.00

Source: Field Survey.

TABLE 4.4   Cropping Pattern (Cultivable Area in Bighas) before and after Intervention

Crops	Bad Bagpura		Bapu	
	Before	After	Before	After
Rabi				
Wheat	112.5	25.0	170.5	159.5
Barley	24.0	5.0	27.0	23.0
Gram	4.0	3.0	0.0	0.0
Mustard	242.5	345.5	114.5	119.5
Groundnut	19.0	30.0	25.0	14.0
Total	402.0	408.5	314.5	316.0
Kharif				
Bajra	194.0	185.0	271.0	261.5
Guar	17.5	19.0	3.0	0.0
Maize	2.0	0.0	0.0	0.0
Jowar	147.0	189.0	36.0	39.0
Til	6.5	11.0	0.0	0.0
Total	367.0	404.0	310.0	300.5

Source: Field Survey.

due to recharge (regeneration) in Bapu made all the difference. The construction of tank for collecting rainwater and of the medbandis in more than 500 bighas of land arrested the decline of area especially under wheat production in Bapu as compared to Bad Bagpura. In other words, villagers of Bapu took better care to prevent aggravation of the agroecological rift. The area under wheat production in respect of small and marginal farmers did not decline much in Bapu in the recent past despite having severe water scarcity (Table 4.5). However, it declined

TABLE 4.5   Cropping Pattern per Poor Household on an Average before and after Intervention in Both Villages (Area in Bighas)

I. Bad Bagpura

Crops	Before		After	
	Poor	Rich	Poor	Rich
Rabi				
Wheat	1.53	3.44	0.18	1.06
Barley	0.21	0.94	0.06	0.17
Gram	0.06	0.11	0.09	0.00
Mustard	2.50	8.89	3.02	13.67
Groundnut	0.30	0.50	0.45	0.83
Total	4.61	13.89	3.80	15.72
Kharif				
Bajra	2.65	5.92	2.44	5.81
Guar	0.06	0.86	0.11	0.86
Maize	0.06	0.00	0.00	0.00
Jowar	1.61	5.22	1.76	7.28
Til	0.03	0.31	0.05	0.53
Total	4.41	12.31	4.35	14.47

II. Bapu

Crops	Before		After	
	Poor	Rich	Poor	Rich
Rabi				
Wheat	1.79	4.91	1.68	4.55
Barley	0.32	0.55	0.31	0.27
Gram	0.00	0.00	0.00	0.00
Mustard	0.98	4.64	0.99	5.00
Groundnut	0.04	0.00	0.05	1.00
Total	3.13	10.09	3.03	10.52
Kharif				
Bajra	2.65	9.00	2.73	7.64
Guar	0.00	0.27	0.00	0.00
Maize	0.00	0.00	0.00	0.00
Jowar	0.26	1.73	0.28	1.91
Til	0.00	0.00	0.00	0.00
Total	2.91	11.00	3.01	9.55

Source: Field Survey.

sharply in Bad Bagpura. The poor in Bad Bagpura did fairly well in mustard production, which requires less water for irrigation.

The prevention of agroecological rift further has implications for the food security of the household in terms of availability of agricultural output. The availability of wheat production of small and marginal farmers increased in Bapu while it declined in the other village during the period under study (Table 4.6). In respect of mustard production, the average availability of mustard per household of the small and marginal farmers increased in both villages.

Although the retention of cereals for home consumption was 70%–80% in both villages, per capita availability of everything that was required minimum, including food, clothing, education, health and housing and, of course, social ceremonies, were found to be inadequate. From this point of view, the situation of Bad Bagpura was precarious for it was not only the availability of cereals for home consumption that was low, but only a meagre amount of mustard was available for sale. However, Bapu, which followed an adaptive strategy more intensively, presented a comparatively better situation, but vulnerability of the small and marginal farmers to food insecurity was no less.

TABLE 4.6 Agricultural Production of Major Crops per Poor Household per Year

Villages / Crops	Before Intervention*		After Intervention	
	Poor	Rich	Poor	Rich
Bad Baghpura				
Wheat	5.51	25.26	0.73	6.67
Barley	0.12	1.70	0.24	1.00
Mustard	3.41	18.41	7.12	22.56
Bajra	6.94	15.09	6.09	13.33
Bapu				
Wheat	8.04	26.26	9.68	24.82
Barley	0.37	0.55	0.92	0.91
Mustard	0.99	8.19	1.84	11.82
Bajra	5.89	17.70	7.75	16.27

Source: Field Survey.
Note: * Crop output before intervention is estimated based on the information on yield rate of each crop and area as given by the sample households.

Agriculture could no longer be considered a dependable source for livelihood even for medium landholders in Bad Bagpura. In this village, it was only the large farming households who could have more than 500 grams (both wheat and bajra together) of cereal per person per day (Table 4.7). A member of a marginal farmer's household could avail only 118 grams of cereal per day from agriculture. However, the situation at Bapu was not as bad as it was at Bad Bagpura. For instance, Table 4.7 shows that a member in the marginal farmer's household could get an average of 474 grams of cereal (both wheat and bajra) per day. For past several years, ever since rainfall became inadequate, villagers continued to confront the same conditions of livelihood generation, with marginal variation.

TABLE 4.7   Per Capita Availability of Agricultural Food for Consumption per Day (kg)

Crops	Bad Bagpura				Bapu			
	Marginal	Small	Medium	Large	Marginal	Small	Medium	Large
Wheat + Bajra total	0.118	0.214	0.244	0.512	0.474	0.723	0.679	1.038
Mustard	0.020	0.044	0.022	0.071	0.016	0.066	0.058	0.063

Source: Field Survey.

Even with respect to stocking rate of livestock, Bapu could achieve more than the other village under study over the years. Livestock, expressed in terms of cattle unit per household in Bapu village, was 3 units before water and soil conservation took place. However, it increased to 4 units, while the same declined in Bad Bagpura from 6 units to 4 units. The noticeable change that had taken place in Bapu village in the wake of intervention was that even small and marginal farmers could grow fodder on their land and sell it to the landless after having retained the required quantity for their animals. This had facilitated the poor of this village to prevent the decline of livestock.

However, gain in terms of milk production, consumption, and sale was too low to depend on as a source of livelihood (see Table 4.8). If cost, including the imputed value of household labour, is taken into consideration, net returns from livestock may turn out to be negative or

TABLE 4.8 Average Production, Consumption, and Sale of Milk per Day (in kg)

Villages	Production		Consumption		Sale	
	Poor	Rich	Poor	Rich	Poor	Rich
Bad Bagpura	5.32	14.11	3.54	5.83	1.79	8.11
Bapu	6.68	20.36	4.02	8.55	2.64	11.82

Source: Field Survey.

too small, especially for the poor. All these observations on the villages under study are pointers to the growing decay of livelihood generation, especially of the poor. Although the poor could gain more in one village, where the village community is engaged in a continuous struggle to bring back resilience in its agroecology, achievement is not sufficient to get them out of the vulnerability trap of food insecurity. This provides the context that gives legitimacy to why employment generation programmes, such as MGNREGA, should be supported. However, as mentioned earlier, the effectiveness of this programme at lessening the food insecurity of the poor needs scrutiny.

MGNREGA: How Important Is It?

A poor household with seven or eight members in the villages could earn in wages from MGNREGA on average Rs 7,547 in Bad Bagpura and Rs 7,283 in Bapu during 2009–10 (Table 4.9). The wage income from MGNREGA was 10% of the gross household income estimated from all sources. If we go by the latest estimate of the planning commission, which considered Rs 700 per person per month as the amount required for a minimal diet, the poor in these villages could be all below the poverty line in the absence of MGNREGA (Table 4.9). With the inflow to the poor household of earnings from MGNREGA, monthly per capita income is Rs 776 in Bad Bagpura and Rs 875 in Bapu. The medium and large landholders, the rich component of the population, could add 4% to 6% to their household income, although the inflow of wages for the rich under this programme was more than for the poor (Table 4.9). In Bad Bagpura, it was Rs 7,722 while it was Rs 8,773 in Bapu.

TABLE 4.9   Contribution of MGNREGA to Household Income of the Poor

Sources	Bad Bagpura		Bapu	
	Poor	Rich	Poor	Rich
MGNREGA	7,547	7,722	7,283	8,773
	(10.12)	(4.24)	(9.91)	(6.22)
Wages	11,548	0	5,246	0
Service	18,648	44,167	14,841	0
Non-farm	25,142	58,111	29,652	43,636
Agriculture (Net)	5,146	55,081	9,159	63,229
Livestock (Net)	6,512	17,208	7,339	25,400
Gross annual income	74,542	182,289	73,520	141,038
Gross income of the HHs per month	6,212	15,191	6,127	11,753
Average income per person per month	776	1,899	875	1679

Note: Figures within parentheses are percentage share of gross annual income.
Source: Field Survey.

No doubt, MGNREGA has made a difference to the livelihood generation of the poor in these villages. Their household economy is now more stable than earlier when the searching cost of wage employment was too high. The livelihood generation scenario has now changed due to the implementation of this programme. But it has led a dichotomy in the rural labour market. It has widened the scope for women to obtain wage employment. And, by doing so, it seems to have injected greater flexibility to the available household labour. Women seek wage employment under MGNREGA while men do the same in other vocations, including agriculture. Men can afford to move anywhere they like for wage employment. However, this is difficult for women, which is why they prefer to work as wage labourers under MGNREGA, nearer to their homestead.

This was corroborated in discussions with villagers, who expressed without ambiguity that the expansion of the scope for livelihood generation, especially by providing wage employment to women under MGNREGA, has positively affected their personal life. They are now also able to send their children to schools. Out of 60 respondents in Bad Bagpura, 53 said that they were now able to send their children to school. In Bapu, 77 respondents out of 80 expressed the same. Also, there had been a marked improvement in housing and sanitary conditions of the villagers in the recent past.

Similarly important is that MGNREGA was linked to restoration of agroecology in these villages. Initiatives taken under this programme, such as the construction of storage tanks and the desilting of farm ponds, appear to have contributed a great deal to the restoration of agroecology of these villages. Farmers now have reasons to expect to gain from agriculture and to bring back stability to their source of livelihood. In addition, the pastureland of the village was revived under this programme. This is a great incentive to increase livestock to provide an additional source of livelihood generation that the poor almost lost.

Strategy for Adaptation

A relevant suggestion, which one may think of, will essentially be a strategy to adapt to climate change. It means that we need to seek adaptive strategies to climate change, especially for the semi-skilled and unskilled poor in land-related activities. Land-related activities include mainly agriculture, horticulture, and livestock. In a dryland context, where the challenge of climate change is very high, one must explore different means of harnessing, in a way that makes maximum use of renewable resources while precipitation is low. While no alternative is available to rainwater conservation, it is necessary to deepen watershed development activities that are undertaken under MGNREGA throughout the state. However, what is not taken up seriously under this programme is the construction of bunds (medbandis) in the agricultural fields for soil and moisture conservation. This is an extremely important step in dryland agriculture that fails to perform well due to continuous loss of soil moisture. Even though such activities are to be taken up in private agricultural land, one needs to work out how they can be brought under the purview of MGNREGA. This will go a long way towards addressing the problem of agroecological rift that leads to a massive fall in crop productivity and a loss of soil nutrients.

The other activity that could be taken up as an adaptive strategy is related to the sustainable development of livestock, especially small ruminants such as sheep. The state with its largest stock of sheep and largest amount of grassland has also the largest potential to generate employment and income opportunities for the poor, unskilled, and semi-skilled villagers (Ray 1997). Grass can grow even under conditions of low precipitation, while agriculture may not. Grass is finally converted into wool, milk, and leather. There is a large scope for grassland development by way of implementing MGNREGA in almost all parts of the state. No such development has taken place as a strategy to adapt to climate change based on other local resources, such as sheep and wool.

In order to develop activities based on sheep and wool in the state, a common facility centre must be developed (Ray 1997).[4] One may need to explore whether MGNREGA could create infrastructure for such activities to come up. The common facility centre will remove market distortions and create space for poor sheep rearers to gain a greater share in the final value addition of their produce. It will also generate income opportunities for the poor by processing activities it takes up. If the damage inflicted on agriculture by faulty practices in a low rain-fed regime is repaired, as is being done in the villages under study, the poor would be able to escape from the vulnerability trap of food insecurity.

References

Altieri, M.A. 1995. *Agroecology: The Science of Sustainable Agriculture*. Boulder: West View Press (from Peter Michael Rosset, Braulio Machin Sosa, Adilen Maria Roque Jamine, and Dana Rocio Avila Lozano. 2011. 'The Campesino-to-Campesino Agroecology Movement of ANAP in Cuba: Social Process Methodology in the Construction of Sustainable Peasant Agriculture and Food Sovereignty'. *The Journal of Peasant Studies* 38(1, January): 161–91.

———. 2002. 'Agroecology: the Science of Natural Resource Management for Poor Farmers in Marginal Environments'. *Agriculture, Ecosystems and Environment* 93(1–24) (from Peter Michael Rosset, Braulio Machin Sosa, Adilen Maria Roque Jamine, and Dana Rocio Avila Lozano. 2011. 'The Campesino-to-Campesino Agroecology Movement of ANAP in Cuba:

[4] The Common Facility Centre (CFC) is a model producers' organization of sheep rearers. It runs on commercial lines in that services related to raw wool processing including (a) sheering, (b) grading, (c) scouring, (d) testing, (e) packaging, and, finally, (f) marketing are provided to the sheep rearers on payment basis. The centre also develops and manages common gazing lands (Ray 1997).

Social Process Methodology in the Construction of Sustainable Peasant Agriculture and Food Sovereignty'. *The Journal of Peasant Studies* 38(1, January): 161–91.

Acharya, Sarthi and Vidya Sagar. 2007. 'Labor Employment and Poverty', in V.S. Vyas, Sarthi Acharya, Surjit Singh, Vidya Sagar (eds), *Rajasthan: The Quest for Sustainable Development*, pp. 129–55. New Delhi: Academic Foundation.

Government of India. 2010. *State Profile: Groundwater Scenario of Rajasthan.* Central Groundwater Board, Ministry of Water Resources. Available at http://cgwb.gov.in/gw_profiles/st_Rajasthan.htm.

Institute of Development Studies. 2008. *Human Development Report, Rajasthan (An update-2008)*, prepared for Government of Rajasthan under Planning Commission, GOI and UNDP assisted project on 'Strengthening state plans for Human Development'.

Jodha, N.S. 2010. 'The Changing Resource Use Dynamics in Arid Lands, Viewed through Water and Livestock Lens', in S. Singh and M.S. Rathore (eds), *Rainfed Agriculture in India*, p. 244. Jaipur: Rawat Publications.

Khan, Yaseen. 1998. *Climate and Dryland Ecology.* Jaipur: Rawat Publications.

Rathore, M.S. 2007. 'Natural Resource Use, Environmental Implications', in V.S. Vyas, Sarthi Acharya, Surjit Singh, Vidya Sagar (eds), *Rajasthan: The Quest for Sustainable Development*, pp. 37–75. New Delhi: Academic Foundation.

Ray, Sunil. 1997. 'Sustainable Livestock Development in Rajasthan: Some Issues', in V.S. Vyas, Sarthi Acharya, Surjit Singh, Vidya Sagar (eds), *Rajasthan: The Quest for Sustainable Development*, pp. 231–53. New Delhi: Academic Foundation.

———. 2008a. 'Is Rajasthan Heading Towards Caste War?' *Economic and Political Weekly* 43(10): 19–21.

———. 2008b. *Management of Natural Resources-Institutions for Sustainable Livelihood: The Case of Rajasthan.* New Delhi: Academic Foundation.

Swaminathan, M.S. 2010. 'Shaping Rajasthan's Agricultural Future', in S. Singh and M.S. Rathore (eds), *Rainfed Agriculture in India*, p. 31–44. Jaipur: Rawat Publications.

COASTAL POVERTY

5

MOHAMMAD YUNUS
BINAYAK SEN

Poverty in Coastal Bangladesh

In this chapter, we analyse poverty in the coastal region of Bangladesh based on a small survey we carried out. Our survey results confirm the intuitive belief that the coastal poor are more exposed to environmental risks. Our data further shows that these risks manifest themselves in food insecurity, ill health, livelihood loss, and homelessness. In coping with natural disaster–related crises, the poor rely more than the non-poor on wage labour, the mortgage or sale of assets, and distress migration, while at the same time receiving less in external assistance. The coastal non-poor are also at risk, but they have better coping capacities, including more access to affordable credit for the poor.

Countries with coastlines have experienced faster long-term economic growth than the landlocked countries. Access to coastlines is associated with reduced import prices and increased export revenues. This 're-export model' is easier to achieve in coastal developing countries due to the lower cost of intermediate products (Arvis, Raballand, and Marteau 2010). The physical and biological diversity at the place where land and sea meet creates opportunities for the people living there, including the poor. Natural resources in the form of 'common property' create opportunities for the poor to make a living using traditional technology. Thus, access to common property and diversity of the environment are boon to the poor living in coastal regions.

From this argument, a question naturally arises: does the difference in growth performance between coastline and landlocked countries hold equally for coastal vis-à-vis non-coastal regions within the same country? Despite wide access to common property, people living near a coast can be poorer than those residing in the interior regions. This is especially true with the additional risks brought about by climate change to countries such as Bangladesh. As the region is subject to at least three types of natural calamity—tidal fluctuations, salinities (soil, surface water, and groundwater), cyclones—which govern the nature and extent of vulnerabilities, diversity of environment in the coastal region of Bangladesh is also a bane for the poor living there.

The coastal households struggle to adapt to the constantly changing nature of coasts. Changes in the coastal environment force many of them, particularly those dependent on natural resources, into increased marginalization and displacement from the common property on which they inseparably depend. Because of the constant flux of the coastal environment (due to natural disasters) and increased human encroachment (due to the expansion of economic activities), the incidence of poverty among the coastal people may be different from the rest of the population. A number of issues follow from the above observations: Is there an additional burden of environmental poverty in the coastal regions over and above the routine poverty that characterize the poor households in non-coastal regions? What are the correlates of the coastal poverty? If so, how do the coastal poor and non-poor cope with the increased vulnerability? How can policies mitigate the adverse environmental effects on the coastal poor?

These questions are addressed with diverse data from Bangladesh—spatial data (geo-referenced poverty and other indicators at sub-district and district level) for 1981, 1991, and 2001 culled from population censuses; nationally representative household income and expenditure survey (HIES) data for rounds 2000 and 2005; and a special-purpose survey on environmental risks and coping methods in 12 coastal districts. Relevant econometric techniques are applied, depending on the nature of information (qualitative and quantitative) available in these data.

The chapter contains six sections. The next (second) section outlines the salient features of the coastal region of Bangladesh. The third section delves into the higher incidence of poverty in coastal region using a spatial poverty map and household survey data. The fourth section characterizes risks related to food security, housing, and health faced by coastal households, and the livelihood choices made by them. The fifth section discusses the coping methods adopted by coastal households. The final section summarizes our findings and presents some of their implications for policy.

Some Features of the Coastal Region of Bangladesh

The coastal region of Bangladesh consists of 147 *upazilas* (geographical sub-area of a district) in 19 administrative districts.[1] These upazilas stretch over 32% of the territory and comprise 28% of population of Bangladesh. The total population of the coastal region was about 35 million in 2002 (Bangladesh Basic Survey [BBS] 2003). The average density of population is 743/sq. km. This is less than the national average of 839/sq. km. However, population density markedly varies across the coastal districts: The district of Chandpur has the highest density, with 1,315/sq. km, while Bagerhat has the lowest density, with 383/sq. km.

As many as 48 upazilas are exposed to coastlines (Uddin and Kaudstaal 2003). About one third of the people of coastal region live in upazilas exposed to the coast. The average density of population in the upazilas exposed to the coast is 482/sq. km. The average population growth rate is 2.1, which is higher than the national average of 1.6. In the coastal zone, 77% of people live in rural areas. Even though this proportion is the same as the national average, variations exist among districts.

The principal sources of livelihood are agriculture and activities related to agriculture. Only 13% of the urban population of the coastal region is employed in the manufacturing sector compared to 17% in the country as a whole (Ahmad 2005). In the offshore islands, many people are dependent on natural resources for their livelihood. More than half of the coastal population is dependent on agriculture as either wage labourers or as small farmers. The coastal region is also vulnerable to natural disasters.[2]

---

[1] The coastal districts are Bagherhat, Barguna, Barisal, Bhola, Chandpur, Chittagong, Cox's Bazar, Feni, Gopalganj, Jessore, Jhalokathi, Khulna, Laxmipur, Narail, Noakhali, Patuakhali, Pirojpur, Satkhira, and Shariatpur. See Uddin and Kaudstaal (2003) for details.

[2] For detail of the opportunities and challenges of people living in the coastal region, see Islam and Ahmad (2004).

For the purpose of the vulnerability assessment of households, 12 coastal districts were selected. In the second stage, 18 upazilas were selected from these districts. These upazilas were selected based on their proximity to the Bay of Bengal. In the third stage, 36 union parishads or *paurashavas* were selected. As such, the selection process in the first three stages was purposive. Finally, 532 households were selected, with an average of 15 households from each union parishad/paurashava.

Table 5.1 presents the distribution of the households. The household questionnaire was designed in a manner to extract the socioeconomic characteristics of a household, the level of exposure to risks, and the experience of catastrophic effects of the last disaster on their lives and livelihood and how they cope with the disaster.

Additional Burden of Poverty in the Coastal Region

Regional Variation in Poverty

There is a variation in poverty across regions of Bangladesh.[3] This is evident even from the poverty data available at the divisional level (see Table 5.2). Poverty is highest in the Rajshahi division (in the north-west)—an area marked by river erosion, unpredictable char dynamics, and remoteness. The coastal divisions of Barisal (in the south) and Khulna (in the south-west) come next in the poverty ranking. The two coastal divisions do not have as same level of poverty, largely because of the differential performance on account of non-agricultural and export sectors. Thus, Khulna outperforms Barisal in terms of higher industrial concentration due to the legacy of the industrial belt in Khalishpur, Khulna, and Noapara (Jessore) and a greater concentration of export-oriented shrimp cultivation. The least poverty is observed in the eastern regions of the country, namely, Chittagong, Dhaka, and Sylhet.

Across the divisions, the pace of poverty reduction was the highest in Dhaka (15%), followed by Chittagong (12%), Sylhet (9%), and Rajshahi (6%). While poverty situation in Barisal showed marginal improvement at 1%, that in Khulna appeared to have worsened by the same magnitude. While the eastern and north-western regions experienced faster annual

---

[3] For a comprehensive documentation of spatial variations insocial progress see Sen and Ali (2009).

TABLE 5.1 Spatial Distribution of Sample Households

Districts	Upazila	Union Parishad/Paurashava
Bagerhat	Sharankhola	Dakshinkhali (15)
		Royenda (15)
Barguna	Amtali	Amtali Sadar (15)
		Haldia (13)
	Patharghata	Patharghata Sadar (15)
		Kalmegha (15)
Bhola	Char Fashion	Char Kalmi (15)
		Char Manika (14)
	Tazumuddin	Chandpur (15)
		Chanchra (15)
Chittagong	Banshkhali	Katharia (15)
		Saral (14)
	Port Thana	Paurashava (Two Wards) (29)
	Sitakunda	Barabkunda (15)
		Muradpur (15)
Cox's Bazar	Cox's Bazar Sadar	Khurushkul (15)
		Chaufaldandi (15)
	Maheshkhali	Dhalghata (14)
		Kutubjhum (15)
Feni	Sonagazi	Sonagazi Sadar (14)
		Char Chandia (15)
Khulna	Dakope	Banishanta (15)
		Sutarkhali (15)
Laxhmipur	Ramgati	Char Ramiz (15)
		Char Alexander (15)
Noakhali	Companyganj	Char Fakira (15)
		Char Kakra (15)
Patuakhali	Dashmina	Dashmina (15)
		Banshbaria (15)
	Kala Para	Khaprabhanga (15)
		Lata Chapli (15)
Pirojpur	Mathbaria	Tushkhali (15)
		Bara Machhua (15)
Satkhira	Shyamnagar	Buri Goalini (14)
		Atulia (15)
Total		(432)

Note: The size of the sample in each union parishad/paurashava is in parentheses.

TABLE 5.2 Incidence of Regional (Upper) Poverty Lines (HCR) in Bangladesh

Scope	Year	National	Barisal	Chittagong	Dhaka	Khulna	Rajshahi	Sylhet
All	2000	48.9	53.1	45.7	46.7	45.1	56.7	42.4
	2005	40.0	52.0	34.0	32.0	45.7	51.2	33.8
	Change	−8.9	−1.1	−11.7	−14.7	0.6	−5.5	−8.6
Rural	2000	52.3	55.1	46.3	55.9	46.4	58.5	41.9
	2005	43.8	54.1	36.0	39.0	46.5	52.3	36.1
	Change	−8.5	−1.0	−10.3	−16.9	0.1	−6.2	−5.8
Urban	2000	35.2	32.0	44.2	28.2	38.5	44.5	49.6
	2005	28.4	40.4	27.8	20.2	43.2	45.2	18.6
	Change	−6.8	8.4	−16.4	−8.0	4.7	0.7	−31.0

Sources: BBS (2000, 2005).

rates of poverty reduction, Barisal and Khulna experienced a worsening of the poverty situation, especially in the urban areas between 2000 and 2005. Narayan, Yoshida, and Zaman (2007) attributed the higher rates of poverty reduction in the eastern and north-western regions to higher growth in per capita consumption as well as a sharp reduction in intra-region inequality. In contrast, Barisal and Khulna hardly register any reduction in poverty due to anaemic growth in per capita consumption along with increasing inequality within each division.[4]

Poverty in the Coastal vis-à-vis Non-coastal Upazilas

As administrative divisions consist of relatively impoverished and afflu-ent areas, poverty statistics at the divisional level mask the intra-divi-sional variation. Hence, it is important to look at the poverty situation at the sub-divisional level to gauge some of the intra-divisional varia-tion. Although the accuracy of poverty estimates below division level is lower and therefore need to be treated with caution, poverty mapping data obtained through the courtesy of BBS, provide some hint of the stark divide between coastal and non-coastal upazilas in terms of head count ratio (BBS 2009). It was found that that poverty in coastal upazilas was 47.7% compared to 41% in the non-coastal upazilas (see Table 5.3). Thus, poverty incidence in the coastal upazilas was 6.7 percentage points higher than in the non-coastal upazilas, and the difference is at the statistically significant 1% error level.[5]

Does the difference found above still persist even after some of the meso-level factors influencing upazila level poverty are controlled for? To assess these hypotheses, the upazila-level poverty rates were regressed on two types of meso-level determinants of poverty: basic literacy and popu-lation, together with a dummy for coastal status. Basic literacy is pur-ported to capture the level of human capital endowment in the upazila,

---

[4] Recent evidence (based on HIES 2010) however shows contrary trends with faster reduction in poverty in the western region (Rajshahi, Khulna, and Barisal) compared to the eastern region (Chittagong and Dhaka) even though the level is still much higher.

[5] The difference of means test was conducted under the assumption of equality of population variance. The standard error was found at 2.531. There-fore, the *t* statistic was −2.648.

TABLE 5.3   Average Poverty Incidence by Coastal Area Status

Upazila	Number	Headcount Index (%)	Standard Deviation
Coastal	47	47.7	19.5
Non-coastal	461	41.0	16.2

Source: Estimates are based on upazila-level unpublished poverty data from the BBS (2009).

while population (density and growth) is used to capture the concentration of economic activities in the upazila. Higher levels of basic literacy and/or population densities are expected to lower poverty incidence.

The results under three different specifications (through three mutually non-exclusive sets of covariates) are reported in Table 5.4. The results confirm that the poverty level is indeed higher in the coastal upazilas; 7%–8% even after controlling for basic literacy and the concentration of economic activities.

TABLE 5.4   Proximate Determinants of Poverty by Coastal Upazila Status

Covariates/Specifications	I	II	III
Dummy (Coastal Upazila = 1)	0.07*	0.08**	0.07*
Literacy Rate 2001	−0.33**	−	−
Literacy Rate 1991	−	−0.42**	−0.43***
Population Density 2001 (Natural Logarithm)	−0.05***	−0.05***	−
Population Density 1981 (Natural Logarithm)	−	−	−0.05***
Population Growth Rate 1981–2001 (Annual Average)	−0.96*	−0.92*	−1.46***
Constant	0.96***	0.92***	0.95***
Number of Observations	467	466	466
Adjusted R^2	0.25	0.25	0.25

Note: Figures with one, two, or three asterisks indicate significance at 10%, 5%, and 1% error probability levels, respectively. Clustered standard errors are used in assessing the level of significance.

Poverty in the Coastal vis-à-vis Non-coastal Districts

Living in coastal environments has adverse well-being implications. Using the HIES data, we explore correlates of per capita consumption expenditure that include a district-level coastal area dummy along with standard demographic controls, educational human capital, access to infrastructure (power), land and non-land assets, urban residence, and divisional characteristics (see Table 5.5). However, the coefficient of the coastal dummy was significant only with HIES 2000 data. The per capita consumption expenditure of Barisal and Khulna are not higher than that of the Rajshahi division (considered as the reference category in the model). It may be recalled that Barisal and Khulna comprise most of the coastal districts.

TABLE 5.5 Correlates of Monthly Per Capita Consumption Expenditures by Coastal District Status

Variables	Per Capita Consumption Expenditures	
	HIES, 2005	HIES, 2000
Dummy (Coastal District = 1)	−586.37	−707.31***
Dummy (Urban = 1)	1,289.85***	1,702.40***
Division Dummy (RC–Rajshahi)		
Barisal = 1	280.17	206.54
Chittagong = 1	4,219.97***	3,566.89***
Dhaka = 1	3,954.75***	2,873.51***
Khulna = 1	−254.82	724.43***
Observations	10,070	7,140
Adjusted R^2	0.35	0.39

Note: The socio-demographic characteristics of the households controlled in the regressions are not reported, for the sake of brevity. Figures with one, two, or three asterisks indicate significance at 10%, 5%, and 1% error probability levels, respectively. Robust standard errors are used in assessing the level of significance.

Environmentally Poor Areas or Poor People?

Does the higher incidence of coastal poverty reflect the fact that more people with disadvantaged assets reside in coastal areas, or does it simply indicate 'environmental poverty adversities', such as higher environmental risks? Ravallion and Wodon (1997) provide a first-cut answer to this question. Following these authors, non-coastal households were matched with coastal households using the propensity score matching (PSM) method.

The results confirm the hypothesis of 'environmental poverty adversities' (see Table 5.6). For the unmatched sample, the coastal district has 0.01% lower per capita expenditure than the non-coastal districts, but the difference is not statistically significant. For the matched sample under the kernel method, the coastal district has a 9.1% lower per capita expenditure than the non-coastal districts and this difference is statistically significant. For the matched sample under the nearest neighbour method, the coastal district has a 9.6% lower per capita expenditure than the non-coastal districts. The results confirm the hypothesis of 'environmental poverty adversities': Even for households with similar attributes, per capita expenditure is likely to be lower (and consequently poverty likely higher) in coastal areas.

Characterization of Coastal Poverty

Food security is used as a proxy for the incidence of poverty in the coastal region.[6] In this analysis, food security refers to the number of calendar months per year a household can provide 'sufficient' food for its members. It is a household perception indicator and a measure of subjective well-being. The estimation results are presented in Table 5.7.

TABLE 5.6 PSM Impact Estimates of ATT for per Capita Consumption Expenditures by Coastal Area Status

Sample Type	Treatment	Control	Difference	S.E.	T-statistic
Unmatched	13,804.025	13,935.625	−131.599	220.585	−0.60
Matched by Kernel Density	13,804.025	15,187.813	−1,383.788	224.636	−6.16***
Matched by Nearest Neighbour	13,791.887	15,256.121	−1,464.234	242.946	−6.03***

Note: Figures with one, two, or three asterisks indicate significance at 10%, 5%, and 1% error probability levels, respectively. Estimated from the pooled HIES 2005 and 2000 data. A caliper value of 0.005 has been considered for judging the treatment-control difference in the 'nearest neighbour' method.

[6] While food security used in this analysis may take into account of the availability and access aspects, it ignores the utilization aspect. Thus the figures should be treated with caution.

TABLE 5.7   Correlates of Household Poverty in the Coastal Region

Dependent Variable	HH Food Security Status
Estimation Method	Ordered Logit
Distance from Sea (km)	−0.006 (0.005)
HH Received Remittance = 1	0.703* (0.367)
HH Is Rural = 1	−0.644* (0.367)
HH Is Exposed to Sea = 1	−0.786** (0.322)
HH Is Cyclone Prone = 1	1.003*** (0.335)
HH Head Has Environment Dependent Occupation = 1	0.356 (0.301)
HH Head Does Not Have Environment Dependent Occupation = 1	0.875*** (0.302)
LR Test $\chi^2(k)$	102.99[0.00]
Pseudo R^2	0.054
Observations	532

Source: Authors' compilation.

Notes: (a) The reference category for 'rural' is 'urban'; for 'exposed to sea' is 'interior'; for 'cyclone prone' is 'flood prone'; and for 'environment dependent' and 'not environment dependent' major occupational categories it is 'other occupational categories'. (b) Figures in parentheses are cluster (union) robust standard errors, where applicable. Figures with one, two, or three asterisks indicate significance at 10%, 5%, and 1% error probability levels, respectively. Figures in square brackets are *p*-values. (c) The socio-demographic characteristics of the households controlled in the regressions are not reported, for the sake of brevity.

The food security variable is treated as an ordinal variable under the assumption that the levels of food security have a natural ordering (low to high), but the distances between adjacent levels are unknown. Hence, an ordered logit model is used for estimation.

It may be noted that within the coastal region, distance from sea, as such, may not be the crucial correlate or defining characteristic of poverty. However, households exposed to the sea appear to have low food security during disaster. The ordered logit for households that are exposed to sea and are in a higher food security category is 0.786 less than for households in the interior areas when the other variables in the model are held constant.

Households not dependent on environmental resources are less vulnerable. The ordered logit for households that are not dependent on natural resources and are in a higher food security category is 0.875

more than for households belonging to any other groups when the other variables in the model are held constant. Households receiving remittances appear to have high food security. Rural households are poorer than their urban counterparts. One paradoxical finding is that cyclone-prone households appear to have higher food security than flood-prone households.

Characterization of Household Vulnerabilities

Households in the coastal region are subject to four types of vulnerability or risk—related to food security, livelihood, health, and housing (shelter). These risks can be assessed either separately under livelihood approach following Chambers and Conway (1992) or through an integrated vulnerability index following Hahn, Reiderer, and Foster (2009). Toufique and Yunus (2013) estimated livelihood vulnerability indices for the coastal and interior districts based on household survey data. Even though livelihood vulnerability index approach combines several components into a single indicator it does not focus on the factors driving the variations in the components. Thus, these four risks are *separately* analysed to assess the proximate factors that propel or hinder the extent and pace of these vulnerabilities.

Food Security Risks

One of the proxies used for assessing food security risks was the daily number of meals taken during a disaster. The estimation results are presented in Table 5.8. The daily number of meals is treated as ordinal under the assumption that the number of meals taken has a natural ordering (low to high), but that the distances between adjacent numbers are unknown. Hence, an ordered logit model is used for estimation.

As expected, rich households far from the coast appear to have afforded more number of meals during the disaster. In particular, the ordered logit for households far from the sea affording more number of meals is 0.01 more than households residing closer to the sea coast. Similarly, the ordered logit for households with higher levels of food security affording more number of meals a day is 0.096 more than households with lower levels of food security. Rural households that are exposed to sea and cyclones could afford fewer number of meals during disaster.

TABLE 5.8   Characterization of Food Security Risks of Households

Dependent Variables	Number of Meals the HH Afforded during Disaster
Estimation Method	Ordered Logit
Distance from Sea (km)	0.010*** (0.003)
HH Food Security Status	0.096*** (0.025)
HH is Rural = 1	−0.657*** (0.242)
HH is Exposed to Sea = 1	−0.312* (0.183)
HH is Cyclone Prone = 1	−0.467** (0.228)
LR Test $\chi^2(k)$	46.51[0.00]
Pseudo R^2	0.046
Observations	532

Source: Authors' compilation.

Notes: (a) The reference category for 'rural' is 'urban'; for 'exposed to sea' is 'interior'; for 'cyclone prone' is 'flood prone'; and for 'environment dependent' and 'not environment dependent' major occupational categories it is 'other occupational categories'. (b) Figures in parentheses are cluster (union) robust standard errors, where applicable. Figures with one, two, or three asterisks indicate significance at 10%, 5%, and 1% error probability levels, respectively. Figures in square brackets are *p*-values. (c) The socio-demographic characteristics of the households controlled in the regressions are not reported, for the sake of brevity.

Livelihood Risks

Vulnerability in the coastal region also manifests itself in different livelihood conditions. It may be recalled that most of the households in the coastal areas live on natural resources, which are vulnerable to natural disaster. When natural disaster occurs, it disproportionately affects the population living close to the coastline. Some of the livelihood-related risks are presented in Table 5.9.

It was found that households living closer to the sea have lost less in crops (Tk 131) and household effects (Tk 118), but lost more in livestock/poultry (Tk 91) and homestead trees (Tk 550). As expected, households with higher food security lost more in values in almost all livelihood sectors than the poor: crops (Tk 2,201), livestock/poultry (Tk 912), fish and shrimp (Tk 4,682), and household effects (Tk 1,871). Similarly, households exposed to sea lost in almost all livelihood sectors: crops (Tk 9,281), livestock/poultry (Tk 7,037), homestead trees (Tk 30,138), and household effects (Tk 8,164). Rural households lost more in agri-

TABLE 5.9 Characterization of Livelihood-Related Risks of Households

Dependent Variables	Damage to		
	Crop	Livestock/Poultry	Fish and Shrimp
Estimation Method	Tobit	Tobit	Tobit
Distance from Sea (km)	131.622** (59.979)	−91.415** (41.014)	−216.181 (146.540)
HH Food Security Status	2,201.985*** (481.968)	912.620*** (304.148)	4,682.138*** (1,144.301)
HH Is Rural = 1	8,168.033 (5,010.102)	4,352.319 (3,021.814)	2,717.806 (9,466.463)
HH Is Exposed to Sea = 1	9,281.648*** (3,448.909)	7,037.382*** (2,266.878)	11,517.402 (7,560.503)
HH Is Cyclone Prone = 1	−4,416.822 (4,195.717)	71.352 (2,765.965)	−18,156.964** (8,846.577)
LR Test χ²(k)	42.02[0.00]	22.13[0.00]	31.14[0.00]
Pseudo R²	0.014	0.003	0.021
Observations	532	532	532

Dependent Variables	Damage to		
	Equipment	Homestead Trees	Household Effects
Estimation Method	Tobit	Tobit	Tobit
Distance from Sea (km)	168.494 (119.312)	−549.945*** (188.975)	118.143* (67.760)
HH Food Security Status	999.711 (912.102)	1,699.646 (1,354.360)	1,870.563*** (524.618)
If HH Is Rural	19,674.611* (10,577.603)	10,322.084 (13,576.792)	−22,684.773*** (4,688.422)
If HH Is Exposed to Sea	1,411.050 (7,046.010)	30,138.330*** (10,312.713)	8,164.604** (3,808.743)
If HH Is Cyclone Prone	−14,821.783* (8,384.833)	−8,349.921 (12,411.045)	1,235.961 (4,633.466)

		LR Test $\chi^2(k)$		
LR Test $\chi^2(k)$	17.40[0.03]	33.07[0.00]	48.14[0.00]
Pseudo R^2	0.006	0.004	0.012
Observations	532	532	532

Source: Authors' compilation.

Notes: (a) The reference category for 'rural' is 'urban'; for 'exposed to sea' is 'interior'; for 'cyclone prone' is 'flood prone'; and for 'environment dependent' and 'not environment dependent' major occupational categories it is 'other occupational categories'. (b) Figures in parentheses are cluster (union) robust standard errors, where applicable. Figures with one, two, or three asterisks indicate significance at 10%, 5%, and 1% error probability levels, respectively. Figures in square brackets are p-values. (c) The socio-demographic characteristics of the households controlled in the regressions are not reported, for the sake of brevity. (d) Only agricultural and fishing equipment are considered under the broad category of 'equipment'.

cultural and fishing equipment (Tk 19,674), but less in household effects (Tk 22,684) than their urban counterparts.

Health Risks

It was found that considerable health risks are experienced by households residing in environmentally risky coastal environments. Such health risks apply to the poor and non-poor alike; in fact, given the health-seeking behaviour, the non-poor experience higher health risk-related coping costs. Thus, more food security status causes sickness costs to increase by Tk 141 (see Table 5.10). The marginal cost of sickness for a member of the household appears to be about Tk 3,900, while the matched figure in case of injury is Tk 5,800. Sickness costs increase with distance from the coastline: Tk 16 for every kilometre. This gain indirectly suggests the concentration of the poor nearer to the coastline. The sickness costs of cyclone-prone households appear to be

TABLE 5.10   Characterization of Health-related Risks of Households

Dependent Variables	Direct Costs Incurred Due To	
	Sickness	Injury
Estimation Method	Tobit	Tobit
Distance from Sea (km)	15.853** (7.220)	3.862 (11.378)
HH Food Security Status	141.067** (55.135)	−95.502 (87.032)
HH Is Rural = 1	−298.635 (555.822)	1,030.698 (944.393)
HH Is Exposed to Sea = 1	389.994 (420.102)	1,116.972 (709.529)
HH Is Cyclone Prone = 1	980.674** (480.954)	1,205.146 (811.617)
LR Test $\chi^2(k)$	327.22[0.00]	220.43[0.00]
Pseudo R^2	0.094	0.132
Observations	532	532

Source: Authors' compilation.

Notes: (a) The reference category for 'rural' is 'urban'; for 'exposed to sea' is 'interior'; for 'cyclone prone' is 'flood prone'; and for 'environment dependent' and 'not environment dependent' major occupational categories it is 'other occupational categories'. (b) Figures in parentheses are cluster (union) robust standard errors, where applicable. Figures with one, two, or three asterisks indicate significance at 10%, 5%, and 1% error probability levels, respectively. Figures in square brackets are p-values. (c) The socio-demographic characteristics of the households controlled in the regressions are not reported, for the sake of brevity.

Tk 1,000 higher than their flood-prone counterparts. In contrast, costs due to accident and injury do not vary by distance or by food security status. However, the marginal cost of injury of a member escalates to a staggering amount of Tk 5,800, and each person-day of sickness costs Tk 9 when due to illness and Tk 21 when due to injury (not shown in the results of Table 5.10).

Homelessness in the Coastal Region

One of the vulnerabilities related to shelter is the number of days any member of a household remaining homeless. The results are presented in Table 5.11. It may be noted that the number of days remaining homeless is over-dispersed but does not have an excessive number of zeros. Hence, a negative binomial regression model is estimated.

It was found that homelessness decreases with distance from sea. If a household were to increase its location from the coastline by 1 km,

TABLE 5.11   Characterization of Homelessness-related Risks of Households

Dependent Variable	Number of Days Remained Homeless
Estimation Method	Negative Binomial
Distance from Sea (km)	−0.009*** (0.003)
HH Food Security Status	−0.018 (0.021)
HH Is Rural =1	0.722*** (0.206)
HH Is Exposed to Sea =1	−0.614*** (0.157)
HH Is Cyclone Prone =1	0.843*** (0.195)
Strength of House	−0.355*** (0.096)
LR Test $\chi^2(k)$	97.36[0.00]
Pseudo R^2	0.034
Observations	532

Source: Authors' compilation.

Notes: (a) The reference category for 'rural' is 'urban'; for 'exposed to sea' is 'interior'; for 'cyclone prone' is 'flood prone'; and for 'environment dependent' and 'not environment dependent' major occupational categories it is 'other occupational categories'. (b) Figures in parentheses are cluster (union) robust standard errors, where applicable. Figures with one, two, or three asterisks indicate significance at 10%, 5%, and 1% error probability levels, respectively. Figures in square brackets are p-values. (c) The socio-demographic characteristics of the households controlled in the regressions are not reported, for the sake of brevity.

the difference in the logs of counts could be expected to decrease by 0.009 units. Similarly, households with strong houses had lower level of homelessness.[7] If the strength of household's house were to increase by one unit, the difference in the logs of expected counts of homelessness would be expected to decrease by 0.355 units. It was also found that the difference in the logs of expected counts of homelessness is expected to be 0.722 units higher in rural households than in urban ones. Similarly, the difference in the logs of expected counts of homelessness is expected to be 0.843 units higher for cyclone-prone households than for flood-prone households. In contrast, the difference in the logs of expected counts of homelessness is expected to be 0.614 units lower for households living closer to coastline than for households living in interior areas. One explanation for this finding may be related to the availability of cyclone shelters built by the government.

Coping with the Environment

It was found that households living farther from sea sought more assistance (including loans) and widened the sources of such assistance, offered fewer days of wage labour, and were less prone to distress migration (see Table 5.12). Households with higher food security resorted to the use of savings, took loans from diverse sources, sold assets, and borrowed from NGOs. Many of these mechanisms gave them enough of a cushion to decrease the sale of labour. Rural households, generally poorer, used less of their savings, received more assistance (but less in loans) from several agencies, and had fewer mortgage-related assets. They also borrowed much less from NGOs. In short, even though natural disasters such as cyclones hit the poor and the non-poor in coastal environments alike, in coping with crisis the poor have less access to formal support and greater dependence on wage labour and distress migration.

Households exposed to the sea received less assistance and relief from the government or NGOs. They also mortgaged out and sold more

[7] The strengths of houses were measured by assigning a zero weight separately for floor, wall, and roof not made of tin or brick and a unit weight for these dimensions made of tin or brick. In the second stage, all three dimensions were added together. Thus, the outcome is a discrete variable ranging between zero and three.

TABLE 5.12 Characterization of Coping Mechanism of Households

Dependent Variables	Coping with Risks Through			
	Use of Saving	Number of Sources of Help Received	Number of Sources of Loan Received	Number of Types Assets Mortgaged
Estimation Method	Logit	Poisson	Poisson	Poisson
Distance from Sea (km)	0.002 (0.006)	0.003** (0.001)	0.004** (0.001)	0.006 (0.005)
HH Food Security Status	0.322*** (0.056)	0.014 (0.011)	0.041*** (0.011)	0.227*** (0.044)
HH Is Rural = 1	−1.345** (0.643)	0.371** (0.148)	−0.230* (0.135)	−0.958** (0.438)
HH Is Exposed to Sea = 1	0.420 (0.388)	−0.431*** (0.089)	0.177*** (0.088)	0.703** (0.311)
HH Is Cyclone Prone =1	−0.336 (0.285)	−0.171* (0.102)	−0.202** (0.099)	−1.040*** (0.291)
HH Received Remittance =1	0.660 (0.449)	−0.347** (0.165)	−0.274* (0.160)	0.123 (0.429)
Extent of Amenity in the Village	−0.232** (0.100)	−0.023 (0.023)	−0.059** (0.024)	−0.200** (0.089)
LR Test $\chi^2(k)$	67.47[0.00]	76.90[0.00]	41.65[0.00]	80.63[0.00]
Pseudo R^2	0.207	0.049	0.030	0.208
Observations	532	532	532	532

(Cont'd)

TABLE 5.12 (Cont'd)

Dependent Variables	Coping with Risks Through			
	Sale of Assets	Sale of Labour	Distress Migration	GO/NGO Relief/Assistance
Estimation Method	Negative Binomial	Poisson	Poisson	Poisson
Distance from Sea (km)	0.002 (0.003)	−0.015*** (0.004)	−0.011** (0.004)	0.002 (0.002)
HH Food Security Status	0.096*** (0.022)	−0.110*** (0.023)	−0.026 (0.025)	0.010 (0.013)
HH Is Rural =1	−0.048 (0.265)	−0.147 (0.292)	−0.471 (0.329)	0.176 (0.169)
HH Is Exposed to Sea = 1	0.515*** (0.166)	0.145 (0.174)	−0.026 (0.201)	−0.307*** (0.105)
HH Is Cyclone Prone = 1	−0.844*** (0.172)	−0.675*** (0.180)	−0.879*** (0.206)	−0.419*** (0.113)
HH Received Remittance = 1	0.245 (0.250)	−0.663 (0.429)	−0.611 (0.470)	−0.734*** (0.235)
Extent of Amenity in the Village	−0.090* (0.047)	−0.059 (0.051)	−0.101* (0.061)	−0.014 (0.027)
LR Test $\chi^2(k)$	71.64[0.00]	88.82[0.00]	52.04[0.00]	76.05[0.00]
Pseudo R^2	0.081	0.123	0.087	0.059
Observations	532	532	532	532

Source: Authors' compilation.

Notes: (a) The reference category for 'rural' is 'urban'; for 'exposed to sea' is 'interior'; for 'cyclone prone' is 'flood prone'; and for 'environment dependent' and 'not environment dependent' major occupational categories it is 'other occupational categories'. (b) Figures in parentheses are cluster (union) robust standard errors, where applicable. Figures with one, two, or three asterisks indicate significance at 10%, 5%, and 1% error probability levels, respectively. Figures in square brackets are p-values. (c) The socio-demographic characteristics of the households controlled in the regressions are not reported, for the sake of brevity.

in assets to cope with disasters. While cyclone-prone households sold less in the way of assets, they also received less external assistance than their flood-prone counterparts did. Households receiving remittances appeared to be less dependent on external assistance. Households in villages with better amenities (local public goods) coped better with crises. They required less external assistance.

Main Findings and Implications for Policy

Even though there are abundant opportunities for eking out a livelihood in the coastal region of Bangladesh, the opportunities are replete with various types of vulnerability due to environmental adversities associated with living in the coastal belt. That this accentuates poverty is evident from results obtained from spatial and HIES data. The PSM results confirm the maintained hypothesis of 'environmental poverty adversities'. This excess burden of poverty comes from the higher exposure to environmental risks in the coastal region.

The micro-survey evidence further shows that these risks are manifest in several areas of household existence—food insecurity, ill health, and sickness, the loss of natural resource dependent livelihoods, and increased homelessness. The poor, especially those living near the sea, have to rely more on wage labour, mortgage/sales of assets, and distress migration. And they also get less assistance from the government and NGOs. Although the non-poor are also vulnerable to risks while residing in these environments, they tend to have better coping capacities and more access to formal credit and other forms of support. These results have implications in the context of climate change in terms of developing short-term coping strategies within the current 'natural habitat' of the poor, and in terms of long-term exit policies through human capital and migration to urban areas.

References

Ahmad, M. 2005. *Living in the Coast: Urbanization*. Dhaka, Bangladesh: Program Development Office, Integrated Coastal Zone Management Plan, Water Resources Planning Organization, Ministry of Water Resources, Government of the People's Republic of Bangladesh.

Arvis, J., G. Raballand, and J.F. Marteau. 2010. *The Cost of Being Landlocked: Logistics, Costs, and Supply Chain Reliability*. Washington D.C.: World Bank.

BBS. 2000. *Report on the Household Income and Expenditures Survey, 2000*, Bangladesh Bureau of Statistics, Dhaka.

———. 2003. *Population Census, 2001*. National Report (Provisional). Dhaka: Bangladesh Bureau of Statistics.

———. 2005. *Report on the Household Income and Expenditures Survey, 2005*. Dhaka: Bangladesh Bureau of Statistics.

———. 2009. *Updating Poverty Maps of Bangladesh*. Dhaka: World Bank, Bangladesh Bureau of Statistics, and World Food Programme.

———. 2010. *Report on the Household Income and Expenditures Survey, 2010*. Dhaka: Bangladesh Bureau of Statistics.

Chambers, R. and G. Conway. 1992. *Sustainable Rural Livelihoods: Practical Concepts for the 21st Century*. Sussex, UK: Institute of Development Studies.

Hahn, M.B., A.M. Reiderer, and S.O. Foster. 2009. 'The Livelihood Vulnerability Index: A Pragmatic Approach to Assessing Risks from Climate Variability and Change—A Case Study in Mozambique'. *Global Environmental Change* 19: 74–88.

Islam, M.R. and M. Ahmad. 2004. *Living in the Coast: Problems, Opportunities, and Challenges*. Dhaka: Program Development Office, Integrated Coastal Zone Management Plan, Water Resources Planning Organization, Ministry of Water Resources, Government of the People's Republic of Bangladesh.

Narayan, A., N. Yoshida, and H. Zaman. 2007. *Trends and Patterns of Poverty in Bangladesh in Recent Years*. Washington D.C.: World Bank.

Ravallion, Martin and Quentin Wodon. 1997. 'Poor Areas, or Only Poor People?' Policy Research Working Paper, Series 1798, World Bank, Washington D.C.

Sen, B. and Z. Ali. 2009. 'Spatial Inequality in Social Progress in Bangladesh'. *Bangladesh Development Studies*: 32(2): 53–78.

Toufique, K.A., and M. Yunus. 2013. 'Vulnerability of Livelihoods in the Coastal District of Bangladesh', Bangladesh Development Studies 36(1): 95–120.

Uddin, A.M.K. and R. Kaudstaal. 2003. *Delineation of the Coastal Zone*. Dhaka: Program Development Office, Integrated Coastal Zone Management Plan, Water Resources Planning Organization, Ministry of Water Resources, Government of the People's Republic of Bangladesh.

6

MOHD. SHAHADT HOSSAIN MAHMUD

Climate Change and Coastal Poverty in Bangladesh

One-third of Bangladesh is close enough to the Bay of Bengal to be considered as a coastal zone. This area is especially vulnerable to climate change. Its vulnerability increases daily, and daily the poverty of coastal population is aggravated. The Government of Bangladesh (GoB) has initiated some measures to address this problem. Although the initiatives have implications for coastal poverty, they are insufficient. Bangladesh needs to scale up those initiatives and explore other possibilities. In this chapter, I

- present an overview of coastal areas of Bangladesh and the livelihood pattern of its people;
- explain the poverty situation of coastal population and the problems that will be caused by climate change;
- depict disaster management approach of Bangladesh, including its climate risk management framework; and
- talk about initiatives taken by the GoB to address coastal poverty, achievements, lessons learnt, and the way forward.

Overview

Bangladesh is the largest low-lying deltaic country in the world. It was formed by the deposits of mud and sand left behind by three gigantic river systems, namely the Brahmaputra, the Ganges, and the Meghna. It is crisscrossed by over 270 rivers and tributaries. It covers an area of 143,998 sq. km and has 156 million people. According to the 2001 population census, the coastal zone of the country has 6.85 million households with 35.1 million people. The average per capita yearly income is US$574. This densely populated, agrobased, very poor country is prone to natural disasters due to its geographical location and the monsoon climate. During last 20 years, 5 devastating floods and 4 catastrophic cyclones hit the country, causing deaths of about half a million people and economic damage equivalent to US$5.6 billion (Mahmud 2010).

The 'coastal zone' of Bangladesh is made up of the 19 districts (out of the country's 64) that are closest to the Bay of Bengal. These 19 districts cover about a third (32%) of the county's area and more than one-fourth (28%) of the total population. The social and ecological setting of this zone differs from rest of the country. It is more vulnerable to global warming–linked climate changes. And that vulnerability is increasing day by day, aggravating the poverty of coastal population (PDO-ICZMP 2004b).

Although the coastal zone possesses a wide range of opportunities for contributing to national development, those opportunities were unexplored and did not received much attention until the mid-1990s. Accordingly, a context of insecurity was created there, which discouraged investment and squeezed the economic activities of coastal people. The coastal vulnerabilities attracted the attention of the government after the mid-1990s, when the government realized the reality. It declared the zone to be one of three 'neglected regions' (MoP 1998) and acknowledged it was 'vulnerable to adverse ecological processes' (ERD 2003). Later, the government formulated the Coastal Zone Policy, 2005 and the Coastal Development Strategy, 2006. It also established the Estuary Development Programme and other initiatives to address coastal vulnerabilities.

Climate Change

Changes to the climate that are the result of natural climatic evolution normally happen slowly. But due to effects of global warming, the trend of climate change has had added impetus in recent decades. The result has been a rapid alteration of the patterns of rainfall and temperature across the globe. One of the most negative consequences of global warming is melting of ice. That melting of snow from the Himalayans is the main cause of flooding and inundation of coastal areas of Bangladesh. Global warming–linked climate changes are hindering the livelihoods of millions of people by generating natural disasters of various types and magnitudes. Poor communities dependent on natural resources and women with limited assets and limited involvement in decision making are especially susceptible to such changes in the climate (Mahmud 2010).

The threat that climate change poses to animals and wildlife has made combating it one of the top priorities of nature conservancy. Some experts expect one-fourth of the earth's species to be extinct by 2050, if the warming trend continues at its current rate. Conservation scientists see climate change as the biggest threat to the biosphere, lands, and water. As temperatures rise, the heat-related illness, flooding, severe storms in coastal areas, and insect-borne diseases will increase.

Bangladesh is susceptible to climate change because of its geographical location. Its deltaic shape at the funnel of sea has made it vulnerable to all sorts of hazards related to the ocean storms and river flooding. Other reasons are:

- monsoon climate and topography,
- huge network of rivers and channels,
- enormous discharge of water heavily laden with sediment,
- large number of islands between the channels,
- shallow funnelling to the coastal area, and
- strong tidal and wind action.

Coastal Zone and Coastal Poverty

In Bangladesh, the coastal zone is quite different from rest of the country. This chapter indicates that the natural resources of the coastal zone are so different from the rest of the country so as to require special forms of management. The coastal zone contains terrestrial and aquatic habitats, such as mangrove forests, wetlands, and tidal flats, which are critical for human and nature's survival in those areas. It has the world's largest mangrove forest (the Sundarbans), the longest sandy beach (Cox's

Bazar), and 72 offshore islands (including the attractive coral landmass, Saint Martin). The coastal zone has a lower population density, higher literacy rates, better gender balance, special livelihood groups (marine fishers, salt farmers, *bawali*, and *mawali*), large disadvantaged groups (erosion victims, island dwellers), and distinct ethnic communities (Rakhaine, Pundra-Khatrio, Munda, and Mahato).

The coastal zone of Bangladesh has diverse resources, including mangroves, coastal and marine fisheries, coastal agriculture, shrimp, crab, and salt. There is also land generated through accretion that may provide settlement facilities for the growing coastal population. Some employment opportunities for coastal population can be created by the management of (a) on-shore and offshore oil and gas fields and other energy sources (e.g., wind, tidal energy), (b) seaports at Mongla and Chittagong and surrounding industrial infrastructure, and (c) tourism opportunities at coastal beaches, islands, and the Sundarbans. Yet vast the population residing in the coastal zone have distressing lives as victims of cyclone, storm surge, drainage congestions, salinity intrusion, land erosion, and climate changes. The major livelihood groups are presented in Table 6.1.

TABLE 6.1   Major Livelihood Groups of Coastal Bangladesh

Livelihood Group	% of HHs	Remarks
Rural Areas:		
Farm labour	25.5	Estimates are based on the 2001
Small farmer	25.2	Population Census and Census of
Medium and large farmer	6.7	Agriculture. Population Census of 2001 indicates that rural households
Fisherman	7.5	are 76.7%. In this table the same
Salt farmer	0.6	is calculated 81.2%. The reason of
Shrimp fry collector	2.7	slightly higher percentage is some
Forest resource collector	1.7	groups (salt farmer, shrimp fry collector and forest resource collector)
Others	11.3	are included in other groups.
Urban Areas:		
Poor	11.7	The 2001 Population Census indicates
Non-Poor	11.7	that urban households are 23.3% equally divided into poor and non-poor.

Source: PDO-ICZMP (2004b).

A unique feature of the coastal zone is its distinct vulnerabilities that many people face. Coastal people are vulnerable to climate change induced hazards because they live in a volatile estuarine environment facing all threats that originate from the ocean. Besides, there are threats of climate change from upstream land and water uses. These threats affect almost every aspect of live and limit livelihood choices of the people. Major vulnerabilities are described in Table 6.2.

The coastal zone is slightly more income-poor than the rest of the country. Average per capita GDP of coastal population in 1999–2000 (at current market price) was BDT 18,198 compared to BDT 18,291 outside the coastal zone. Here, poor and extreme poor account for 52% and 25% against national average of 49% and 23% respectively. Despite the rich sources of marine food, the calorie intake of the poor is lower than that of the population residing outside the coastal zone. Out of

TABLE 6.2   Overview of Vulnerabilities in Coastal Bangladesh

Vulnerabilities	Vulnerable Areas	Present Status	Aggravation
Cyclone, storm surge	Islands, exposed areas	Devastating but seasonal	Increasing
Land erosion	Estuaries, islands, rivers	Serious but seasonal	Increasing
Flood	Exposed areas	Serious but seasonal	Increasing
Drainage congestion	Khulna, Jessore, Noakhali	Localized but year round	Increasing
Salinity Intrusion	Exposed areas	Localized and seasonal	Increasing
Drought	Satkhira	Localized and seasonal	Increasing
Earthquake	Chittagong	Unpredictable	Increasing
Arsenic contamination	All over	Serious and year round	Increasing
Ecosystem degradation	Marine, the Sundarbans	Serious and year round	Increasing
Pollution	Chittagong, Khulna	Serious and year round	Increasing
Climate change	All over	Serious and year round	Increasing

Source: PDO-ICZMP (2004b).

19 coastal districts, extreme poverty is the main feature in 3, with much lower GDP per capita in seven districts and higher GDP per capita in two districts. Among the livelihood groups, incidence of poverty is highest among agricultural labourers. In the coastal zone, poverty is mainly due the lack of employment and income opportunities, which is aggravating by the high population increases (BBS 2002).

To overcome coastal poverty, a quarter of a million new jobs need to be created annually, and about four-fifths of these jobs should be in urban areas (PDO-ICZMP 2004b). As in other areas of Bangladesh, women on the coast are poorer than the men. A widespread gender gap is prevalent in all spheres and at all levels, including health, nutrition, education, employment, and political participation. The coastal zone lacks physical facilities with respect to market infrastructure that is critical for economic life. Distances between economic potential areas are very high: for example, cities outside the coastal areas typically serve population situated in 66 sq. km, while in the coastal region it is 80 sq. km. This lower number of growth centres in the coastal areas also implies lesser market access for women and men, less economic participation, and restricted mobility (PDO-ICZMP 2004c).

Services with respect to water, sanitation, health, and electricity are poor in the coastal zone. The density of running tubewells per square kilometre is 7, compared to 8 for whole Bangladesh. Only 11% of households possess water-sealed latrine, compared to 14% nationally. One hospital bed (run by government) is available for 4,637 persons compared to 4,276 persons nationally. Access to the national electricity grid is limited to only 31% of households. It is apprehended that some parts of coastal zone, particularly remote and inaccessible offshore islands, will not be connected with the national electricity grid in the foreseeable future (PDO-ICZMP 2003).

In the coastal zone, the average area under a union parishad (UP, an administrative sub-disrict) is 35 sq. km compared to 32 sq. km outside coastal zone. Since proximity to a UP office is assumed to be positively correlated with services rendered by a UP in respective jurisdictions, we can reasonably assume that coastal people are enjoying lesser services compared to the people living outside coastal zone. Most rural households in the coastal areas are either landless or small farmers, despite social structures are mainly based on land holdings (PDO-ICZMP 2004a).

Anticipated Climate Change Impact

Climate changes have resulted in an increasing frequency and severity of natural disasters. These have harmed the ecosystem and the quality of human life. The major risks in coastal Bangladesh are as follows:

- Sea-level rise that might increase: floods and river bank erosion; salinity intrusion in agricultural lands; the shortage of pure drinking water; water logging; undesired change in bio-diversity; and loss of wildlife.
- Unpredicted rainfalls might be responsible for: droughts and decreased productivity in agriculture; deforestation and changes in cropping patterns; unemployment among agricultural labourers.
- Harm to health that might derive from: increased incidence of water-borne and air-borne diseases; bacteria and parasites of warmer and wetter conditions.
- Loss/lack of entitlements that might cause: loss of standing crops; loss/damage of livestock, dairy, poultry, and fisheries; loss of trees and fruits; loss/damage of vegetable garden.
- Disruption of social network that may create: unemployment, poverty, insecurity, crime, violence, migration.

Global temperature will have risen 1.8°C to 4.0°C by the last decade of the 21st century. This may result in 0.18 to 0.79 metres of sea-level rise.[1] Sea level is expected to rise in Bangladesh by about 88 cm by 2075.[2] This may cause inundation of 17% of the land and a salinity move up to 60 km north, heavy water logging, severe drainage congestion, disruption in coastal polders, strong cyclones and tidal surges, bigger floods, more river erosion, change in coastal morphological dynamics, and the migration of 35 million people to cities. Bangladesh is the most vulnerable country in the world to tropical cyclones and the sixth most vulnerable country to floods.[3]

---

[1] See the projection of Intergovernmental Panel on Climate Change (IPCC).

[2] According to the National Adaptation Programme of Action (NAPA).

[3] According to UNDP.

Disaster Management Approach in Bangladesh

Bangladesh has created a simple model to guide disaster risk reduction and emergency response management efforts. There are two major components of the comprehensive disaster management model: (a) risk reduction and (b) emergency response. Risk reduction has another two elements: (a) defining risk environment and (b) managing the risk environment. The key characteristics of this model are as follows:

- It provides a framework to guide the achievement of the Hyogo Framework for Action commitments.
- It articulates the elements of disaster management and their interactive relationships.
- It facilitates a transition from generic hazard-based programmes to specific risk-based programmes through the inclusion of technical inputs.
- It provides guidance for the design of policy, planning, and training.
- It provides a mechanism for achieving consistency in process and methodology.
- It ensures preparedness and response strategies that are influenced by technical and traditional considerations.

In Bangladesh, disaster risk reduction and climate change adaptation are instrumental for reducing the vulnerability of communities and for achieving sustainable development. This is because climate change is altering disaster risk, not only through increased weather-related risks, sea-level rise, and temperature and rainfall variability, but also through increases in societal vulnerabilities from stresses on water availability, agriculture, and ecosystems. While climate change adaptation is an adjustment in natural and human systems, disaster risk reduction is the development and application of policies and practices that minimize risks to vulnerabilities and disasters. Thus, disaster risk reduction, as an essential part of adaptation, is providing the first line of defence against climate change effects. Bangladesh developed a climate risk management framework to overview the links between mitigation, climate risk management, and disaster risk reduction and their relationship with development and sector planning Figure 6.1.

In Bangladesh, climate change threatens both previous achievements and future efforts to reduce poverty. In order to address this problem,

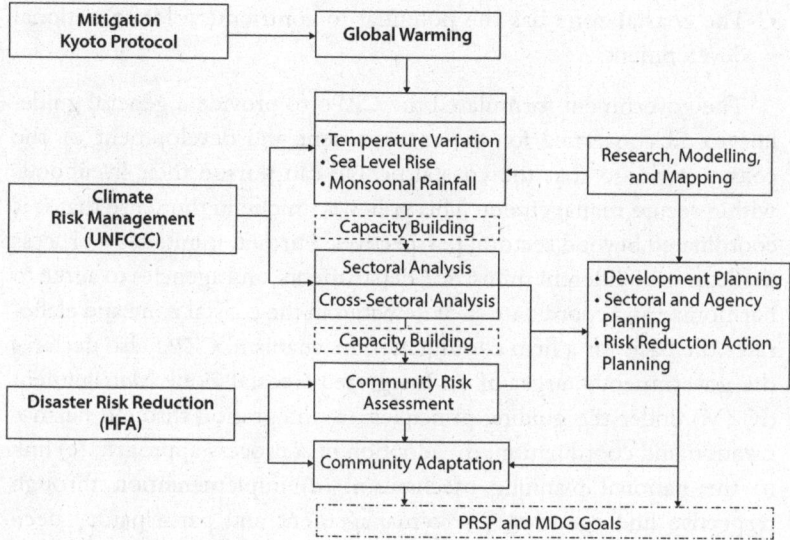

FIGURE 6.1   Climate Risk Management Framework

the government initiated the Comprehensive Disaster Management Programme (CDMP) in 2004 as a way of achieving the government's Vision and Mission on Disaster Management. Meanwhile CDMP developed a framework model for mainstreaming disaster risk reduction in government programmes through promoting community-level adaptation that at the same time create sustainable livelihood activities, thereby contributing to poverty reduction.

Coastal Zone Policies in Bangladesh

The GoB developed Coastal Zone Policy (CZPo) in 2005, reflecting new thinking about the role of policy in development. The government gave the following three reasons for initiating the CZPo:

- The coastal zone is lagging behind the rest of the country in socio-economic development.
- Weak number and quality of initiatives in the coastal areas to cope with different disasters and gradual deterioration of the environment.

• The coastal zone has the potential to contribute a lot to national development.

The government formulated the CZPo to provide a general guideline to all concerned for the management and development of the coastal zone, so that the coastal people can pursue their livelihoods within secure management. This policy is unique in the sense that it is coordinated beyond sectoral perspectives. Further, it initiates a process that commits different ministries, departments, and agencies to agree to harmonize and coordinate their activities in the coastal zone and elaborates the basis for a firm coordination mechanism. CZPo also declares the government's target of an Integrated Coastal Zone Management (ICZM) under the guiding principles: (a) integration through harmonization and coordination; (b) adoption of a process approach; (c) link to the national planning mechanism; (d) implementation through respective line agencies; (e) co-management and participatory decision; (f) gender equality; (g) participatory monitoring and evaluation; (h) supporting the national policies of decentralization and the development of the private sector; (i) interventions based on the best available knowledge; (j) efforts to fill knowledge gaps; and (k) priority setting on issues of the coastal zone. The goal of ICZM is to create conditions in which the reduction of poverty, the development of sustainable livelihoods, and the integration of the coastal zone into the national process can take place (MoWR 2005).

Coastal Policy Framework and Development Strategy

The GoB has made its coastal zone policy statements in relation to development objectives. They provide general guidelines for coastal people to pursue their livelihoods under secured conditions. The policy framework covers economic growth, basic needs, opportunities for livelihoods, the reduction of vulnerabilities, sustainable management of natural resources, equitable distribution, empowerment of communities, women's development, gender equity, and the conservation and enhancement of critical ecosystems. Measures will be taken to realize the objectives and poverty reduction through enhancing economic growth in the coastal zone. In this regard, the available economic opportunities of the coastal zone will be further enhanced through sustainable management practices in order to improve the living standards of the coastal communities. This is done by investing in different sectors, such as marine fisheries, salt production, shrimp culture, crab culture, shell culture, pearl culture, livestock development, area-based agriculture development and agrobased industries, transport, ship building, ship-breaking, tourism, extraction of beach minerals, and renewable and non-renewable energy.

With regard to basic needs and opportunities for livelihood, the coastal zone was lagging behind the areas of water and sanitation, energy, health, agriculture, and biodiversity adopted in 2002 World Summit on Development. To address this unexpected situation, GoB prescribed policies to alleviate poverty through creation of job opportunities; finding options for diversified livelihoods; increase coverage of primary education, health care, sanitation, and safe drinking water facilities; increase production of diversified high-value export goods; and introduce collateral-free credit under easy terms for livelihood enhancement programme. In coastal zone, agriculture continues to be a major source of employment, which is seasonal in nature. To tackle this, GoB considers that the reduction in vulnerability to natural disasters would be an integral aspect of the national strategies for poverty reduction and integration will be made with 'Comprehensive Disaster Management Plan' on aspects concerning the coastal zone (MoWR 2005).

The GoB has given adequate importance on diverse natural resources of coastal zone, such as inland fisheries and shrimp, marine fisheries, mangrove and other forests, land, livestock, salt, minerals, sources of renewable energy like tide, wind, and solar energy. Government has also adopted medium- and long-term policies to ensure sustainable management of both biotic and abiotic coastal resources. The policies shall lead to possible steps to secure just share from all international rivers reaching the coastal zone of the Bay of Bengal and suitable measures for sustainable use of renewable resources and, to that end, limit harvesting, extraction or utilization to the corresponding cycles of their regeneration. However, optimum utilization of resources will be ensured by taking advantage of the complementarities and trade-offs between competing uses and rigid enforcement of conservation regulations will affect the livelihoods of many people and such conservation efforts will be linked, as far as possible, with alternative opportunities of employment.

It is delineated that different kind of social, economic, and technical barriers limit the access of poor people to opportunities. Since the disadvantaged cannot get their justified share due to ineffective access mechanism, actions are designed to reach the poorest and the remote rural areas, which are vulnerable to adverse ecological processes with high concentrations of socially disadvantaged. It is planned to ensure equitable distribution of natural economic benefits to exposed coastal islands and increase access of natural resources for the disadvantaged. Coastal policy framework is included with policies of equal participation of all stakeholders in establishing effective cooperation between the government agencies and non-governmental organizations along with initiatives to keep up the cultural heritage of different communities living in the coastal zone. It also includes a gender sensitive and participatory approach that focuses on the reduction of gender inequalities and differences in needs and interests between men and women. Necessary measures are planned to conserve and develop aquatic and terrestrial including all ecosystems identified by the Bangladesh National Conservation Strategy.

GoB considering the need for an area specific programme in coastal Bangladesh firstly endorsed Integrated Coastal Zone Management Plan (ICZMP) to be implemented by Water Resources Planning Organization (WARPO) to provide directives for the development of CZPo. Later, the GoB enacted the Coastal Development Strategy (CDS) focused on the implementation of CZPo. The CDS was approved at the second meeting of the Inter-Ministerial Steering Committee on ICZMP held in 2006. It was prepared through multi-level and multi-sectoral dialogues. It describes priorities and targets based on coastal zone policy objectives and available resources. It represents a departure from 'business as usual' in the management of coastal zone using the potentials. It is in fact, a home-grown document that presents aspirations of the coastal people, developed through an extensive process of consultation, review and endorsement.

The objectives and methodologies of CDS are consistent with 'National Strategy for Accelerated Poverty Reduction' known as 'PRSP', which supports not only ICZMP but also implementation of 'Priority Investment Programme (PIP)' developed under Integrated Coastal Zone Management Plan Project (ICZMPP). CDS takes into account the strength of coastal zone that includes untapped and less explored resources, comparatively higher literacy and location of two seaports with other ancillary infrastructures. However, CDS does not represent overall framework and recipe for all development actions for the whole coast. It is a targeted process and the targeting is identified with respect to regions, disadvantaged groups, issues and opportunities. The strategic priorities of CDS evolved through a consultative process, guided interventions, and investments. These are: (a) ensuring fresh and safe water availability, (b) safety from man-made and natural hazards, (c) optimising use of coastal lands, (d) promoting economic growth emphasising non-farm rural employment, (e) sustainable management of natural resources, (f) improving livelihood condition of people, (g) environmental conservation, (h) empowerment through knowledge management, (i) creating an enabling institution (MoWR 2006).

Initiatives to Address Coastal Poverty

Coastal poverty and coastal opportunity in Bangladesh are not hidden issues; rather it is exposed to policymakers as well as development activists in many ways. But those issues were not given proper attention in the past. Recently the GoB has initiated some measures to address this problem. These are:

- PDO-ICZMP: stands Programme Development Office for Integrated Coastal Zone Management Plan, which is a programme under Water Resources Planning Organization (WARPO) of the Ministry of Water Resources (MoWR) jointly financed by the Netherlands and the UK.
- Land Reclamation: an initiative of the Bangladesh Water Development Board (BWDB) to recover accredited char and offshore lands.
- Green Belt Creation: initiative of the Department of Forest (DoF) to protect cyclone and storm surges through protection of trees.
- Char Livelihood Project: BWDB leaded initiative supported by five relevant departments to distribute khas lands among landless poor and uphold their livelihoods.
- Coastal Rehabilitation Programme: BWDB initiated programme to construct polders at different places.
- Empowerment of Coastal Fisheries Community: an initiative of the Ministry of Fisheries (MoF) to uphold the livelihood of fisher folk community.

- Coastal Afforestation Programme (on-going): a programme of the Ministry of Environment and Forest (MoEF) to create a forest on the bank of sea and coastal embankment.
- RR schemes for Sidr- and Aila-affected people: schemes of risk reduction adopted at Sidr- and Aila-affected areas by GO-NGO-INGOs and development partners.

Achievements

It is difficult to mention any significant achievement with regard to addressing coastal poverty in Bangladesh since no substantive measure was taken in this regard. Although the GoB, in addition to national-level regular safety-net programmes, has initiated some measures to address this problem, most of those were indirect in nature and had limited implications. Yet, the following steps may be treated as a first-stage achievement in the way to address coastal poverty in Bangladesh:

- CZPo, 2005: establishes the goal of ICZM to create conditions, in which the reduction of poverty, development of sustainable livelihoods and the integration of the coastal zone into national processes can take place.
- CDS, 2006: the linking pin in the ICZM process, dedicated to linking the CZPo with concrete development programmes and interventions.
- Polders, embankments, and shelters: constructed 123 polders, more than 5,000 km of embankments and more than 2,000 multi-purpose cyclone shelters.
- Land Reclamation: more than 50,000 ha of land was reclaimed along the Noakhali coast through Meghna cross dam.
- Mangrove Plantation: vast areas in newly accreted chars and islands have been put under mangrove plantation.
- Cyclone Preparedness Programme (CPP): Bangladesh Red Crescent Society (BDRCS) initiated CPP in the early 1970s that eventually developed into a world model of physical and institutional infrastructure for disaster management in cyclone prone areas.
- Promotion of Saline Tolerant HYV (BR 47, 15 types of vegetables) and implementation of various RR schemes in Sidr- and Alia-affected areas.

Lesson Learned

It is perceived that the unique development opportunities of the coastal zone are instrumental in reducing vulnerability and poverty of coastal communities. This strategy is an attempt to unlock the potentials of the coastal zone along with strategies to mitigate natural and man-made hazards and to preserve, restore, and enhance coastal ecosystems. It describes priorities and targets based on CZPo objectives and available resources. However, the following lessons are realized through different initiatives taken by GoB in addressing coastal poverty in Bangladesh:

- Favourable mindset of relevant stakeholders is essential.
- Needs horizontal-vertical integration at national, sectoral, and local levels.
- Should be emphasized in Annual Development Planning.
- Requires integration of DRR and CRM through effective partnerships among wide range of actors.
- Commitment, motivation, and financial support are very much needed to address coastal poverty.

The Way Forward

On the basis of the Coastal Zone Policy, the GoB approved the Coastal Development Strategy at the second meeting of Inter-Ministerial Steering Committee on ICZMP held in February 2006. The Coastal Development Strategy is the linking pin between the Coastal Zone Policy and concrete interventions. It prepares coordinated actions and arrangements for the implementation through selecting strategic priorities and setting targets. The government should scale up the above-mentioned initiatives. It should also scale up the management of

- land generated through natural accretion,
- diverse resources of the Sundarbans,
- coastal and marine fisheries,
- coastal agriculture, shrimp, crab, and salt,
- on-shore and offshore gas fields,
- coastal wind and tidal energy,
- sea ports located at Mongla and Chittagong, and
- tourism at beaches, islands, and the Sundarbans.

The most sensitive issue is that coastal poverty is getting worse in Bangladesh due to the negative consequences of climate change. This has occurred because of unplanned technological development and the high CO_2 emissions in developed and rapidly developing countries. Hence, the developed nations responsible for climate change should contribute to reducing coastal poverty of Bangladesh.

References

BBS. 2002. *Statistical Yearbook of Bangladesh 2001*, Bangladesh Bureau of Statistics, Dhaka.

ERD. 2003. *Bangladesh—A National Strategy for Economic Growth, Poverty Reduction and Social Development*. Dhaka: Ministry of Finance.

GoB. 2008. *Bangladesh Climate Change Strategy and Action Plan*. Dhaka: Ministry of Environment and Forest (MoEF).

Mahmud, Mohd. Shahadt Hossain. 2010. 'Disaster Management and Climate Change: Bangladesh Perspective', paper presented in the Climate Change Science-Policy Dialogue organized by BCAS in collaboration with EU, UNEP, IPCC, and some other international organizations on 9–11 February 2010 at Pan-Pacific Sonargoan Hotel, Dhaka, Bangladesh (Dialogue report is available at http://start.org/download/2010/ccmap-bangladesh-final.pdf).

Ministry of Water Resources (MoWR). 2005. *Coastal Zone Policy*, Ministry of Water Resources Organization. Dhaka: Ministry of Water Resources, Government of the People's Republic of Bangladesh.

———. 2006. *Coastal Development Strategy*. Water Resources and Planning Organization, Dhaka: Water Resources Planning Organization (WARPO).

PDO-ICZMP. 2003. *Coastal Livelihoods—Situation and Context, Programme Development Office for Integrated Coastal Zone Management Plan*. Dhaka: Water Resources Planning Organization (WARPO).

———. 2004a. *Living in the Coast—People and Livelihood, Programme Development Office for Integrated Coastal Zone Management Plan*. Dhaka: Water Resources Planning Organization (WARPO).

———. 2004b. *Living in the Coast—Problems, Opportunities and Challenges, Programme Development Office for Integrated Coastal Zone Management Plan*. Dhaka: Water Resources Planning Organization (WARPO).

———. 2004c. *Women of the Coast—A Gender Status Paper of the Coastal Zone, Programme Development Office for Integrated Coastal Zone Management Plan*. Dhaka: Water Resources Planning Organization (WARPO).

7

SHANILA ATHULATHMUDALI
AMILA BALASURIYA
KARIN FERNANDO

Adapting to Climate Change in the Coastal Areas of Sri Lanka*

Climate change threatens to affect developing countries mainly due to larger populations, less economic development, and greater levels of poverty. The situation challenges developing countries to meet economic and social development agendas with minimum impact on the natural environment, thereby advocating sustainable pathways to development. This requires building 'adaptive capacity' that encompasses a country's capabilities, resources, and institutions. Building adaptive capacity would support adapting the country's practices to achieve a sustainable balance between human and environmental well-being. In Sri Lanka, efforts to address climate change are in the early stages. The interventions are advocated, tried, and tested from policy to practice, involving a range of actors and sectors that address climate change directly. In this chapter we examine how different levels of actors attempt to address climate change. It uses an actor-based approach to

* This chapter is based on a study entitled 'Exploratory study on adapting to climate change in coastal areas of Sri Lanka' by Shanila Athulathmudali, Amila Balasuriya, and Karin Fernando, published in 2011.

analysing elements that aid and impede adaptation. We highlight issues that can aid better climate change adaptation. The study focuses on agriculture, fisheries, and tourism livelihoods that are important to the poor coastal communities in Sri Lanka.

Setting the Context: Climate Change, Coastal Zones, and Livelihoods

For Sri Lanka, climate change is expected to have a significant effect on sectors such as water, agriculture, fisheries, and health (GSL 2000). As the country is a small island, its coastal areas become a geographic impact zone at risk from sea-level rise, storms, coastal erosion, and inundation (Jayatilake 2008). Coastal areas are inhabited by 25% of the population (MoE 2010b), and large tracts of the coastal belt are already under pressure from a host of human-induced environmental degradations, which will be exacerbated by climate change (Pallewatta 2010). Tourism, fisheries, and agriculture play a significant role in the livelihoods of coastal communities who share the coastal vulnerability.

The agricultural sector employs 33% of the nation's labour force as landed farmers and casual and wage labourers (DCS 2009). Rice is a widespread crop and is essential for food security. It is one of the crops vulnerable to climate change threats, such as prolonged droughts, weather variability, and high temperatures (MoE 2010d). Temperature rise and reduced rainfall can lead to reduced productivity because of spikelet sterility, soil moisture stress, and salinization (Punyawardena 2007). Further, sea-level rise can lead to salt water intrusion and erosion that will exacerbate land scarcity (Punyawardena 2007).

So far, the effects of climate change on fisheries have not been assessed, but climate change is expected to have a wide range of effects on the production, availability, and breeding patterns of aquatic life (Jayatilake 2008). Rising temperatures in the oceans result in sea-level rise, frequent storm surges, increase in coastal erosion, and coastal flooding that will bring changes to coastal and marine habitats. Changes to the habitats can affect the breeding grounds (that is, mangroves, wetlands, coral reefs) of both coastal and marine species that will, in turn, affect the fisheries industry and coastal communities who depend on these resources (MoE 2010d).

Sri Lanka's tourism sector is driven by coastal attractions. According to a visitor survey conducted by the Sri Lanka Tourism Development Authority (SLTDA), 62% of visitors cited the beach as the main reason for them to visit the country (SLTDA 2009a). For the tourism sector, climate change can lead to loss of beach areas, more frequent storms and flooding, and degradation of coastal habitats that then reduce the appeal of the destination, the value of assets, and revenue (MoE 2010b).

Conceptual Framework and Methodology

Coping versus Adaptation

Coping is an immediate to short-term reactive response to changes in the immediate spatial environment. It is a way of getting by in uncertain situations (Berkes and Jolly 2001). It is a temporary adjustment. Adaptation is a medium- to long-term response to climate stimuli. It is a quasi-permanent adjustment. It can be a response to changes that have already happened or it can be a response to expected future changes. It can reduce negative effects and capitalize on opportunities created by particular phenomenon (IPCC 2007). Initial coping may give way to longer term adaption as a way of dealing with recurring events.

Adaptive Capacity

Adaptive capacity of a country is the ease with which it can position itself to make changes that will offset the effects of climate change. This depends on a country's skills and resources to make these changes (UNEP 2009). Adaptive capacity has the following four elements:

- Ecosystem resilience—the ability of different stakeholders to use and work within the natural ecosystem without damaging what is already in existence.
- Knowledge chains—access by different stakeholders to information and systems in place for information sharing, to appropriate training that will provide the necessary skills, and use of technical innovations.

- Supportive governance structures—how adaptation is integrated and prioritised in development planning and implementation.
- Socioeconomic conditions—the ability for interventions (or adaptive measures) to bring about livelihood security and the suitability of interventions to social/cultural norms.

Increasing adaptive capacity involves a range of stakeholders—policymakers, government, non-government, private sector, community groups, and individuals. It is described as a cascading system where there are different levels (local, national, and international) and different stakeholders/institutions whose cooperation and commitment determines how decisions are taken to adapt to climate change (Adger, Arnelll, and Tompkins 2005). This process increases in complexity also due to the fact that different stakeholders tend to respond to the same climate stimuli with different perspectives, depending on their capacities, experiences, social interactions, agendas, and power dynamics (Long 2001).

Hence, the conceptual framework illustrated in Figure 7.1 examines how the four elements of adaptive capacity are addressed amongst four large stakeholder categories (policymakers, sectoral/institutional actors, civil society, and the community/individuals) to understand

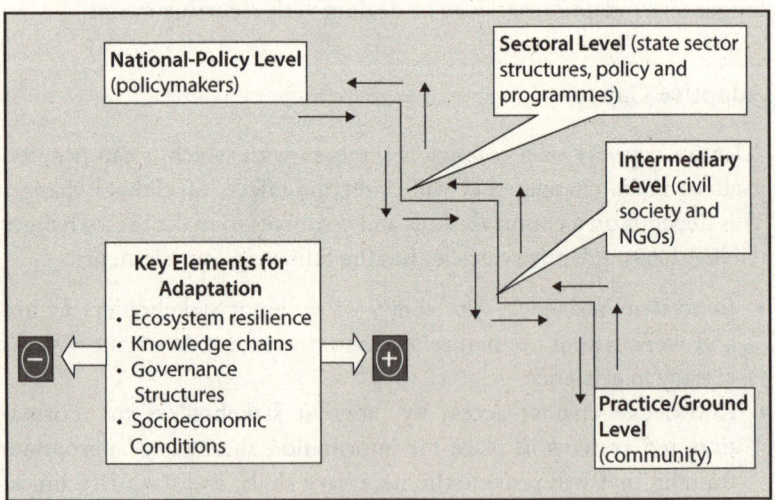

FIGURE 7.1 Illustrated Conceptual Framework
Source: This was constructed by CEPA for this study.

interactions that affect how adaptive measures are taken up. In this frame, the idea that there are levels at which different stakeholders interact are visualized as a cascading process with policy decisions at the macro level being placed at the top and decision taken to put things into practice—at the ground level or, in other words, at the micro level at the lower end. There are also intermediate levels in this process. At each level there are different interactions and the interplay of stakeholders. The arrows indicate that the interactions flow in both directions influencing both policy and practice.

The study aims to answer the following questions:

- What simulates adoption of adaptation strategies?
- How do different stakeholders aid adaptation?
- What issues should be addressed if we want to aid scale-up?

Methodology

This study used a qualitative approach, based on literature reviews, focus groups' discussions, and key person interviews to review policies and implementation processes that captured the stakeholder perspective. One sample site was selected for each of the livelihood groups (agriculture, fisheries, and tourism). At each site we traced the chain of interactions down to a community-centred implementation level. The sample sites were selected based on a vulnerability mapping (MOE 2010b; 2010d) that mapped climate threats with social and economic indicators. This was also matched with district poverty data (DCS 2008) to choose sites in districts with high levels of poverty. Specific livelihoods groups were selected based on livelihoods that show a greater degree of poverty, such as small-scale agriculture, fisheries, and tourism activities.

The sites were elected to capture communities engaged in rain-fed rice farming (in the village of Bundala on the south coast), coastal fisheries (in Kalpitiya, on the north-west coast), and small-scale tourism enterprises, such as small guest houses and tour operations (in Bentota on the south-west coast).

Fifteen interviews were conducted in the three sectors. Focus group discussions were conducted in the fisheries community. The president of the farming society was interviewed in the agriculture sector and randomly selected individuals involved in tourism were interviewed to get micro-level information from the tourism sector.

The study was designed to capture links moving from macro to micro, looking at how various actors affected implementation. The limitations to this study were that it focused only on primary actors and links and did not capture auxiliary links. It was also limited to one case study application and the insights are set within these parameters.

Modalities of Addressing Climate Change Adaptation

Actions at National-Policy Level

Tackling climate change and integrating it into development policy is at its infancy in Sri Lanka, but it is supported by the government. The President's *Ten-year Development Framework* recognizes the need for sustainable development (MoFP 2006). Furthermore, the *Action Plan* of the National Council for Sustainable Development has been established to promote sustainable practices amongst multiple sectors such as solid waste management, water management, and conservation (NCSD 2009). The main government entity entrusted with developing policy for climate change, adaptation, mitigation, and clean development mechanism is the Ministry of Environment (MoE). While the government at the highest level has affirmed the importance of environmental and climate change–related problems, the resultant programmes often lack sectoral buy-ins, and as a result do not reach the people in need.

Sectoral Policies and Implementation

Climate change will affect a variety of sectors. Dealing with climate change requires integrating this fact into policies and plans. A brief overview of how stakeholders in the three selected sectors are dealing with climate change is presented in the following paragraphs.

Agriculture Sector

The policy directives of the agriculture sector are driven by the objectives of socioeconomic development and increased productivity linked to food security. The policy also highlights the need to apply sustainable principles, such as sustainable cultivation, water management, organic fertilizer, and climate-resistant seed varieties. Furthermore, it acknowledges the need for livelihood support, such as information, technology, credit, and insurance. The departments of agriculture and agrarian development link policies to practice. The Department of Agriculture is involved in achieving an equitable and sustainable agricultural development through the development and dissemination of improved agricultural technology. The Department of Agrarian Development provides services and facilities to farmers. There are other institutions such as non-governmental organizations (NGOs) that provide information, technical assistance, raw material supply, infrastructure support, experimentation with crops, and processing and marketing techniques that aim to promote sustainable farming.

Rice, being the staple food in Sri Lanka, has seen the most adaptations. Most of the assistance provided to farmers is based on livelihood support, while a few directly target climate change. Farmers have also been changing their practices over time to capitalize on markets and adjust to changing conditions by using both traditional and new techniques.

A case study of traditional seeds that could overcome salinity was conducted in the Bundala village located in the semi-arid coastal area of Hambantota District, in southern Sri Lanka. The area features a wetland ecosystem. The average annual rainfall is 1,074 mm, which allows for one good rain-fed rice cultivation season per year. The primary income source in the village is from rice cultivation and salt production.

Salinity was one of the main deterrents to the rice industry in Bundala, leading to large areas of rice lands remaining uncultivated for over 20 years. In 2005, there was renewed interest in cultivating these lands spurred on by a government programme. However, attempts were not successful, and the Rice Research Institute (RRI) deemed the area unsuitable for cultivation. Some of the villagers were determined to find a solution. The National Federation for Conservation of Traditional Seeds and Agriculture Resources (NFCTSAR) carried out a series of programmes to convince the community to experiment with traditional varieties. One farmer experimented with two traditional varieties in several abandoned rice fields. At the end of the season, one of the traditional varieties produced a good yield. This proved to be a catalyst for other farmers leading to support from agriculture services. The Department of Agrarian Development worked with the farmer society and NGOs to enact the provisions of the Agrarian Development Act (number 46), which allowed farmers cultivating on abandoned lands to have the sole rights to the rice harvest for five years. They assisted landless farmers to sign a Memorandum of Understanding with landowners for the use of abandoned rice lands. The Department of Agriculture provided the seed and the abandoned rice fields have now been revived.

Fisheries Sector

The fisheries policy has five objectives: increasing national fish production, increasing employment opportunities and aquatic product exports, while minimizing post-harvest losses, improving the quality and safety of fish products, and conserving aquatic environment (MOFAR 2006). The thrust of the latest policy is also implicit in tackling environmental problems through the conservation of coastal and aquatic environments in its 10-year development plan (MOFAR 2007). With the end of the three decades of civil war,[1] the restrictions and controls on fishing activities have been removed, and the policy is encouraging a shift towards offshore fishing and aquaculture as a way of promoting alternative livelihoods. Information on new technology and sustainable practices are channelled to the fishermen through the ministry's research arms. The role of NGOs in developing sea fishing is not widespread and can be location-specific. In the following paragraph is an example of how a fisheries community is dealing with changes in their livelihoods.

A case study on how small-scale fishermen find new ways of adapting to climate change is the Kalpitiya region, a peninsula that separates the Puttalam lagoon from the Indian Ocean. The area hosts a marine

---

[1] The Civil War in Sri Lanka between the government and the militant separatist group—the Liberation Tigers of Tamil Eelam (the LTTE)—was fought over a separate state in the north and the east of the island. Due to the armed conflict, there were restrictions on fishing in the coastal areas surrounding the north and the east of the country. Fishing times and areas, especially offshore, were restricted. In addition, destructive fishing practices were also not regulated. With the end of the armed conflict in May 2009, the restrictions have been removed and new regulations have been enforced.

sanctuary and a variety of coastal habitats. This area was historically a fishing community, with some members engaged in home gardening. Most women practised animal husbandry as a secondary livelihood. During the war, the Navy had considerable control over the community's fishing activities and imposed security restrictions. This led to the use of destructive fishing techniques that went unregulated. After the war, restrictions on going out to sea have been removed. However, the community reports that the change to more environmentally safe practices is difficult. Tighter regulations and a lack of equipment for engaging in offshore fishing have reduced incomes. Coastal erosion is another threat to their livelihoods, with villagers finding it difficult to land their boats. The lack of landing sites is threatened by tourism projects, which have recently sprung up in the area. The prevailing environmental and economic conditions have led to alternative livelihoods, such as aquaculture and aloe vera cultivation. These receive aids from skills development and awareness projects carried out by the Ministry of Fisheries and NGOs. The community has also switched to tourism-related activities. The fishermen see tourism as a good income source and an employment generator for the future, but they find that poor infrastructure, inadequate lodging, and regulations by the Department of Wildlife are hindrances. In addition, the community's lack in English language skills hinders its ability to communicate with tourists. This area has also been earmarked for tourism investment by the government.

Tourism Sector

The tourism sector is one of the largest foreign exchange earners. It is highlighted in the President's *Ten-year Development Framework* as a sector of high priority. The tourism strategy, reformulated after the civil conflict, has set ambitious targets of greater economic value by opening up investment opportunities to both local and foreign investors, and intends to develop new tourism areas that remained undeveloped during the civil conflict (SLTDA 2009b). Sustainable interventions are seen in terms of niche markets, green buildings, and waste management but not as a core component of its development orientation. Beach tourism on the south coast is where a large informal tourist sector is concentrated. Though there is no data available on the number of poor households engaged in tourism, the poor are more likely to be employed as local guides, guest house owners, and souvenir vendors (Fernando and Meedeniya 2009). These are informal and unregulated jobs which can be more vulnerable to shocks. Extension services for climate change activities do not fall under the mandate of the Ministry of Tourism, which works mainly on licensing and regulating ground-level activities. The current tourism development strategy does not give priority to gearing these communities for environmental shocks.

A case study on how climate change affects tourism-related livelihoods of the poor is Beruwela, a national holiday resort located south of Colombo. The resort, which opened in 1969, has become the unofficial water sport capital of Sri Lanka. It is a popular destination for tourists. The main livelihood of this area used to be fishing. However, since the tourist resort was established, many livelihoods involve support for the tourism industry. The younger generation stays in this sector because of the good earnings. The greatest environmental concern is pollution, for which responses from local authorities are not forthcoming. Some guesthouse owners have resorted to making private arrangements to collect and dispose of waste.

For tour boat operators, pollution of the waterways and surrounding areas is a major deterrent to their business. They are not directly hurt by coastal erosion. They reported a reduction in beach erosion after a sea wall was built to protect beaches from erosion in front of high-end resort hotels. While the civil war acted as deterrent to tourism, new global threats like the financial crisis of 2008/09 also had impacts on tourism. The perceived repercussion is that there are now fewer tourists spending money on lodging, tours, shopping, and water sports. Other threats are 'beach boys' (touts) and souvenir sellers who harass guests along the beach and outside hotel premises. The tourist police have taken steps to address this problem.

For both small guesthouse owners and tour boat operators there has been limited livelihood assistance through the government tourism arms or civil society groups. The guest houses are inspected by the Tourist Board, but no assistance has been given when changes are required. Tour operators who own boats need to be registered with the port and the Navy and have relevant identification and insurance arrangements. The Water Sports Association arranges meetings every two or three months to provide safety training for water sports and its equipment.

Since the war ended, guesthouse owners and tour boat operators have been positive about the future of the industry. They expect a rise in foreign and local tourists to the area. They hoped to welcome tourists from more non-traditional regions as part of the 'Visit Sri Lanka 2011' campaign. They are gearing up to capitalize on the increase in tourism and for the moment do not feel that they are going to be adversely affected by climate change in the future and therefore do not feel the urgency to put in place any protective measures.

Findings

Enablers and Hurdles of Adaptive Capacity

Adaptive capacity requires a combination of four components—environmental resilience, knowledge chains, socioeconomic conditions, and supportive governance structures. This section discusses the enablers and hurdles based on these components within different levels of actors (Tables 7.1 and 7.2).

At the policy level, attempts have been made to highlight the need to bring in principles of sustainable development into development planning and put in place suitable frame conditions. There is a small push towards sustainable development through national initiatives. Climate change policies and strategies have been initiated to provide overall direction. In order to formulate these polices and strategies, consultative approaches were used to share technical information, provide a space for dialogue and to influence sectoral policies to integrate climate change issues into their working areas.

Despite these favourable conditions, and the attempts to get sectoral buy-in, applying the principles of these policies and strategies is not mandatory. In addition, while the MoE is responsible to push this agenda, they do not have structures for implementation except on a demonstration scale. The Ministry's role is limited to coordinating, lobbying, and relying on other ministries to filter adaptation activities and programmes through their institutional structures and administrative systems. This is hindered by a lack of incentives and financial resources that can be utilized for implementation, leaving it up to each sector to provide the stewardship needed for adaptation. At the sectoral levels, sector-specific research, extension, and information services allow for

TABLE 7.1 Enablers to Adaptive Capacity

	National-Policy Level	Sectoral Level	Intermediary Level	Practice / Ground Level
Ecosystem resilience	International concern on climate change	Overall focus recognizes the need	International concern and support; Priority given to increase sustainable practices; Can put in place location-/threat-specific interventions	Prevailing conditions leading to innovations
Knowledge chains	Better understanding of climate change and its cross-cutting impacts at the policymakers / decisionmaker level; Using consultative methods to get stakeholder / sectoral buy-in	Ability to carry out sector-/product-based research (not for tourism); Access to information; Availability of technology	Access to wider knowledge and resources; Bottom-up information flow; Bridging gap of new technology and traditional; Applying the research in the field; Use of media to disseminate	Champions—to be catalysts to take the risk to demonstrate to others; Able to use existing skills and knowledge—to convert known practices
Governance structure	Presidential backing for sustainable development; Flexibility within the policy to consider the uncertainty of climate change; Sectoral buy-in and focus areas through climate change strategy	Existing implementation arms (not the same for all sectors); Institutional structures and developed administrative	Ability to work at different levels—lobby for policy change, pilot at ground level; Influencing local and provincial decisionmakers to support CCA activities	Support from extension services (to a limited extent for sustainable practices)

	Institutional structures and developed administrative systems that can be used	systems that can be used for information, support etc. (top-down)	Building collective voice through networks and lobbying for change	Support from external organizations—guidance, finances, technology (old /new)
Socioeconomic	The focus is on creating win-win situations that balance development/growth needs with environmental protection/conservation needs	Post-war context has created new opportunities for income and employment	Financial resources	Area- and problem-specific interventions
			Promoting it as a supplementary or complementary activity	Capitalizing on niche markets
				Promotions of other benefits—environmental, health—externally driven

Source: KPIS and FGDs in sample sites.

TABLE 7.2 Hurdles to Adaptive Capacity

	National-Policy Level	Sectoral Level	Intermediary Level	Practice/Ground Level
Ecosystem resilience	Uncertainty in the science Location- and threat-specific (hence action cannot be generalized)	New, not well-understood, complex nature of the science Uncertainty in the science	Needs to be coupled with economic incentives	Although climatic threats are understood the need to act now, taking preventative action is not priority (that is, sea-level rise)
Knowledge chains	Very new subject Not well-understood, knowledge confined to academic levels Poor coordination between the ministries to share information	Sectoral agendas determine type of work of information that flows to the ground level (Alternatives get low priority) There are few mechanisms to feed information from the ground up to influence sectoral policy	Mainstream not supportive Technology that is introduced not always practical or relevant Information flow to influence policy not well structured	Types of information in the mainstream promotes status quo (agri-extension, fisheries) applications are scattered and long-term success is not high, hence lack of interventions to promote/learn from
Governance Structure	Climate change policy cannot be generalized No implementation arm—can only promote and lobby The decision-making process doesn't focus on	Mis-match between policy and what is practically possible Balancing of objectives—between food security, economic growth and sustainability	NGO/environmental lobby perceived as negative Certain government policies—that is, fertilizer subsidy act as deterrents Short-term nature of planning	Existing sectoral priorities and subsidies counter argue climate change adaptation Limited support to promote climate change adaptation

	financial allocation for climate change–related interventions Poor coordination between the ministries Cross-cutting nature of climate change requires ownership and buy in beyond the scope of the climate change policy	New area, not properly incorporated into existing structures, therefore limited knowledge and capacity Short-term planning that is also changing with successive ministers	Mainstream not supportive—have to be convinced and sustainability requires their buy-in Time-bound projects, ownership, ability to build sustainable structures is problematic Scattered nature of interventions make is hard to scale-up	Economic needs drive decisions and prevent risk-taking, even if they understand the negative/long-term effects Limited links with green markets Limited access to raw material Can be labour intensive requiring time and effort Time needed for experimenting as well as to yield results—therefore no immediate gains—hence risky.
Socioeconomic	Very limited finances to promote ground-level adaptation	Limited designated financial resources or fiscal incentives	Working with the most vulnerable so not easy to find risk-takers	

Source: KPIS and FGDs in sample sites.

knowledge generation and sharing.[2] This has aided the absorption of specific environmental issues into the research agenda, and those innovations that look to increase environmental resilience have been taken to the grassroots through existing extension and implementing arms. However, the bulk of research and knowledge shared is focused on increasing production. In addition, the systematic information flow is one-way. This leaves a situation where learning and experiences at the micro level do not get absorbed into programmes.

The major hurdle at the sectoral level is that although sector-specific policies acknowledge the need for sustainable practices, the sectoral objectives take priority and override the incorporation of climate change adaptation. Adaptation is hampered by limited technical knowledge of climate change issues, the uncertainty in the science, and the specificity of actions that impede generalized solutions that can be easily main-streamed. Furthermore, the short-term vision in the planning process, and changes to structures and leadership, hinder the long-term commitment needed to undertake climate change adaptation. Poor coordination between the ministries with respect to the sharing of information and collaboration reduces the push needed to apply the policy.

At the intermediary level, civil society groups are a key stakeholder. They have flexibility in scope and function and are able to give priority to environmental resilience. They are also aided through access to funds and technology that aid adaptation and give specific training, education, and awareness to various groups. The greatest asset this group of actors has is their ability to work across different levels from policy to practice.

Hurdles to adaptation for civil society groups is the fact that actors working specifically on sustainability issues are small in number, geographically scattered, and not adequate to generate a critical mass that can enable scaling-up climate change adaptation. In addition, the civil society lobby is perceived as a negative force that opposes certain government policies. This perception limits their ability to influence change. Short-term project cycles are another problem, as the projects only continue as long as they are backed by an NGO and are not absorbed into the mainstream.

---

[2] Extension services and local technical support exist in the agriculture and fisheries sectors, but not in the tourism sector.

At the local level, changes in livelihood patterns can be classed as coping as opposed to adapting. The enabling factor for all three cases has been economic benefits. However, the agriculture case study shows signs of adaptation. Prevailing environmental conditions have stimulated a change that also has economic benefits. However, at present this has not led to a complete change from conventional practices, but is done as a supplementary activity. It also shows that adaptation required a range of external actors with their infusions of funds, training, and marketing links.

Barriers to adaptation at the ground level are economic risks that poor farmers may not be willing to take. Further, the information and support for adaptation within the existing sectoral structures is limited due to sectoral agendas taking priority over sustainability. Hence the impetus to change is not created.

Way Forward for Building Adaptive Capacity

At present when looking at how decisions are made at different levels (from policy to practice) and how adaptive capacity is perceived, ecosystem resilience is the one that is given the least importance. Economic benefits override the need to put in place efforts to manage the environment, while other elements such as information available also tend to be skewed to a conventional growth model and not towards a sustainable model. Hence, building adaptive capacity requires a better understanding of this term and its components amongst the various stakeholders. It also needs to consider how different stakeholders can commit to making changes in a way that complements the different cascading levels that are in place. It is important to unravel the context, vested interests, competing agendas, capacities, and resources that exist amongst the stakeholders and to reconcile specific enablers and hurdles at each level—for example by looking to

- balance sectoral agendas and climate change–adaptation agenda— one of the most crucial challenges that needs to be addressed;
- reducing mismatches between policy and practice—where at the policy level a recommendation or a change cannot be put in place at the ground level;

- recommended adaptations at local level must balance livelihood benefits with ecosystem requirements and have to be supported by technical knowledge as well as incentives;
- access to information and better knowledge chains are critical for adoption of sustainable practices—that take information and skills from policy to practice and vice-versa—so that polices can reflect and cater to local realities;

Due to specificity of adaptation to product, location, and climate threat, a more decentralized approach may be appropriate. This may help to localize activity and hence create practical links amongst the actors. Adaptation at different levels needs to be supported by funding, technology, capacity, and experimentation to come up with specific problem solvers. Another important aspect is the time component that adaptation involves. It is a gradual process that has to work through levels of policymakers and stakeholders to get individuals on board and build resilience to climate change effect through trial, error, and research according to the specific climate threats and context.

References

Adger, N.W., N.W. Arnelll, E.L. Tompkins. 2005. 'Successful Adaptation to Climate Change across Scales', *Elsevier* 15: 77–86. Available at: http://research.fit.edu/sealevelriselibrary/documents/doc_mgr/422/UK_Successful_Adaptation_to_CC_-_Adger_et._al.,2005 pdf (accessed on 15 September 2010).

Berkes, F. and D. Jolly. 2001. 'Adapting to Climate Change: Social-Ecological Resilience in a Canadian Western Arctic Community', *Conservation Ecology*, 5(2): 18. Avialble at http://www.consecol.org/vol5/iss2/art18 (accessed on 18 August 2010).

DCS (Department of Census and Statistics). 2008. *Household Income and Expenditure Survey 2006/07*. Department of Census and Statistics. Available at: http://www.statistics.gov.lk/HIES/HIES2006.pdf (accessed in September 2010).

———. 2009. *Sri Lanka Labour Force Survey, Annual Report-2009*, Department of Census and Statistics, Colombo.

Fernando, K. and A. Meedeniya. 2009. 'Tourism Fall Out in Sri Lanka Due to Global Recession and Other Reasons, and Its Implications for Poverty Reduction', Centre for Poverty Analysis, unpublished.

Government of Sri Lanka (GOSL). 2000. *Initial National Communication under the United Nations Framework Convention on Climate Change*. Colombo: GOSL.

IPCC (International Panel on Climate Change). 2007. *Fourth Assessment Report of the Intergovernmental Panel on Climate Change*, Summary for Policymakers. Contribution of Working Group II. Available at: http://www.ipcc.ch/pdf/assessment-report/ar4/wg1/ar4-wg1-spm.pdf (accessed on 20 August 2010).

Jayatilake, A. 2008. 'Climate Change due to Global Worming: A Global Challenge in Sri Lanka Perspective', *Economic Review*, June/July 2008.

Long, N. 2001. *Development Sociology: Actor perspectives*. Routledge, USA.

Ministry of Agriculture (MoA). n.d. *National Agriculture Policy*. Available at: http://www.mimrd.gov.lk/upload/docs/1277294350E%20NATIONAL%20AGRICULTURAL%20POLICY.pdf (accessed in November 2010).

———. 2010a. 'National Climate Change Adaptation Strategy for Sri Lanka 2011 to 2016' (Final Draft), unpublished.

———. 2010b. 'Strengthening Capacity for Climate Change Adaptation Sector Vulnerability Profile: Urban Development, Human Settlements and Economic Infrastructure', Climate Change Secretariat Sri Lanka, ADB TA 7326 (SRI), Draft, unpublished.

———. 2010c. 'Strengthening Capacity for Climate Change Adaptation Sector Vulnerability Profile: Water', Climate Change Secretariat Sri Lanka, ADB TA 7326 (SRI), Draft, unpublished.

———. 2010d. 'Strengthening Capacity for Climate Change Adaptation Sector Vulnerability Profile: Agriculture and Fisheries', Climate Change Secretariat Sri Lanka, ADB TA 7326 (SRI), Draft, unpublished.

Ministry of Fisheries and Aquatic Resources (MOFAR). 2006. *The National Fisheries and Aquatic Resources Policy*, Government of Sri Lanka.

———. 2007. *Ten Year Development Policy Framework of the Fisheries and Aquatic Resources Sector*, Government of Sri Lanka.

MoFP (Ministry of Finance And Planning). 2006. 'Mahinda Chintana: Vision for a new Sri Lanka: A Ten Year Horizon Development Framework 2006-2016', Discussion Paper.

NCSD (National Council For Sustainable Development). 2009. *National Action Plan for Haritha Lanka Programme: 2010–2016*.

Pallewatta, N. 2010. 'Impacts of Climate Change on Coastal Ecosystems in the Indian Ocean Region', pp 3–16. In *Coastal Zones and Climate Change*, edited by D. Michel and A. Pandya, A. Washington: The Henry. L. Stimson Centre.

Punyawardena, B.V.R. 2007. 'Impacts of Climate Change on Agriculture in Sri Lanka and Possible Response Strategies: Impacts, Adaptation and Mitigation, National Conference on Climate Change 2007', Centre for Climate Change Studies.

Schipper, L. 2009. 'Expanding the Community of Community based Adaptation',
    SEI Stockholm Environmental Institute Policy Brief. Available at http://sei-
    international.org/publications?pid=1283 (accessed in September 2010).

Sri Lanka Tourism Development Authority (SLTDA). 2009(a). *Survey on
    Departing Foreign Tourists from Sri Lanka: Statistical Tables.* Sri Lanka Tourism
    Development Authority. Available online at http://www.sltda.lk/statistics
    (accessed in September 2009).

Sri Lanka Tourism Development Authority (SLTDA). 2009(b). *Tourism for all:
    National Strategy for Sri Lanka Tourism.* Available online at http://www.sltda.
    lk/node/431 (accessed in November 2010).

United Nations Environment Programme (UNEP). 2009. *IEA Training Manual
    Volume 2: Vulnerability and Impact Assessments for Adaptation to Climate Change,*
    UNEP DEW/1251/NA.

FLOODLAND POVERTY

8

SANTADAS GHOSH

Coping with Natural Disaster in the Sunderban Delta of India

The Sundarbans in India

The Sundarbans is the largest mangrove delta[1] in the world. It is spread across both India and Bangladesh. The Indian side contains 48 forested and 54 densely populated islands. People on these islands have very few livelihood choices due to their remoteness and a lack of infrastructure. The region is highly vulnerable according to climate change predictions. This chapter is based on a primary survey of a dispersed set of island-households on their socioeconomic conditions. It also sheds light on the coping behaviour of households after a cyclonic disaster devastated the single crop in the region. I found that with a single annual crop, households usually augmented their living by engaging in multiple earning activities, such as fishing, prawn-fry collection, and migrant labour. Sundarban islanders are not much worse off than people on the rural mainland. They have easy access to river waters for fishing. However, after a natural disaster, the coping behaviour of the households has been identified as (a) temporary migration of income

---

[1] A mangrove delta is a set of low-lying islands on a river mouth which is exposed to saline water and where mangroves are the only natural vegetations.

earners and (b) non-farm day labour. Data shows that pressure on forest and rivers had actually gone down after the disaster.

Location and Geography

The Sundarbans is the largest mangrove forest tract in the world, the largest tiger reserve, and a World Heritage Site (because of its biodiversity). It is located in the Gangetic delta, at the southern corner of the eastern state of West Bengal in India and spreads over neighbouring Bangladesh. It comprises of a large number of low-lying deltaic islands, large parts of which are periodically drowned by tidal saline water from the Bay of Bengal. On the Indian side, 48 such islands constitute the reserve forest that is home to the famous Royal Bengal Tiger, while 54 other islands are inhabited and contain a large population of tigers. The reserve forest and settlements are on two mutually exclusive sets of islands. There is no human habitation inside the reserve forest.

Officially, the Sundarban Biosphere Reserve extends beyond these islands and covers part of the mainland now. It is spread over two southern districts of West Bengal. As per the 2001 census, the total population of the Sundarban region was 3.7 million. The decennial growth rate during 1991–2001 was 17.4% (close to the state average of 17.8%). The population density as per the 2001 census was 845 per sq. km, greater than rural West Bengal's average of 676 per sq. km.[2]

This chapter deals exclusively with the Sundarbans' island population. In the absence of any estimates from secondary sources, I estimated the population of the islands to be 1.5 million. Due to their remoteness and lack of infrastructure, livelihood choices are limited compared to other 'coastal' people in the mainland. These people reside in a delicate ecological site and biodiversity hotspot. Their livelihood practices and exploitation of natural resources have important implications for sustainability and management. These islands are most vulnerable in the face of predicted sea-level rise due to climate change.

In this chapter, I explore the socioeconomic conditions of the population in two parts. First, I estimate the poverty scenario. This cannot

---

[2] Sources are the Department of Sundarban Affairs (available at http://www.sadepartmentwb.org/) and the Directorate of Census Operation, West Bengal (available at http://web.cmc.net.in/wbcensus).

be obtained from secondary sources. Second, I investigate the spontaneous livelihood coping behaviour of the population in face of a natural disaster that could be related to climate change. The findings are based on a primary survey of a large and dispersed set of households carried out after Cyclone Aila (2009), whose salt deposits rendered agriculture impossible in vast stretches of land for at least a year.

Brief History of Settlements

Though historical evidences suggest some population presence in the region, the Sundarbans was depopulated for all practical purposes by the 17th century, probably owing to a series of natural calamities. The present population in the Indian Sundarbans has a history of more than one hundred years. Introducing human settlement in the area was done in a planned way under British rule, with the motivation of increasing revenue collection. The forest on the islands was cleared and divided into plots, which were then leased out to prospective landlords (Hunter 1876; Pargiter 1934).

Agriculture was made possible by erecting earthen embankments. On the Indian side, such embankments run up to 3,500 km. They became lifelines of human existence by blocking the inflow of salt water, which is detrimental to freshwater agriculture. The islands are dotted with tanks of all sizes that store rainwater for the villagers' year-long use. Groundwater is saline in the upper layers of the water table. Lifting groundwater for irrigation is not economically viable. The region is characterized by rainfed, single-crop agriculture.

Data and Sample

A substantial part of the islands' population lives in conditions different from their mainland counterparts. The islands are not always demarcated by administrative units. So, detailed information on the inhabitants is not available from secondary sources. One of my objectives was to arrive at empirical estimates of socioeconomic indicators. My estimates are based on a detailed survey of 618 households, spread over 31 villages scattered over 18 islands in the Indian Sundarbans. The 31 villages were selected to ensure sufficient variation in remoteness and natural resource proximity. They are spread over two administrative blocks in the Sundarbans—Gosaba and Patharpratima—which are located along its northern and southern boundary. For each of the selected villages, a list of all households was prepared with their current landholding status. Then 20 households from each village were selected as random sample maintaining a fixed proportion from each landholding strata.[3] The field survey was carried out from March to June 2010.

Findings

Infrastructure and Livelihood

The populated islands in the Sundarbans are poor in infrastructural provisions, mainly due to their inaccessibility. Only two villages have conventional electricity. Though 90% of the villages have a primary school, only one has a secondary school and only four have a primary health centre. The only source of drinking water is deep tube well. The average number of tube wells is seven per village. The average well serves 348 households and 1,564 people.[4]

Due to the lack of connectivity and electricity, there is no small-scale manufacturing. The list of major livelihoods is limited and excludes industrial work. Among land-based earners, cultivators and agricultural labourers constitute the main workforce. A small proportion of the households had salaried employment. Daily labour, petty trade, and artisanship were other major livelihood options (Figure 8.1).

These land-based practices do not directly put anthropogenic pressure on the surrounding ecosystem and the World Heritage Site. However, one-fifth of households exploit river waters for fishing. Some people sneak into forest creeks for a larger catch. Sometimes they also

---

[3] There were four landholding strata. The proportion of households in each stratum was computed on the basis of the combined list of 31 villages. 20 households from each village was selected such that the same proportions are reflected in the samples of size 20; e.g., 30% landless in the population translated to 6 landless households out of 20 households selected from each village. Subsequently, I dropped information on 2 of the 620 households for incompleteness.

[4] Further information regarding the remoteness and infrastructural provisions may be obtained from some other indicators listed in Table 8.1, which are based on the primary survey.

TABLE 8.1 Indicators for Remoteness

Description	Average	Min.	Max.
Average time taken by a student to reach the nearest secondary school (minute)	33	10	90
Average time taken by a student to reach the nearest college (minute)	130	20	270
Average time taken by a patient to reach the nearest Primary Health Centre (minute)	47	15	150
Average time taken by a commuter to reach the nearest mainland bus stop (minute)	110	30	270

Source: Author's own compilation.

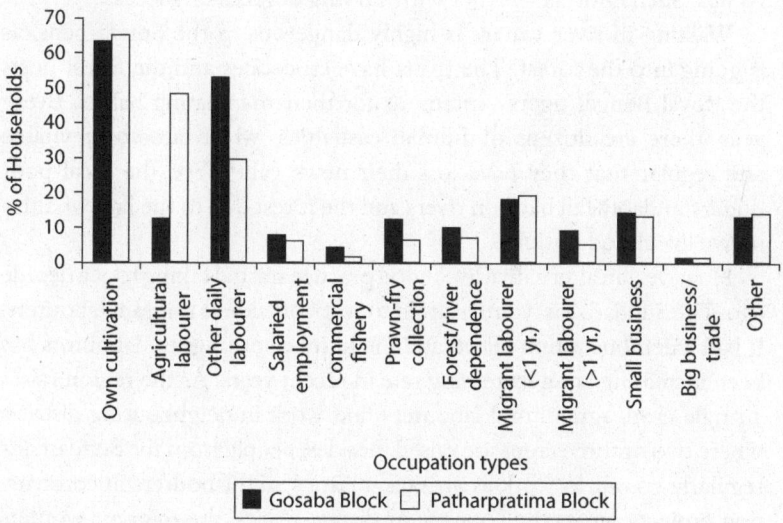

FIGURE 8.1 Livelihood Practices in the Sundarbans and Households'
Participation
Source: Author's estimates.

fetch firewood and collect honey from forest land. On the village side, river waters are also invaded by women and children collecting prawn seedlings. Sundarban waters are nutrient-rich natural hatcheries for many fish species. Collecting prawn seedlings by filtering water with a fine net is a widespread practice even beyond the Sundarbans. The fish seedlings are bought by agents of the large inland fishery owners. The process yields hard cash for villagers. The practice is a highly visible phenomenon along the villages' riverbanks.

Practice of prawn-seedling collection puts huge pressure on the Sundarban ecosystem, as well as on the health of the river embankments. First, in the process of collecting a few prawn seedlings, a large number of the seedlings of other species are wasted. Prawn collection puts a spanner in the natural regeneration of fish stock in the Sundarban waters. Second, villagers walk along river embankments in knee-deep water. This exerts a destabilizing pressure on embankments' bases and destroys the naturally generated mangrove saplings. These ill effects have been recognized for many years, and supplementary employment generation schemes have been floated by the government as well as by NGOs. Such efforts have met with varying degrees of success.

Walking in river waters is highly dangerous in the Sundarbans, as is going into the forest. The rivers have crocodiles and the forest hosts the Royal Bengal tigers—infamous for their man-eating habits. Every year, there are dozens of human casualties, which are so inevitable and regular that they have lost their news value. Yet, the local poor understandably fall back on rivers and the forest due to the lack of alternative livelihood options.

However, an alternative livelihood practice started taking root a decade ago. The Sundarbans' youth started to work outside as migrant labourers. It had a demonstration effect, and the number of migrant labourers has been increasing at an increasing rate in recent years. As the region raises a single crop, agricultural labourers find work in neighbouring districts where two or three crops are raised. Besides, people from the Sundarbans regularly go out to work as artisans, masons, and labourers in construction projects across the country. At distant places, the migrant workers from the Sundarbans generally move in groups headed by a leader and do not return home in less than a year. The major concentration of such workers can be found in the stone quarries of South India, the Andamans, and Delhi. I found that a fifth of the households have sent out at least one working adult (Table 8.4, given under section 'Effects on Livelihood').

Poverty Scenario

In spite of the hardships and limited livelihood opportunities, the islanders of the Sundarbans do not compare badly with their rural counterparts on the mainland in terms of traditional poverty indicators. In the absence of secondary sources, I estimated the incidence of poverty based on a well-dispersed representative sample of households. The estimates use the national and international poverty lines ($1.25 and $2 PPP) (see Table 8.2).

The incidence of poverty in the Sundarban islands is less than in rest of rural India. Since the latest estimates for rural India are half a decade old, the figures for rural India in 2010 can be expected to be lower. The magnitude of the reduction in poverty over these years is difficult to estimate in absence of secondary data. However, it could be said that poverty in the Sundarbans is not as acute as in the rest of rural India or rural West Bengal.

TABLE 8.2   Incidence of Poverty in the Sundarbans

	Criteria	National	$1.25 (PPP adjusted)	$2 (PPP adjusted)
Source: Secondary Data	Year: 2004–05			
	Poverty line: Expenditure per person per month (Rs)	356.3	585	936
	Rural India: population below poverty line	28.3%	41.6%	75.6%
	Year: 2004–05			
	Poverty line: Expenditure per person per month (Rs)	382.2	NA	NA
	Rural West Bengal: population below poverty line	28.6%	NA	NA
	Year 2010 (adjusting for price index for agricultural labourers)			
Source: Primary Survey	(estimated) Poverty line: Expenditure per person per month (Rs)	576.7	882.7	1412.3
	Sundarban islands: population below poverty line	21.4%	40.3%	66%

Sources: World Bank (2008); Reserve Bank of India (2008).

An indirect comparison might be more conclusive in analysing the poverty scenario in the Sundarban islands vis-à-vis rural West Bengal and rural India. This can be carried out with the help of more recent estimates on the pattern of household consumption expenditure in India (NSSO 2010). In these estimates, the rural households are distributed according to the size class of landholdings and the average monthly per capita expenditures (MPCE) for each landholding class. The estimates are available for both rural India and rural West Bengal. From the primary survey, Sundarban households could be distributed in similar landholding classes and their average MPCE could be calculated. Table 8.3 describes it and makes a contrast with the rest of rural India and West Bengal. The MPCE values are adjusted for 2010 using price indices for agricultural labourers.

Table 8.3 shows that except for the lowest landholding class, Sundarban households are better off than their rural counterparts in West Bengal and in India in terms of MPCE. The MPCE calculations took into account an imputed value for self-produced consumption items, mainly rice.

Parts of the lower incidence of poverty in the Sundarbans can be explained by the landholding pattern on the islands. The proportion of landless households is smaller in this region than in rural India and West Bengal for historical reasons. The initial inhabitants, who came to these islands around 100 years ago, all had some amount of land for their own cultivation as part of their invitation package offered by the lease-holders. That was an incentive for them to settle in a hostile environment. So the process of becoming landless—by subdivision and fragmentation of landholding over the generations—has been operative for a shorter time than on the mainland. Also, since almost all the initial settlers came under similar packages, there was not much dispersion in their initial endowment. With the passage of time, households' landholdings became fragmented and some were forced to sell their land, giving rise to the landless class. However, in the absence of varied alternative earning opportunities, many of them did continue with their small holdings. This gave rise to a large proportion of the marginal farmers in the Sundarbans—much larger than the proportion seen in rest of rural India.

Most of the households have a more than one source of income. Since agriculture is not usually a year-long activity, and the average

TABLE 8.3   Distribution of Rural Households by Size Class of Landholding

| | Size Class of Landholding (hectare) | | | | | | | | | |
	0.0–0.01	0.02–0.20	0.21–0.40	0.41–1.00	1.01–2.00	2.01–3.00	3.01–4.00	4.01–6.00	Above 6	Total
% of HH (Rural India)	35	17	12	18	11	4	1	1	1	100
% of HH (Rural West Bengal)	49	26	11	11	3	1	0	0	0	100
% of HH (Sundarban islands)	22	36	22	17	4	0	0	0	0	100
Average MPCE (Rural India, inflation adjusted for 2009–10)	923	924	926	941	1,016	1,197	1,190	1,287	1,468	
Average MPCE (Sundarban islands, 2009–10)	917	1,210	1,722	1,647	1,606	1,800	NA	NA	NA	

Source: Author's own compilation.

landholding is small, most of the working population engages in other activities as well. I estimate that on an average a working adult undertakes 1.5 types of earning activities during a year.

Such small-holders in the Sundarbans could augment their earnings through the surrounding natural resources, such as the rivers and the forests. This is not usually possible in other parts of rural India. Also, many of them have recently resorted to working as migrant labourers. This is not so common in other parts of rural India. All these factors explain an MPCE for the Sundarbans that is higher than similar landholding size classes in rural India.

Climate Change Threats

The coastal population in the Indian subcontinent, particularly in Bangladesh, is vulnerable to flooding as a result of a rise in the sea level (Stern team 2006). As it is a low-lying delta, the Indian Sundarbans will be among the first casualties of sea-level rise. The rise in sea level will not be uniform across all regions, as continental land subsidence is also a phenomenon here. Conducted over a 14-year period ending in 1998, one study estimated an average increase in sea level at the rate of 3.14 mm per year (Hazra et al. 2002) for the region that includes the Sundarbans. This is higher than the average rate in other coastal regions of India.

Sea-level rise is, however, a slow process and its threat to coastal population can be reduced with informed planning and adaptation programmes. The more immediate threat to Sundarban inhabitants from climate change comes from an increased frequency of cyclones and super cyclones in the Bay of Bengal.[5] The effect of such an event is more sudden and disastrous for the island population. These can result in the destruction of their lifeline—the surrounding embankments.

Sundarban embankments are earthen and are traditionally maintained by manual labour. Their height varies between 2 metres and 4 metres depending on the elevation of the site vis-à-vis the surrounding water level. Usually a cross-section view of such an embankment is of

---

[5] Simulation exercises predict an increase in occurrence of cyclones in the Bay of Bengal in the increased Greenhouse Gas scenario (Ali 1999; Unnikrishnan, Rupa Kumar, Fernandes, et al. 2006).

the pyramid type with a flat top. The base of a healthy embankment ranges from 4 metres to 6 metres, with the top being 1.5- to 2-metre wide. Embankments also have village roads on them as well, if the top isn't severely eroded.

The tidal amplitude in this delta region is high. It is even higher on full-moon or no-moon days and in the monsoon season. On special days, the river waters can surge nearly 4 metres from their mean level. Through local knowledge and experience, people maintain the embankments at a height that under normal circumstances can withstand such surges.

Such mud structures face erosion due to daily tidal flows. The erosion is greater when it is stormy and windy. In the monsoon season, when the average river water level becomes higher, a high wind coupled with high tide often eats up the top of weak embankments and saline water overflows into nearby agricultural fields. Such failures are frequent, but they usually affect only a small part of the island. Normally, village roads, which create barriers to the incoming water, confine such inundations within narrower boundaries.

The situation, however, can be disastrous if a cyclone occurs when the rivers are also at their maximum height. In such a situation, even healthy embankments cannot act as protection against high waters. Incidentally, in the 100 years' settlement history of the Sundarban islands, a cyclone's landfall has so far never coincided with the highest river water level—until Cyclone Aila in May 2009.

Cyclone Aila and the Disaster Aftermath

On 25 May 2009, a no-moon day with deltaic rivers reaching their extreme high-tide mark, Cyclone Aila blew directly over the Sundarban islands throughout the day. Though it was forecasted, the people and the administration had no clue what a 100–120 kmph wind speed could mean for this inter-tidal zone when its landfall coincided with an extremely high tide. The result was unseen in the region's history.

Going by the conventional statistics on damages after such a disaster, Aila might not be counted as an unprecedented calamity. The human death toll was around 100 in the Sundarbans, with 50,000 huts partially or fully damaged. Almost all the islands were submerged in salt water. Aila damaged an overwhelming 400 km of the embankments, of which

139 km were washed away with their bases. The damage was fairly uniformly distributed across all the islands. Only a few pockets in few islands survived intact.

The cyclone devastated the islands' all-important agriculture for at least one year. The major freshwater sources on these islands—the village tanks—were overrun by saline water. The immediate aftermath of Aila was a huge shortage of drinking water and food, trailed by a phase of widespread diarrhoea. These consequences are common to such disasters and were addressed by reasonable provisions from various government departments and a large number of NGOs and civil society organizations. But the event had cast its shadow on the normal life of the local population. The dynamics of livelihood adjustment, after such a disaster, is still unfolding. Given climate change predictions, there is an increased probability of a re-occurrence of such events.

Effects on Livelihood

Existing literature tells us that disasters generally have a negative effect on the environment. In a direct way, they can physically damage the environment by their intensity. In an indirect way, the loss of usual livelihood may lead to additional anthropogenic pressures being put on the natural resources. In the case of the Sundarbans, the effect of the disaster was not so much on the environment as was on the livelihood of the poor people. It was seen that during the cyclone, mangrove forests could withstand wind speeds of 100–120 kmph. There was no sign of physical damage to the forest. No tiger was reported to have died. There was no perceivable damage to biodiversity or the ecosystem.

Post-disaster livelihood adjustments are better described when the surveyed villages are grouped across two administrative blocks. This is because the loss in agriculture—the indicator for livelihood disruption—has not been uniform across them. The southern block (Patharpratima) suffered the lesser blow. The islands in this block are situated amidst wide rivers, and they had a more stable embankment network, with more mangrove cover around them. They were submerged by the saline water overflow through the top of embankments, but such waters went back to the rivers at subsequent low tides. The damage to the embankments was less and it could block fresh inflows during subsequent high tides. The average amount of salt deposits on agricultural lands was less, and some cultivation was undertaken in this block in the ensuing monsoon months.

The islands in the northern block (Gosaba), however, are located amidst narrow river channels through which tidal water passes more rapidly. The consequent erosion and damage to the embankments had been greater. In many parts, such embankments were washed out during the cyclone, and the islands remained exposed to tidal water inflows for days and months. The loss in agriculture in the Gosaba block was severe, and this is evident in the intensity of livelihood changes across these two blocks. Primary data show the details in Table 8.4.

A closer look at Table 8.4 reveals that the loss of agriculture naturally caused job losses for agricultural labourers. In turn, a significant increase can be observed for short-term migration and other daily labour. Even estimates in the table under short-term migration could be underestimates. Some of those reporting themselves to be agricultural day labourers also do work on the nearby mainland for short periods.

One finding relates to the status of people's natural resource dependence after such a disaster. One might expect a greater pressure on the rivers and the forest exerted by the local people as their agriculture was lost. This is supported by empirical evidence from other parts of the world. There are a number of studies examining rural household coping strategies in response to natural disasters (McSweeney 2005; Pattanayak and Sills 2001; Takasaki, Barham, and Coomes 2004). The studies suggest that agricultural households living close to a forest can fall back to collecting non-timber forest products or to clearing forests for new agricultural land. Such options could provide an insurance against livelihood shocks. Surprisingly, the findings reveal a different story after Aila in the Sundarbans. It was found that forest and river dependence has marginally declined after the disaster. This is evident in Table 8.4, where the percentage of households engaged in 'prawn-fry collection' and 'forest/river dependence' has gone down after Aila. This paradoxical phenomenon might be explained partly by the prevailing management scenario of the reserve forest. Being a World Heritage Site, the reserve forest is managed by an exclusionist policy. Forests are strictly guarded by the forest department and there is little scope for the villagers to fall back on the forest. Also, there has been an effort in

TABLE 8.4 Livelihood Practices in the Two Survey Blocks: Before and After the Cyclone

Occupation	Block Gosaba			Block Patharpratima		
	% of HH Pre-Aila	% of HH Post-Aila	Change in % of HH due to Aila	% of HH Pre-Aila	% of HH Post-Aila	Change in % of HH due to Aila
Own cultivation	63	16	−47	65	43	−22
Agricultural labourer	12	8	−4	48	47	−1
Other daily labourer	53	57	4	29	30	1
Salaried employment	8	8	0	6	7	1
commercial fishery	4	1	−3	1	1	0
prawn-fry collection	12	10	−2	6	5	−1
forest/river dependence	10	8	−2	7	6	−1
short-term migration	18	22	4	19	23	4
Long-term migration	9	7	−2	5	5	0
small business	14	13	−1	13	14	1
big business/trade	1	1	0	1	1	0
Other	13	12	−1	14	16	2

Source: Author's own compilation.

recent years by the government and NGOs to reduce the practice of prawn-fry collection and forest intrusion. The same agencies undertook large relief initiatives in the aftermath of Aila. They also tried to keep an eye on their beneficiaries so that they did not put more pressure on the ecosystem. But a more convincing reason can be traced to the fact that a sizable chunk of the poor have gone out as migrant labourers. They have been supplementing their agricultural income with fishing and forest collection. It might be concluded that nature of natural resource, as well as the prevailing institutional setup, can be crucial in deciding whether anthropogenic pressure increases or not after disaster.

In the case of migration, for the most part, households as a whole don't migrate, just members of households. Barring exceptions, the households themselves remained planted on the islands after Aila, protecting whatever land they had. Perhaps they knew from experience that such a loss in agriculture was temporary and that land generally regains its productivity after one or two monsoons. Going by field observations, the most explicit post-disaster coping strategy in the Sundarbans had been to engage in migrant labour. Villages were found where more than three quarters of the households had sent at least one working adult to the mainland after Aila.

The importance of migration as a coping strategy is even more evident when the villages are grouped according to the extent of agriculture loss. There was enough variation in the number of days of their exposure to saline water and consequent agricultural loss. Thirteen villages reported a total loss in agriculture. If they are grouped and contrasted with others whose loss was partial, the difference in livelihood changes becomes more pronounced.

Table 8.5 shows the differences with a few key indicators. Where the disaster left agriculture impossible, there was a large reduction in the number of agricultural labourers. People turned to other labour jobs which were more readily available in the mainland. Prawn-fry catching and fishing are mostly resorted to by people with marginal landholding. When agriculture was possible, they stayed in villages. With small landholding, there was a lot of surplus time to exploit open access rivers and venture into the forests. But when there was no agriculture, working adults moved out, reducing the pressure on the rivers and forest.[6]

---

[6] The 48 islands totally covered by mangrove vegetation and without any human settlement are together considered as one single forest.

TABLE 8.5   Livelihood Changes across Two Groups of Villages

	Villages which Reported Total Loss in Agriculture	Villages which Reported Partial Loss in Agriculture
No. of villages	13	18
Average number of days of saline water intrusion	24	7
% of HH reporting no agriculture after Aila	100	21
% change in the number of HH earning from agricultural labour	−27	−3
% change in the number of HH earning from daily labour	13	2
% change in the number of HH earning from migrant labour	58	13

Source: Author's own compilation.

Who Migrates?

It is interesting to explore the profile of households which resorted to temporary migration for at least one of their members. The possible link between migration and the reduction of anthropogenic pressure on the forest and rivers might be validated if landless and poorly endowed households were dominant contributors to migrant labour. It can be seen in Table 8.6 that the highest proportion of households resorting to migration is in the lowest landholding class. This is in spite of their average household size being the lowest. It might be noted that the MPCE estimates, coupled with the observations in Table 8.3, indicate that money earned from the outside may have helped Sundarban villagers maintain a respectable standard of consumption. It appears that in a region that has weak infrastructure and low gross productivity of land, the disaster might have stirred up the population enough to induce a greater mobility in a large labour force that had been severely under-employed.

TABLE 8.6   Migration across Landholding Class

	Landholding Classes (hectare)				
	0–0.01	0.02–0.20	0.21–0.40	0.41–1.00	More than 1 ha
Number of HH in the study	141	201	114	85	25
% of HH contributing to migrant labourer (after Aila)	44	34	35	33	36
Average HH size	4.5	5.0	5.3	5.5	6.4
Average MPCE (Rs)	917	1,210	1,722	1,647	1,606

Source: Author's own compilation.

Government Initiative: The Adaptation Strategy

In light of climate change threats and of the probability of increasing of recurrences of cyclones, the state government had come up with long-term adaptation measures to protect the island population by building several cyclone relief centres. Such measures protect life, but not livelihood. To protect livelihood, the government planned to build bigger and stronger embankments along the boundaries of islands with wide mangrove covers. The plan is to clear land along riverbanks, build embankments with much wider bases and a margin of land on the riverside for growing mangroves. Such plans of in situ protection of islanders against natural disasters involve huge costs. I found that many islanders are willing to move to the mainland. It might make more economic sense to relocate part of population on to the mainland.

* * *

The vast island population in the Sundarbans lives with poor infrastructural provisions caused mainly by location disadvantages. The households are mainly agricultural and the region is characterized by mono-crop, rainfed agriculture. Households augment their earning by engaging in multiple activities, such as fishing, prawn-fry collecting, and migrant labour. However, going by their expenditure data, islanders are not worse off than their rural counterparts in rest of India.

Climate change vulnerability arises mainly from cyclones. The coping behaviour of households has been identified as (a) temporary migration of working men and women, and (b) resorting to non-farm daily labour. However, pressure on forest and rivers has decreased. A sizable number of the poor have been supplementing their agricultural income loss by migrant labour. Their experiences can help in devising long-term coping strategies. Beyond sudden disasters such as cyclones, sea-level rise scenarios envisage a doomsday for islands between 50–100 years from now. There is a growing support for preserving and even increasing the area under mangroves, which is an important tiger habitat. The ever-increasing trend of outmigration might be a sign that the islands are no longer capable of sustaining the economic life of all their inhabitants. An alternative plan of relocating some people to the mainland might be more economically rational than trying to preserve their livelihoods in their present location.

References

Ali, A. 1999. 'Climate Change Impacts and Adaptation Assessment in Bangladesh', *Climate Research* 12: 109–116.

Hazra S., T. Ghosh, R. Dasgupta, and G. Sen. 2002. 'Sea Level and Associated Changes in the Sundarbans', *Science and Culture* 68(9–12): 309–21.

Hunter, W.W. 1876. *A Statistical Account of the Sundarbans* (reprint 1998). Kolkata: West Bengal District Gazetteers, Government of West Bengal, Higher Education Department.

McSweeney, K. 2005. 'Natural Insurance, Forest Access, and Compounded Misfortune: Forest Resources in Smallholder Coping Strategies before and after Hurricane Mitch, Northeastern Honduras', *World Development* 33(9): 1453–71.

NSSO. 2010. *Household Consumer Expenditure in India, 2007–08*. NSS 64th Round (July 2007–June 2008), Report No. 530. National Sample Survey Organization, Ministry of Statistics and Programme Implementation, Government of India, March.

Pargiter, F.E. 2002 [1934]. *A Revenue History of The Sundarbans: Volume I*. Kolkata: West Bengal District Gazetteers, Govt. of West Bengal, Higher Education Department.

Pattanayak, S.K. and E.O. Sills. 2001. 'Do Tropical Forests Provide Natural Insurance? The Microeconomics of Non-Timber Forest Product Collection in the Brazilian Amazon', *Land Economics* 77(4): 595–612.

Stern team. 2006. *Stern Review: The Economics of Climate Change*. The United Kingdom: H M Treasury, The UK's Economics and Finance Ministry. Available at http://www.hm-treasury.gov.uk/media/4/3/Executive_Summary.pdf.

Takasaki Y., B.L. Barham, and O.I. Coomes. 2004. 'Risk Coping Strategies in Tropical Forests: Floods, Illnesses, and Resource Extraction', *Environment and Development Economics* 9: 203–24.

Unnikrishnan, A.S., K. Rupa Kumar, Sharon E. Fernandes, G.S. Michael, and S.K. Patwardhan. 2006. 'Sea Level Changes along the Indian Coast: Observations and Projections', *Current Science* 90(3): 362–68.

9

RAJESH JAISWAL

Watershed Development as a Way of Creating Sustainable Livelihoods in Rural India

This chapter argues that watershed development can be used to reduce poverty by creating livelihoods in the rural rainfed (non-irrigated) agricultural areas of India. Land is a natural asset and is the base for livelihood of human beings. Because of increased population, land is being over-exploited. This has resulted in soil erosion.[1] Soil

---

[1] 'Soil erosion is one form of soil degradation. Other kinds of soil degradation include salinisation, nutrient loss, and compaction' (available at: http://soilerosion.net/).

Soil is naturally removed by the action of water or wind: such 'background' (or 'geological') soil erosion has been occurring for some 450 million years, since the first land plants formed the first soil. Even before this, natural processes moved loose rock, or regolith, off the Earth's surface, just as has happened on the planet Mars. In general, background erosion removes soil at roughly the same rate as soil is formed. But 'accelerated' soil erosion—loss of soil at a much faster rate than it is formed—is a far more recent problem. It is always a result of mankind's unwise actions, such as overgrazing or unsuitable cultivation practices. These leave the land unprotected and vulnerable. Then, during times of erosive rainfall or windstorms, soil may be detached, transported, and (possibly travelling a long distance) deposited. Accelerated soil erosion by water or wind may affect both

erosion has degraded land. Soil erosion has been a major constraint on agriculture and food security in most parts of India. Soil degradation on large tracts of cultivable land is undermining millions of people's livelihoods. With climate change aggravating water scarcity, soil erosion, and the expansion of dryland areas, a different strategy is urgently needed for India's (rainfed) drylands vis-à-vis the irrigation agriculture. This could be watershed development.

Poor Agriculture Is the Main Reason for Persisting Poverty and Hunger

India's economy has grown tremendously in recent years. But the benefits of growth in India have not been evenly distributed between social income groups (vertically) or geographical areas (horizontally). Along with a growing middle class, there are persistently impoverished people. According to recent World Bank figures for 2008, an estimated 41.6% of the Indian population lives below the $1.25 international poverty line and 75.6% below the $2 international poverty line; and according to the National Statistical Office, an estimated 27.5% lives below the Indian national poverty line of $0.3 per day. Furthermore, three-fourths of Indian children under three years are anaemic and half of them suffer from moderate to severe malnourishment. This is in addition to the nearly 90% of pregnant women who are anaemic. Scores of starvation-related deaths are reported across the country. Many parts of India were not included in the development schemes. Some sectors more than others; and some geographical areas have benefited more than others. However, the main reason for the country's high poverty rates and persistent hunger is the poor performance of Indian agriculture. In the 1990s, food grain production grew slower than the population for the first time. The funds flow from the government to the agriculture

---

agricultural areas and the natural environment, and is one of the most widespread of today's environmental problems. It has impacts which are both on-site (at the place where the soil is detached) and off-site (wherever the eroded soil ends up). More recently still, the use of powerful agricultural implements has, in some parts of the world, led to damaging amounts of soil moving downslope merely under the action of gravity: this is so-called tillage erosion. (http://soilerosion. net/doc/what_is_erosion.html)

sector has been pathetically low. Only 2.72% of the total plan expenditure has gone to agriculture in 2012–13 (BE). In the absence of adequate funds from the government, the farmers often need to take the initiative to procure basic farming inputs on their own—be it better quality seeds, minor irrigation facilities, or investment in capital goods. Thus, it results in indebtedness and finally the poor performance of the agriculture.[2]

The Dryland and Rainfed Areas Provide the Livelihoods for the Poor

In India, 60% of arable (fit or used for growing crops) land is rainfed (non-irrigated), and only 40% of the arable land is irrigated.[3] There is little scope to expand the area under irrigation, and the land area for irrigated agriculture even declined mainly due to urbanization. Hence, with growing population and growing demand for higher value food because of increasing spending opportunities and changing consumption patterns, the increasing demands for food (for humans) and feed (animal food) need to be met from increased production from rainfed (non-irrigated) areas. The rainfed (non-irrigated) areas of Indian agriculture

---

[2] Datt and Ravallion (2002) find that differences in trend rates of poverty reduction are attributed to differing growth rates of farm yield per acre, and differing initial conditions.

[3] The term *rainfed agriculture* is used to describe farming practices that *rely on rainfall for water*. It provides much of the food consumed by poor communities in developing countries. For example, rainfed agriculture accounts for more than 95% of farmed land in sub-Saharan Africa, 90% in Latin America, 75% in the Near East and North Africa; *65% in East Asia and 60% in South Asia*. Levels of productivity, particularly in parts of sub-Saharan Africa and South Asia, are *low due to degraded soils, high levels of evaporation, droughts, floods and a general lack of effective water management*. [There is] a close correlation between hunger, poverty and water. However...there [is] much opportunity to raise productivity from rainfed farming.... managing rainwater and soil moisture more effectively, and using supplemental and small-scale irrigation, held the key to helping the greatest number of poor people. It called for a new era of water investments and policies for upgrading rainfed agriculture that would go beyond controlling field-level soil and water to bring new freshwater sources through better local management of rainfall and runoff. (http://en.wikipedia.org/wiki/Rainfed_agriculture)

are the weakest and provide the greatest potential for growth. Thus, to achieve food security, rainfed (non-irrigated) areas must be developed.

Another reason for focusing development efforts on dryland areas is the high concentration of poverty and distress in those drylands of India. A study carried out for the Ministry of Finance, Government of India, and the United Nations Development Programme (UNDP) provides statistical data to establish the macroeconomic significance of watershed programmes for food security and employment guarantee in India (Shah et al. 1998). While incentives for dryland farming were often neglected by the mainstream development policies of India, these dry agricultural regions depend on a natural resource base which forms the lifeline for rural people to provide them with meagre livelihood and income opportunities.

Water Scarcity and Soil Erosion

The adoption of a water-intensive Green Revolution[4] package was made possible by substantial public investment in irrigation. As a result, the gross irrigated area (GIA)[5] went up significantly through the construction of large irrigation projects (for non-rainfed areas), and b) intensive tapping of groundwater through tube wells.[6] However, water policies for

---

[4] Green Revolution refers to a series of research, development, and technology transfer initiatives, occurring between the 1940s and the late 1970s, that increased agriculture production around the world, beginning most markedly in the late 1960s. The initiatives...involved the development of high-yielding varieties of cereal grains, expansion of irrigation infrastructure, modernization of management techniques, distribution of hybridized seeds, synthetic fertilizers, and pesticides to farmers. (http://en.wikipedia.org/wiki/Green_Revolution)

[5] The net irrigated area (NIA) as defined by India's Directorate of Economics and Statistics (DES) is the total area that is irrigated at least once per agricultural year. It does not include areas that were left fallow or that were entirely rainfed during the year of statistics. GIA as defined by DES is *the area irrigated under various crops during a year, counting the area irrigated under more than one crop during the same year as many times as the number of crops grown and irrigated.* (http://www.iwmigiam.org/info/GMI-DOC/GIAM-India-Stats.pdf)

[6] A tube well is a type of water well in which a long 100–200 mm (5 to 8 inch) wide stainless steel tube or pipe is bored into the underground *aquifer*. The lower end is fitted with a strainer, and a pump at the top lifts water for

agricultural purposes seem less successful: There is a growing crisis in the water sector. Larger reservoirs[7] in India have lost over one-third of their storage capacity due to siltation.[8] Siltation is the pollution of water by fine particulate terrestrial plastic material, with the particle size dominated by silt or clay. It refers both to the increased concentration of suspended sediments, and to the increased accumulation (temporary or permanent) of fine sediments on bottoms where they are undesirable. Siltation is most often caused by soil erosion or sediment spill. This has resulted in a reduction in the areas irrigated and in lower electricity generation, thereby rendering large investments in irrigation projects unviable.[9]

Furthermore, there has been excessive groundwater[10] withdrawal by people via wells, resulting in a rapid fall of water tables.[11] Over the last two decades, 84% of addition to the net irrigated area (NIA)[12] has

---

irrigation. The required depth of the well depends on the depth of the water table. (http://en.wikipedia.org/wiki/Tube_well)

[7] A reservoir, artificial lake or impoundment from a dam is used to store water. Reservoirs may be created in river valleys by the construction of a dam or may be built by excavation in the ground or by conventional construction techniques such as brickwork or cast concrete. (http://en.wikipedia.org/wiki/Reservoir)

[8] Planning Commission (2004).

[9] Planning Commission (2004).

[10] 'Groundwater is water located beneath the ground surface in soil pore spaces and in the fractures of rock formations. A unit of rock or an unconsolidated deposit is called an aquifer when it can yield a usable quantity of water' (http://en.wikipedia.org/wiki/Groundwater).

[11] The water table is the surface where the water pressure head is equal to the atmospheric pressure (where gauge pressure = 0). It may be conveniently visualized as the 'surface' of the subsurface materials that are saturated with groundwater in a given vicinity. However, saturated conditions may extend above the water table as surface tension holds water in some pores below atmospheric pressure.[1] Individual points on the water table are typically measured as the elevation that the water rises to in a well screened in the shallow groundwater. (http://en.wikipedia.org/wiki/Water_table)

[12] The net irrigated area (NIA) as defined by DES is the total area that is irrigated at least once per agricultural year. It does not include areas that were left fallow or that were entirely rainfed during the year of statistics. The GIA as defined by DES is the area irrigated under various crops during a year, counting the area irrigated under more than one crop during the same year as many

been groundwater-linked. This means that the water used for irrigation is increasingly being taken from the groundwater rather than brought from outside the area. As a result, groundwater levels further drop causing even more salinization. Groundwater now provides for 70% of the irrigated agricultural area and serves 80% of domestic food production. Already 15% of aquifers[13] are in a critical condition; that is, they are unable to trap sediment and other particles (like bacteria) and provide natural purification of the groundwater flowing through them and the figure will rise to 60% over the next two decades if no remedial action is taken soon.

Watershed Development: Addressing Poverty Reduction and Climate Change in Rural Dryland Areas of India

A watershed is the area of land where all of the water that is under it or drains off of it goes into the same place. In development economics, the term is also being used to cover the drainage basin or catchment area; that is, the extent of land where surface water from rain and melting snow or ice converges to a single point, usually the exit of the basin, where the waters join another water body, such as a river, lake, reservoir, estuary, wetland, sea, or ocean. Watersheds, therefore, include both the streams and rivers that convey the water as well as the land surfaces from which water drains into those channels. Each drainage basin is separated topographically from adjacent basins by a geographical barrier such as a ridge, hill, or mountain.

Developing watersheds means making running water walk, walking water stop, and forcing stopped water underground—by means of ridges and bunds from ridge to valley—stopping soil erosion and thereby the flooding and siltation of the rivers. Watershed development thereby solves two immediate problems, namely drought and flooding. Developing a watershed involves preventing soil runoff (erosion), regenerating natural vegetation, harvesting rainwater, and recharging

---

times as the number of crops grown and irrigated. (http://www.iwmigiam. org/info/GMI-DOC/GIAM-India-Stats.pdf)

[13] 'An aquifer is a wet underground layer of water-bearing permeable rock or unconsolidated materials (gravel, sand, or silt) from which groundwater can be usefully extracted using a water well' (http://en.wikipedia.org/wiki/Aquifer).

(raising) groundwater tables. These modifications enable multi-cropping and diverse agriculture-based activities. Projects or programmes that involve developing a watershed have the potential for allowing residents to survive during droughts, causing agriculture to grow, protecting the environment, and generating jobs.[14]

The main goals in developing watershed are to restore (a) the ecological balance by harnessing and conserving soil and water and (b) natural resources, such as soil, vegetative cover, and water, to their un-degraded states. The benefits of watershed development include reduction in (soil) runoff, rise in the water table, increase in number of wells dug by villagers, increase in the proportion of irrigated land, increase in area sown under various seasons, switch to higher value crops, bringing of potentially arable wasteland that is barren under crop production, increase in fuel wood off take, increase in dry fodder production, increase in milk production, increase in soil fertility, and some increase in round-the-year availability of drinking water. Areas that have watershed development programmes areas are more productive than areas without them. All this can result in the creation of income opportunities for agricultural labourers and farmers. Table 9.1 provides an overview on the impact of watershed management on productivity of arable land, employment, and the economy.

History of Indian Watershed Development

Since the early 1980s the government, NGOs, and international agencies have implemented watershed development programmes in various states of India. However, it took up to 1995 until investments in watershed development have been substantially increasing (Table 9.2). In 2005–06, investments in integrated watershed management programmes were US$114 million and it increased to nearly US$463 million in 2011–12. If one analyses year-wise release of funds under DDP since 1995–96 to 2010–11, one observes that the funds released have risen from 101

---

[14] Kerr and Chung (2001) provide a summary of the operational indicators of the impact of watershed programmes. While there is clear lack of rigorous methodology in most studies. The quality of the data is also highly variable across projects. However, there are some studies and evaluations that do provide an assessment of the potential of watershed programmes for the poor.

TABLE 9.1 Impact of Watershed Management on Productivity of Arable Land, Employment, and Economic Viability

State	Wasteland	Increase in Cropping Intensity (%)	Increase in Productivity (%)	Increase in Employment (%)	Benefit-cost Ratio
Haryana	Sukhomajri	82.0	210.0	29.4	2.06
Haryana	Nada	78.0	165.0	18.6	1.97
Haryana	Bunga	110.0	170.0	28.2	2.05
Punjab	Rel Maira	32.0	52.0	24.0	–
Himachal Pradesh	Behdala	17.0	12.0	Negligible	–
Haryana	Bajra-Ganiyar	21.0	58.0	160	1.58
Haryana	Siha	23.0	67.0	27.0	–
Rajasthan	Kharkhna Kalan	17.0	15.0	Negligible	6.07
Rajasthan	Kishangarh	10.0	12.0	Negligible	2.35
Rajasthan	Chhajawa	32.0	45.0	36.0	2.24
Rajasthan	Mandvarsa	31.0	13.0	3.0	1.90
Uttar Pradesh	Matatila	41.0	21.0	4.0	3.80
Uttar Pradesh	Tejpura	97.0	180.0	40.0	3.40
Uttar Pradesh	Gomti (Gyii)	68.0	52.0	18.0	3.90
Uttar Pradesh	Gomti (GK3a)	41.0	24.0	6.0	2.00
Gujarat	Rebari	20.0	56.0	3.0	2.60
Karnataka	Joladarasi	18.0	56.0	5.0	1.50
Andhra Pradesh	Chinnatekur	25.0	62.0	7.0	1.80
Karnataka	GR Halli	12.0	42.0	3.0	1.50
Gujarat	Shankarpura	60.0	82.0	14.0	–
Maharashtra	Ralegan-Siddhi	62.0	185.0	21.0	–

Source: Sarma and Dhyani (1998), adapted from Kadekodi (1998, 182).

TABLE 9.2   Distribution of Watershed Projects in Selected States: From 1994 to 1999

State	State Share of Nationwide Watershed Projects
Andhra Pradesh	24.0
Madhya Pradesh	17.0
Uttar Pradesh	10.0
Gujarat	8.6
Tamil Nadu	7.0

Source: Rao (2000).

crore in 1995–96 to 304.17 crore in 2009–10 (Table 9.3). This was mainly because the Government of India intensified watershed development programmes in high-risk ecosystems, such as in the states of Uttar Pradesh, Madhya Pradesh, Maharashtra, Andhra Pradesh, Rajasthan, Gujarat, Himachal Pradesh, Karnataka, Tamil Nadu, Assam, Nagaland, and other states, where farm incomes had declined massively due to excessive soil erosion and moisture stress. Until today about 1,500–2,000 watershed development projects have been developed in various states of India (Table 9.4). In the financial year 2001/2002 nearly 6.2 million hectares of rainfed land was under 5,200 micro-watersheds programmes with an estimated cost of 175 million. And up to December 2010 more than 15,000 watershed development projects have been implemented in India (Table 9.4).

Attempts to overcome the problem of degradation of the soil of large tracks of cultivable land (which is undermining millions of livelihoods) have been made through large investments in watershed management.[15] There are five major types of watershed programmes operating in the country. They differ in administration, planning, and system composition as follows (Shridara 2002):

- The National Watershed Development Programme, assisted by the central government and implemented by the state governments, financed 75% of the total watershed investments.
- State governments in states sponsored 25%.

[15] Lal (2000). This has also been done in other parts of Asia, and in Africa and Latin America.

TABLE 9.3   Year-wise Release of Funds under DDP from 1995–96 to 2010–11

Year	Amount released (Rs crore)
1995–96	101.00
1996–97	65.37
1997–98	70.01
1998–99	79.80
1999–00	84.99
2000–01	134.98
2001–02	149.88
2002–03	184.99
2003–04	214.80
2004–05	214.99
2005–06	267.98
2006–07	269.00
2007–08	265.44
2008–09	395.96
2009–10	304.17
2010–11 (as on 31 December 2010)	200.82
Total	3,004.18

Source: Ministry of Rural Development, Department of Land Resources, Government of India. Available at ww.dolr.nic.in/budget1.htm dated 1 December 2011 (accessed on 1 December 2011).

- In India, the World Bank has supported 11 watershed development projects since FY 1981 for a total commitment of US$808 million.
- NGOs also supported watershed development programmes. The NGO and NGO-government collaborative projects devoted time and resources to organizing communities to establish locally acceptable social arrangements for watershed interventions. They selected villages where people had demonstrated ability and willingness to work collectively to solve common problems. Since the budget was limited so it made sense.
- Furthermore, the Indian Council of Agricultural Research has taken up watershed development programmes and provides operational research on those.

TABLE 9.4 Watershed Projects Sanctioned under DDP from 1995–96 to 2010–11 (as on 31 December 2010)

S. No.	State	1995–96	1996–97	1997–98	1998–99	1999–2000	2000–01	2001–02	2002–03	2003–04	2004–05	2005–06	2006–07	Total
1	Andhra Pradesh	96	10	0	100	96	60	80	110	110	110	134	148	1,054
2	Gujarat	345	0	0	100	250	400	304	277	298	298	370	420	3,062
3	Haryana	107	6	0	100	76	144	100	121	118	118	140	159	1,189
4	Himachal Pradesh	80	0	0	0	48	75	95	73	49^e	38	46	48	552
5	Other States	94	49	36	0	96	73	111	77	41	40	50	62	729
6	Karnataka	130	0	0	100	51	226	160	165	166	166	198	220	1,582
7	Rajasthan	841	0	0	0	883^a	681^b	509^c	779^d	780^f	830^g	1,062^h	1,213^i	7,578
	Total	1,693	65	36	400	1,500	1,659	1,359	1,602	1,562	1,600	2,000	2,270	15,746

Source: Ministry of Rural Development, Department of Land Resources, Government of India. Available at: www.dolr.nic.in/budget1.htm dated 1 December 2011 (accessed on 1 December 2011).

Notes: No new projects were sanctioned under DDP from 2007–08 onwards. A project under DDP generally covers an area of 500 hectares.

'a' Includes 614 special projects for sand dune stabilization, shelterbelt plantations, and so on during 1999–2000.

'b' Includes 293 special projects for sand dune stabilization, shelterbelt plantations and so on during 2001–02.

'c' Includes 264 special projects for sand dune stabilization, shelterbelt plantations, and so on during 2001–02.

'd' Includes 362 special projects for sand dune stabilization, shelterbelt plantations, and so on during 2001–02.

'e' Includes 11 special projects sanctioned to the cold desert areas of Lahaul and Spiti districts.

'f' Includes 362 special projects for sand dune stabilization, shelterbelt plantations, and so on during 2003–04.

'g' Includes 387 special projects for sand dune stabilization, shelterbelt plantations, and so on during 2004–05.

'h' Includes 498 special projects for sand dune stabilization, shelterbelt plantations , and son on during 2005–06.

'i' Includes 572 special projects for sand dune stabilization, shelterbelt plantations, and so on during 2006–07.

Economic Benefits of Watershed Development: Productivity Enhancement through Changed Cropping Patterns

Areas with watershed development programmes substantially improve their productivity. To give a few examples:

- A study conducted by Dryland Development Board, Karnataka in Kabbalnala Watershed of Bangalore district in 1986 (Anonymous, 1997) showed an increase in the yield of ragi from 5.3 quintals to 18.0 quintals per hectare. For groundnut, the yield was 3.9 quintals per hectare outside watershed in contrast to 10.9 quintals per hectare inside the watershed.

- Singh and Jain (2004) studied the Kandi Watershed and Area Development Project (KWADP) of Punjab in which two periods, 1979/80 and 2000/01, were taken into account, and reported that the cultivated area increased from 19.4% to 55.3%, cropping intensity increased from 113.7% to 143.1% and the productivity of maize, wheat, and milk was also enhanced.

- Nasurudeen and Mahesh (2006), who studied the Cauvery delta of the Karaikal region of Pondicherry found that the cropping intensity and yield of major crops in watershed system was higher compared to conventional method. Swarnalatha and Yadav (2006) studied the Joharanpur watershed in Solan district of Himachal Pradesh and observed that after adoption of new technology the yield had increased.

- Deshpande and Narayanamoorthy (1999) studied the effect of the National Watershed Development Programme in Gujarat and reported that the cost structure of agricultural operations underwent changes in favour of cash inputs. The watershed treatment induced more consumption of fertilizers, high-yielding variety (HYV) seeds, farm yard manure (FYM), and increased area under irrigation.

Watershed Development for Poverty Reduction

In India, most of the rural poor depend, directly or indirectly, on a watershed for their livelihood. As in many parts of the country, poor people depend mostly on rainwater to meet agriculture needs. In these harsh conditions, poor farmers often turn to lower-value crops, which yield poor returns. Development in these rural areas is further hampered by increased demands on limited natural resources. Improved watershed management has helped communities in Indian states to improve agricultural productivity and income, and to establish sustainable access to water for agriculture, drinking, and other daily needs.

Watershed projects are the main intervention for (way of) managing natural resources and improving the living conditions of farmers. The livelihood base of rural poor and marginal farmers is primarily income from livestock and farm work. They also benefit from casual, unskilled jobs created by construction requirements. Therefore, most watershed projects also include among their aims the improvement of the livelihoods of the rural poor by providing sustainable livelihoods to the people residing in the watershed areas (Figure 9.1).

Especially small farmers gain from watershed development programmes. As poor farmers in absence of water, often turn to lower-value crops, which yield poor returns. However, access to water for agriculture, drinking, and other daily needs results in overall benefits to them.

Many studies show that beneficiaries of watershed development programmes enjoyed higher gross income than those in common dryland areas. Also employment opportunities are higher. For example, Deshpande and Rajashekaran (1997) in their study on the National Watershed Development Programme of Maharashtra found an increase in gross household income from 17% to 42%. And a study by Singh and Jain (2004) on the KWADP watershed programme of Punjab showed new employment generation from crops and dairy productions of 82.7 days and 135.2 days, respectively.

Watershed development programmes can be done by employing a large number of people in labour-based activities. India's recent Mahatma Gandhi National Rural Employment Guarantee Scheme (MGNREGS) is one of the programmes that make use of poor people's labour to develop watersheds, thereby improving the environment and enriching the water level for better agricultural outputs, making the areas more resilient against climate change, and—most importantly—providing stable income sources for the poor.

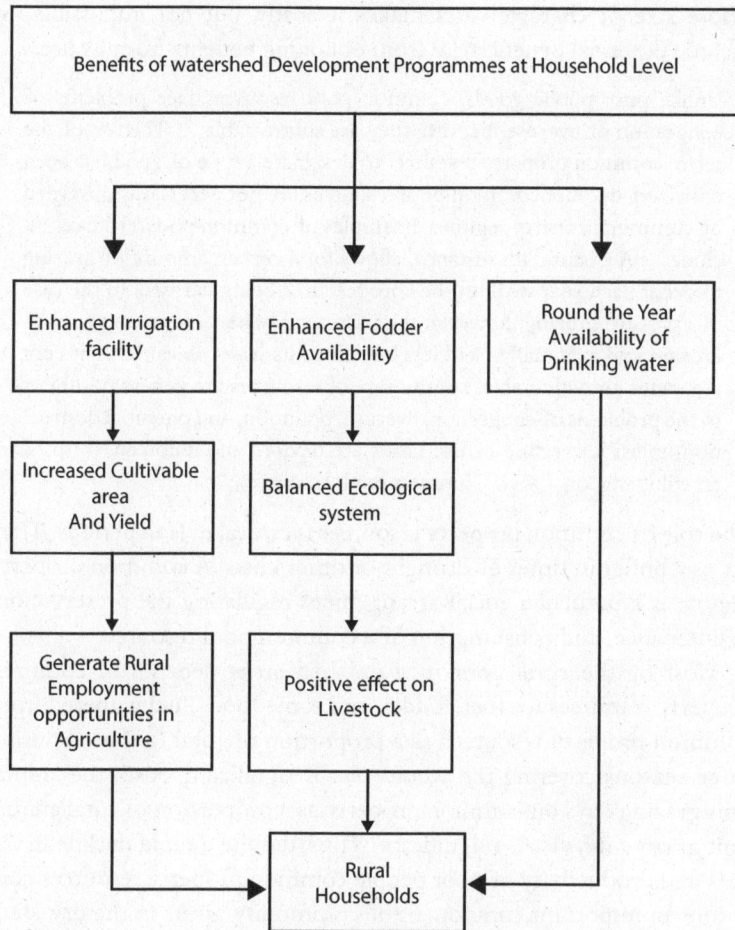

FIGURE 9.1   Household-Level Benefits of Watershed Development
Programmes

Common Property Resources

Watersheds are often common-property resources with little—if any—individual ownerships of land. Common property resources are goods consisting of a natural or human-made resource system (e.g., irrigation systems, fishing grounds, pastures, forests, water or the atmosphere), whose size or characteristics makes it costly, but not impossible, to exclude potential beneficiaries from obtaining benefits from its use.

> Unlike pure public goods, common pool resources face problems of congestion or overuse, because they are subtractable.... The use of the term 'common property resource' to designate a type of good has been criticized, because common-pool resources are not necessarily governed by common property regimes. Examples of common-pool resources include.... A pasture, for instance, allows for a certain amount of grazing to occur each year without the core resource being harmed. In the case of excessive grazing, however, the pasture may become more prone to erosion and eventually yield less benefit to its users. Because their core resources are vulnerable, common-pool resources are generally subject to the problems of congestion, overuse, pollution, and potential destruction unless harvesting or use limits are devised and enforced. (http://en.wikipedia.org/wiki/Common-pool_resource)

The role of common property resources is critical in lean periods. They act as a buffer in times of drought or other crisis. A common property regime is a particular social arrangement regulating the preservation, maintenance, and consumption of a common-pool resource.

Most of the rural poor in watershed areas depend on common property resources for fuel, fodder, and some food. Fuel gathered from common property resources as a proportion of total fuel used during three seasons covering the whole year is significant. Also, the animal unit grazing days on common property as a proportion of total animal unit grazing days is also significant. Thus, despite a rapid decline in the area and productivity of poor people common property resources constitute an important component of community assets in the dry areas of India (KAWAD 1995).

Excludable and Non-excludable Goods

Excludable	Non-Excludable
Private goods food, clothing, cars, personal electronics	**Common goods (common-pool resources)** fish stocks, timber, coal
Club goods cinemas, private parks, satellite television	**Public goods** free-to-air television, air, national defense

Conclusions and Policy Lessons

This chapter found that watershed development—paired with common-property rights—is a useful tool to address climate change and rural poverty at the same time. First, the watershed development programmes involving the entire community and natural resources influence productivity and production of crops, changes in land use and cropping pattern, adoption of modern technologies, increase in milk production, etc. Second, it invokes changes in attitude of the community towards project activities and their participation at different stages of the project. Third, it changes socioeconomic conditions of the people, such as income, employment, assets, health, education, and energy use. In addition to these, there is an impact on environment, use of land, water, human and livestock resources, and development of institutions for implementation of watershed development activities. It is thus clear that watershed development is key to sustainable production of food, fodder, and fuelwood and meaningfully addresses the social, economical, and cultural status of the rural community.

To ensure this, there is a need to bring the three relevant ministries (rural development, agriculture, and environment and forests) under a single umbrella. They are driven by different policy priorities. There is no effective policy-level communication on effective watershed programmes at either the central or the state levels. There is a need to manage watershed development programmes on scientific lines under the direct supervision of a competent committee. Unless these are managed in this way, access by poorer groups may remain low.

Lastly, fiscal decentralization and community empowerment are necessary steps to promote improved community management of natural resources. More work is needed to strengthen the institutional framework at the local level.

References

Anonymous. 1997. *Turning Challenges into Opportunity*. Bangalore: Dry Land Development Board, Government of Karnataka.

Datt, Gaurav and Martin Ravallion. 2002. 'Is India's Growth Leaving the Poor Behind?' *Journal of Economic Perspectives* 16(3): 89–108.

Deshpande, R.S. and A. Narayanamoorthy. 1999. 'An Appraisal of Watershed Development Programme across Regions', *Artha Vijyan* 41(4): 415–515.

Deshpande, R.S. and N. Rajashekaran. 1997. 'Impact of Watershed Development: Experience and Issues', *Artha Vijyan* 34(3): 374–90.

KAWAD. 1995. *ODA Karnataka Watershed Development Project*, Final Report, November, Overseas Development Administration, London.

Kerr, John and Kimberly Chung. 2001. 'Evaluating Watershed Management Projects', *Water Policy* 3(6, August): 537–54.

Lal, R., Ed. 2000. *Integrated Watershed Management in the Global Ecosystem*. Florida, CRC Press.

Nasurudeen, P. and N. Mahesh. 2006. 'Socioeconomic and Environmental Perspectives of Sustainable Watershed', *Agricultural Economic Research Review* 19: 49–58.

Planning Commission. 2004. *Report of the Inter-Ministry Task Force on Integrating Ongoing Schemes*. New Delhi: Government of India.

Rao, Hanumantha. 2000. 'Watershed Development in India: Recent Experiences and Emerging Issues', *Economic and Political Weekly* 35(45), 4 November.

Shah, Amita. 2000. 'Who Benefits from Watershed Development? Evidence from Gujarat', Working Paper No. 118, Gujarat Institute for Development Research, Ahmadabad.

Shah, Mihir, D. Banerji, P.S. Vijayshankar, and Pramathesh Ambasta. 1998. *India's Drylands: Tribal Societies and Development through Environmental Regeneration*. New Delhi: Oxford University Press.

Singh, N. and K. K. Jain. 2004. 'Long term Impact Evaluation of Watershed Development Projects in Punjab', *Indian Journal of Agricultural Economics* 59(3): 321–30.

Shridara, K. 2002. 'An Evaluation of Watershed Programme in Pavagada Taluk of Tumkur District in Karnataka', M. Sc. (Agri.) Thesis, University of Agricultural Sciences, Bangalore.

Swarnalatha, A. and R.P. Yadav. 2006. 'Economic Viability of Rainwater Harvesting by Renovating Village Ponds in Small Agricultural Watershed of Joharanpur', *Agricultural Economics Research Review* 19(January–June): 71–82.

10

G.M. ARIF
N. IQBAL
S. FAROOQ

Poverty and Pakistan's 2010 Flood

In this chapter, we make a preliminary analysis at the district level of the effect of 2010 Pakistan flood on poverty, as measured by head-count ratio, education, health, and displacement. The flood disproportionately affected regions of the country with high deprivation levels, poor infrastructure, and unfavourable demography. The flood caused damage to crops, infrastructure, public, and private property. Damage to crops and infrastructure has severely affected the well-being of the residents. It has probably pushed 6–7 million people into poverty. If the government is to rehabilitate the flood victims, it must mobilize internal resources.

Environment degradation is one of the major challenges faced by Pakistan. Degraded soil, a decline in forest cover, and rising levels of air and water pollution are the major environmental problems. Environmental degradation is compounded by rapid growth of the cities, largely as a result of people moving to them from the country. This growth has led to creation of slums on peripheries and low-lying areas of the cities (Government of Pakistan [GoP] 2010a). Pakistan is also disadvantaged by its heavy dependence on a single river, the Indus, for surface water. The country is, therefore, highly vulnerable to the effects of basin degradation and water pollution.

In the last several years, Pakistan has faced two disasters: an earthquake in 2005 and the flood in July–August 2010. The 2010 flood has implications at both macro and micro levels. At the macro level, the flood has caused losses to both GDP and capital stock and has thus hampered the growth potential of the country. In the long run, its effects are twofold: capital damages may induce a lower GDP in subsequent years (to the extent of investment losses), and output losses (caused during the flood-affected year) may lower incomes and possibly reduce savings available for financing investments. At the micro level, the flood has direct implications for the affected people. It may have reduced their incomes, thus aggravating the household poverty.

Moreover, the 2010 flood has disproportionately affected the poorest regions of Pakistan; that is, southern Punjab and rural Sindh. The majority of the population in these regions is highly dependent on crop income. The flood has snatched their limited assets and livelihoods, and has pushed them into extreme poverty.

The purpose of this study is to derive district-level implications from the recent flood. Due to a lack of data, the scope of study is limited, and it only focuses on implications at the micro level. This study

- analyses the severity of the flood across districts;
- examines the socioeconomic situation in flood-affected districts before the flood in 2010;
- examines losses caused by the flood and the public policy responses;
- assesses implications of the flood for poverty, health, education, and migration; and
- draws policy implications.

Rest of the chapter is organized as follows: The details on methodology and the sources of data are given in the following section. A discussion on flood-affected areas and systematic issues behind the flood is given in the third section, followed by an analysis of the socio-demographic and economic situation prior to the 2010 flood in the fourth section. The losses of flood are analysed in the fifth section, while the adequacy of public responses is discussed in the sixth section. The implications of 2010 flood for poverty, health, education, and migration are given in the seventh section. Conclusions and policy considerations are given in the final section.

Data Sources and Methodology

This chapter is essentially a review study, based on the existing literature, though data gathered from 83 flood-affected households in Muzaffargarh district has also been used. The flood affected some regions of the country more than others. For this study, the districts in each province are classified into three categories (according to how they were affected by the flood): (a) severely affected; (b) moderately affected, and (c) not affected. The primary source for classifying districts into three categories is the assessments of flood damage made by various organizations. Information on pre-flood socioeconomic and demographic characteristics is mainly drawn from the Pakistan Social and Living Standards Measurement (PSLM) 2008–09 and the Pakistan Demographic Survey (PDS) 2007. The 2000 Agriculture Census has been used to obtain the household status and Population Census 1998 has been used to determine population density. Infrastructure data have been taken at the district level from the *mouza* Statistics 2008, published by the Agriculture Census Organization at the mouza level (GoP 2000, 2010b).[1] The extent of poverty at the district level after the 2010 flood was determined using headcount ratio, health, education, and displacement. In addition to secondary data sources, this study has used micro-data of the Pakistan Panel Household Survey (PPHS) conducted by the Pakistan Institute of Development Economics (PIDE) in 2010. The PPHS covered 16 districts. The district Muzaffargarh was hit by the flood during the survey. The fieldwork had to stop and leftover villages were covered after three months, when people returned to their homes. In total 83 flood-affected households were interviewed. This is a small sample, which is not representative at any level, but it provides useful information about the flood-affected households.

Flood-Affected Areas

In central and northern Punjab, the canal command areas are affected by the flooding of the Jhelum and Chenab rivers, whereas southern

---

[1] A mouza is the lowest administrative unit in rural areas and commonly used for land record, revenue collection, census block, and seat allocations in the local bodies.

Punjab is affected by the Sindh river. The areas affected in the province of Sindh are largely on right bank of the Indus river in upper Sindh. The Indus river changed its course due to a breach of the bund on right bank, but again in central Sindh flows of the Indus river diverted from the right bank to join the main stream of the Indus river. In the province of Khyber Pakhtunkhwa (formerly the North-West Frontier Province), the areas affected by flood are largely in south of the Indus river system. The areas in the north were affected severely, but less than in the south. In Balochistan, the area affected by flood is largely in the eastern side of province on the right bank of the Indus river. More than two-thirds of the districts of Pakistan were affected by the flood: 29 severely and 49 moderately affected. The flood also moderately affected 14 districts in North-Eastern Pakistan areas. The proportion of severely affected and moderately affected districts is greater in Punjab and Sindh than in Khyber Pakhtunkhwa and Balochistan. All severely affected districts of Punjab are located in its southern zone, including Muzaffargarh, Rajanpur, D.G. Khan, and Rahim Yar Khan.

Pre-flood Demographic and Socioeconomic Situation: A District-Level Analysis

The Demographic, Social, and Economic Profile of Flood-affected Districts

Table 10.1 presents data for selected socio-demographic indicators classified into three categories. In population density, severely affected districts are no different from other districts. However, among severely affected districts, the density is much higher in Muzaffargarh and Rahim Yar Khan. One of the most important indicators of demography is household size. If a large household increases the number of earners, it would normally reduce its chances of being poor by increasing the household income. According to the PDS 2007, average household size in Pakistan is 6.65—a bit higher (6.58) in urban areas and a bit lower (6.69) in rural areas. Table 10.1 shows that household size in the severely affected districts of Punjab is generally larger (around 7.5) than in either not-affected or moderately affected districts. To some extent, Table 10.1 indicates relatively high fertility and probably a high dependency ratio in southern Punjab and rural Sindh, the two severely affected flood

TABLE 10.1 Pre-flood Socio-demographic Characteristics by Districts

Districts	Population Density (person per kilometre)	Household Size	Literacy Rate	Infant Mortality Rate	Non-agri Household (%)	Livestock Households	Farm Household	Poverty 2004–05		
								Urban	Rural	Total
Punjab										
Districts Severely Affected by the Flood										
Mianwali	181	7.5	57	54	33.1	22.4	44.4	17	23	22
Layyah	178	7.5	52	80	17.2	16.7	66.1	22	30	29
Rajanpur	90	7.5	27	62	24.7	16.9	58.4	29	34	33
D.G. Khan	138	7.6	41	61	32.7	18.9	48.4	20	35	33
R.Y. Khan	264	7.2	43	82	20.5	12.0	27.8	18	38	34
Muzaffar Garh	320	7.4	44	82	27.3	18.8	54.5	28	38	37
Khushab	139	6.7	58	79	33.6	18.2	48.2	21	26	25
Districts Moderately Affected by the Flood										
Bhakhar	129	6.5	58	80	18.0	18.8	63.2	27	26	26
Sargodha	455	6.6	61	91	44.5	25.5	29.9	18	31	27
Jhang	322	6.6	51	89	32.5	25.3	42.2	26	31	30
Multan	838	7.0	56	70	56.6	18.2	25.3	21	35	30
Districts Not Affected by the Flood										
Islamabad	–	6.3	84	39	75.5	5.2	19.3	3	16	8
Chakwal	166	6.3	76	59	29.5	13.9	56.5	12	12	12

(Cont'd)

TABLE 10.1 (Cont'd)

Districts	Population Density (person per kilometre)	Household Size	Literacy Rate	Infant Mortality Rate	Non-agri Household (%)	Livestock Households	Farm Household	Poverty 2004-05		
								Urban	Rural	Total
Lahore	3,566	6.8	80	50	91.4	4.7	3.9	9	24	12
Rawalpindi	636	6.6	69	40	53.0	5.0	42.1	10	17	14
Jhelum	261	6.5	77	69	41.9	11.5	46.7	11	18	16
Gujrat	642	7.0	73	65	43.6	10.5	45.9	14	18	17
Sialkot	903	7.4	66	70	52.1	14.3	33.6	12	19	17
Attock	186	6.2	61	60	36.7	10.3	53.0	10	19	17
Gujranwala	939	7.5	71	76	64.7	14.8	20.6	16	23	19
Faisalabad	927	7.0	61	58	59.2	16.0	24.8	15	25	21
Toba Tek Singh	499	6.9	65	64	46.7	21.7	31.6	17	23	21
Narowal	541	7.7	63	74	31.2	21.0	47.8	19	24	23
Mondi Bahawal	434	6.6	66	71	35.4	22.7	41.9	18	25	24
Sahiwal	576	6.7	50	65	41.7	22.9	35.4	16	27	25
Sheikhupura	557	7.0	65	87	48.6	17.6	33.9	17	29	26
Hafizabad	352	7.0	58	81	40.5	25.8	33.7	23	27	26
Bahawalnager	232	6.7	43	92	33.7	25.0	41.3	25	28	28
Okara	510	6.5	50	86	40.5	25.2	34.3	23	30	29
Khanewal	476	7.1	52	87	32.3	27.8	39.9	26	30	29
Kasur	595	7.0	56	74	43.9	21.0	35.1	25	31	29
Pakpattan	472	6.2	45	95	35.5	26.9	37.6	21	31	30

Lodhran	422	7.2	46	86	30.9	23.0	46.2	24	31	30
Vehari	479	6.6	44	–	35.7	25.7	38.6	27	32	31
Bahawalpur	98	6.7	54	72	38.9	18.9	42.2	24	34	31
Ghotki	160	6.5	45	57	–	–	–	22	18	19

Sindh

Districts Severely Affected by the Flood

Sukkur	176	8.6	56	35	47.7	26.8	25.5	17	23	19
Khairpur	97	6.9	54	44	29.5	25.5	45.0	18	21	21
Jaccobabad	270	6.8	39	32	32.9	36.6	30.5	20	22	22
Shikhapur	350	6.9	53	32	45.1	18.6	36.3	26	27	26
Thatta	64	6.0	41	38	43.8	32.0	2.4	24	27	26
Dadu	89	7.4	61	36	37.1	30.9	32.1	28	27	27
Larkana	260	7.1	53	57	35.9	28.9	35.2	29	29	29

Districts Moderately Affected by the Flood

Hyderabad	524	6.3	69	43	58.4	22.2	19.4	16	21	19
Nowshero Fero	369	7.5	72	33	45.9	29.0	25.1	19	25	23
Nawabshah	238	7.0	49	44	28.0	38.3	33.7	26	22	24

Districts Not Affected by the Flood

Karachi	2,795	6.1	78	39	97.7	1.8	0.5	8	24	9
Tharparkar	47	6.9	39	48	29.5	25.5	45.0	14	19	18
Mir Pur Khas	536	5.9	45	42	40.8	37.3	21.9	12	29	23
Sanghar	135	6.7	53	41	29.4	28.8	41.8	21	25	24
Badin	169	6.0	40	42	27.4	20.7	51.9	22	26	25

(Cont'd)

TABLE 10.1 *(Cont'd)*

Districts	Population Density (person per kilometre)	Household Size	Literacy Rate	Infant Mortality Rate	Non-agri Household (%)	Livestock Households	Farm Household	Poverty 2004–05		
								Urban	Rural	Total
Khyber Pakhtun Khaw										
Districts Severely Affected by the Flood										
Peshawar	1,606	8.0	53	32	70.5	11.2	18.3	19	33	26
Lower Dir	454	9.9	52	57	8.9	16.3	74.8	27	27	27
Tank	142	8.8	38	47	24.9	23.7	51.4	29	27	28
Nowshera	500	8.8	43	44	52.0	11.6	36.4	25	29	28
D.I. Khan	116	7.3	39	57	32.8	25.0	42.2	20	32	30
Swat	236	8.8	47	50	43.0	10.1	46.8	21	33	31
Charsada	1,026	7.6	43	38	45.4	18.3	36.4	35	34	34
Kohistan	63	10.2	30	47	3.7	9.5	86.8	–	38	38
Upper Dir	156	9.5	49	57	11.8	13.2	74.9	32	41	41
Shnagla	274	8.9	39	61	18.7	12.4	68.9	–	41	41
Districts Moderately Affected by the Flood										
Abbottabad	448	6.6	72	54	25.8	3.9	70.2	12	24	22
Haripur	401	6.8	68	50	30.0	9.1	60.9	10	24	22
Hangu	287	10.4	44	36	22.6	6.8	70.6	23	27	27
Bannu	551	9.4	49	35	38.6	10.3	51.1	20	28	27

Swabi	665	7.8	49	56	36.3	18.4	45.3	28	29	29
Chitral	21	8.5	56	86	3.7	5.0	91.3	17	30	29
Kohat	221	7.0	49	51	41.1	10.4	48.5	22	32	30
Karak	128	10.8	53	51	14.1	8.8	77.1	28	31	31
Lakki Marwat	155	9.2	44	54	24.7	19.2	56.0	19	32	31
Mardan	895	8.0	47	41	45.9	15.8	38.3	29	34	33
Mansehra	252	7.8	57	35	28.3	7.7	64.0	18	34	33
Malakand	475	9.2	56	39	22.3	11.7	66.1	33	34	34
Batgram	236	8.4	47	67	13.0	5.7	79.3	-	36	36
Boneir	271	9.5	37	40	15.8	12.1	72.0	-	40	40
Balochistan										
Districts Severely Affected by the Flood										
Jafarabad	177	8.1	38	34	21.2	21.2	57.6	15	23	22
Nasirabad	73	8.2	31	41	42.4	6.2	51.4	20	26	26
Districts Moderately Affected by the Flood										
Loralai	30	9.9	38	35	20.7	25.4	53.9	17	27	26
Barkhan	29	7.4	29	82	12.7	10.2	77.1	27	27	27
Qilla Saifull	28	8.9	37	62	3.6	12.8	83.6	13	30	29
Musa Khel	23	8.1	23	82	3.6	65.4	31.0	-	31	31
Bolan/Kachhi	38	7.8	52	47	19.0	15.0	65.9	28	32	31
Sibbi	23	8.6	46	32	56.1	14.0	30.0	21	39	34
Jhal Maagsi	30	9.3	23	66	4.9	9.2	85.9	33	37	36

(Cont'd)

TABLE 10.1 (Cont'd)

Districts	Population Density (person per kilometre)	Household Size	Literacy Rate	Infant Mortality Rate	Non-agri Household (%)	Livestock Households	Farm Household	Poverty 2004–05		
								Urban	Rural	Total
Districts Not Affected by the Flood										
Gwadar	15	6.8	61	41	89.6	4.1	6.3	10	21	15
Quetta	281	8.9	67	42	77.7	6.8	15.5	12	31	20
Kalat	36	9.2	42	55	30.2	10.1	59.7	20	21	21
Khuzdar	12	7.4	46	61	21.6	18.4	60.0	21	21	21
Mastung	30	9.8	37	57	57.4	10.6	32.0	15	27	25
Awaran	4	8.1	43	60	15.0	31.4	53.6	–	25	25
Ketch/Turbat	18	7.2	52	44	33.9	18.2	47.8	13	27	26
Panjgur	14	8.6	49	32	7.0	24.7	68.3	6	30	29
Ziarat	22	8.8	65	66	8.8	8.2	83.0	20	30	29
Zhob	14	10.7	41	52	18.1	25.8	56.1	14	32	30
Kharan	4	6.6	33	46	19.0	18.4	62.7	22	32	32
Qillah Abdull	112	9.6	37	32	24.7	23.2	52.1	13	36	34
Lasbela	21	8.4	40	46	23.5	25.6	50.9	23	38	34
Pishin	47	11.2	55	32	35.1	19.0	45.9	29	36	35
Chaghi	4	8.5	43	49	21.2	25.5	53.3	24	43	40
Kehli	–	4.6	7	51	45.1	45.3	9.6	–	–	–

Source: Cheema (2010); GoP (2010b); Jamal et al. (2003).

zones. It suggests a relatively high population pressures in flood-affected districts.

The literacy rate at the national level for population 10 years and above was 57% in 2008–09. The literacy data by district show that situation is worse in flood-affected districts of all provinces (Table 10.1). In Punjab, the severely affected districts, such as Rajanpure, Rahim Yar Khan, D.G. Khan, and Muzaffargarh are amongst the least literate. Similarly, in Sindh, the severely flood-affected districts of Jaccobabad, Thatha, Dadu, and Kashmore fall in the lowest ranks in literacy. Infant mortality rates also show that flood-affected districts in all provinces have higher rates than the nation as a whole or than their respective provinces.

In the nation as a whole, 45% of rural households are non-agricultural, 37% are agricultural, and 18% are livestock owners. There is a variation in the share of pure livestock households among total rural households across the four provinces; it is highest, 22%, in Sindh. The district-level analysis shows relatively high proportion of farm households in severely affected districts of Punjab and Sindh (Table 10.1). These are districts where dependency on the crop sector is high and access to non-agricultural income is lower than in economically better-off regions.

The pre-flood situation (2008–09) of housing units by tenure reveals that 87% of households were living in their own dwelling units while 6% rented, about 6% had rent-free units, and 1% lived in subsidized housing (GoP 2009). The district-level statistics reveal that people predominantly live in their own housing units. There is no significant difference in house ownership between flood-affected districts and other districts of provinces.

Infrastructure

Data on physical infrastructure in the provinces and districts are presented in Table 10.2 including access to metal road, electricity, street soling, drain system, and availability of piped drinking water. The table shows clear differences in infrastructure between the districts. In Punjab, 80% of mouzas have a metal road (roads built with broken stines and bricks) within 1 km of them. In severely flood-affected districts of Punjab, 76.9% of mouzas are located less than 1 km from a metal road.

TABLE 10.2 Percentage of Mouzas Having Infrastructure Facilities

| Province | Physical Infrastructure | | | | | Soft Infrastructure | |
	Distance to Metal Road < 1	Electricity	Soling Street	Drain	Piped Water	Education Institutions	Health Institutions
Overall Punjab	80.0	47.0	66.0	58.0	9.0	34.0	30.5
Severely affected district	76.9	15.9	49.4	33.7	5.5	32.6	28.1
Moderately affected district	79.0	26.8	66.8	53.8	7.0	34.2	31.7
Total affected district	77.6	19.8	55.7	41.0	6.1	33.2	29.4
Overall Sindh	67.0	10.0	30.0	23.0	7.0	37.5	27.3
Severely affected district	64.3	10.3	35.0	29.1	8.0	35.8	26.6
Moderately affected district	70.6	12.1	49.1	34.3	10.6	40.1	30.7
Total affected district	67.1	11.1	41.3	31.4	9.2	37.7	28.4
Overall KPK	38.0	34.0	29.0	19.0	20.0	33.3	24.5
Severely affected district	55.2	38.0	53.1	37.4	30.8	41.7	29.4
Moderately affected district	63.8	36.3	57.8	39.5	30.7	46.3	35.3
Total affected district	60.1	37.0	55.8	38.6	30.7	44.3	32.7
Overall Balochistan	20.0	12.0	8.0	7.0	9.0	22.3	11.3
Severely affected district	36.5	6.5	4.5	3.0	4.5	26.9	12.3
Moderately affected district	22.2	14.3	2.6	1.5	11.7	25.6	11.5
Total affected district	24.6	13.0	2.9	1.8	10.5	25.8	11.6

Source: GoP (2010b).

In Sindh, overall 67% mouzas have access to a metal road within 1 km. In the severely flood-affected districts of Sindh, 64.3% of mouzas are located less than 1 km from a metal road. Access to metal roads within the distance of 1 km is very bad in Khyber Pakhtunkhwa (38% mouzas) and Balochistan (20% mouzas), although the flood-affected districts of these two provinces were better than the average for their respective provinces (Table 10.2).

In terms of electricity, 47% mouzas in Punjab, 10% mouzas in Sindh, 34% mouzas in Khyber Pakhtunkhwa, and 12% mouzas in Balochistan have access to electricity for the whole mouza. The flood-affected districts in Punjab and Sindh have less access to electricity than their provincial averages. In Khyber Pakhtunkhwa and Balochistan, the flood-affected districts have more access to electricity than their province averages. The situation of soling streets, piped drinking water, and drainage systems is not different from the situation of access to a metal road and electricity (Table 10.2).

In Punjab, 34% of mouzas have educational institutions for boys, and 30.5% for girls.[2] The flood-affected districts in Punjab have less access to these facilities (Table 10.2). In Sindh, 37.5% of mouzas have education institutions for boys, and 27.3% for girls. The flood-affected districts have lower figures than their provincial averages.

Pre-flood Poverty Situation

More than one-third of population was living below poverty line in severely affected districts of Punjab before the 2010 flood. The poverty level was relatively low in moderately and not affected districts of Punjab (Table 10.1). In Sindh, the situation is not different; poverty declined between 2001 and 2005 and around one-quarter of households in severely affected districts were living below poverty line in 2004–05 (Table 10.1). With the jump in poverty after 2005–06, approximately 30% of Sindh population was below poverty line just before 2010 flood. The deprivation levels show that districts severely affected by flood

---

[2] Education Institution Index for boys is an index calculated by taking the summation of four indicator of education by equally weighting so: Education Institution Index = ([primary school × 0.25] + [middle school × 0.25] + [high school × 0.25] + [college × 0.25]). Similar index is calculated for girls.

particularly in Punjab and Sindh have high deprivation levels while the majority of districts with low deprivation are not affected by flood or only moderately (Jamal et al. 2003).

The picture that emerges from the pre-flood district-level analysis is that overall Pakistan has not witnessed any reduction in poverty between the 2007 and 2010 because of high inflation and low economic growth. Regional and district-level variations in socio-demographic and economic indicators persist in the country and the flood of 2010 disproportionately affected poor regions and districts, particularly in southern Punjab and rural Sindh.

Losses of the 2010 Flood

The 2010 flood caused damage at an unprecedented level to agriculture, livestock, fisheries, and forestry. It also destroyed primary agriculture infrastructure, including tube wells, water channels, headworks, bunds, storages, animal sheds, seed stocks, and machinery. The flood struck just before the major crops were to be harvested. Table 10.3 shows the cropped areas that were affected and the extent of cattle loss by district. In Punjab, the flood heavily damaged crops in Mianwali, Rajanpur, Muzaffargarh, Sargodha, Rahim Yar Khan, and Jhang districts. Muzaffargarh, Rajanpur, and Rahim Yar Khan are in south Punjab and are part of the cotton belt on which the textile industry heavily depends. Similarly, cropped areas damaged in various districts of Sindh were part of the cotton belt. The loss of cattle was high: 3.2 million heads, 6 million poultry were also lost. Sukker district alone lost 124,000 cattle. The other severely affected districts in Sindh were Gotki, Shahdadkot, Khairpur, and Kashmore. The cattle losses were high in Charsadda and Kohistan districts of Khyber Pakhtunkhwa (NDMA 2010).

The PPHS data collected from 83 households after the flood in Muzaffargarh district show that 54% of households reported serious damages to both their crops and livestock. The rest of the households are likely to be landless, depending on the agriculture sector indirectly. The value of reported crop and livestock losses were Rs 180,000 and Rs 37,000 respectively. Keeping in view small landholdings, it appears that flood-affected households lost all their crop income. Eighty-one per

Table 10.3   Province-wise Damages of Cropped Area and Cattle Head

	Cropped Area Affected (acres)	Cattle Head Lost
Punjab		
Severely affected districts	1,310,255	3,461
Moderately affected districts	401,701	198
Sindh		
Severely affected districts	2,235,045	262,238
Moderately affected districts	218,458	26
Khyber Pakhtunkhwa		
Severely affected districts	423,933	51,327
Moderately affected districts	136,132	1,423
Baluchistan		
Severely affected districts	349,400	NA
Moderately affected districts	281,305	15,031
North-Eastern Pakistan areas		
Moderately affected districts	85,140	4,957

Source: NDMA (2010).

cent of the flood-affected households reported some damage to their dwelling units, and the value of the reported loss was Rs 102,000 per household. District Muzaffargarh is among the poorest districts of the country. The 2010 flood has added to their misery.

Poverty Implications of 2010 Flood

Poverty Levels

In the absence of data for the post-flood period, it is not possible to estimate poverty at the national or district levels. However, it is possible to make some educated guesses about how the recent flood affected poverty levels. The flood hit severely the areas in south Punjab and rural Sindh where poverty has historically been higher than other regions of the country. The data shows that rural households in south Punjab and Sindh are engaged in farming, livestock rearing, and non-agriculture activities. Empirical studies have shown that poverty has been higher in non-agriculture households, followed by livestock households and small farmers. It has been shown that the flood-affected areas lost homes, crops, and livestock. Due to the lack of an industrial base, sources of income for households situated in these severely affected areas are less diversified; with heavy dependence on agriculture, livestock, and casual labour, but negligible flows of remittances. These areas are character-ized by large household size, low literacy levels, higher mortality rates, landlessness, a low level of infrastructure, and poor access to education and health facilities. There also exists more inequality of assets and land ownership (GoP various issues).

Through the destruction of roads, the flood hurt the commodity market. As a result, the functioning capacity of transporters, proces-sors, wholesalers, and retailers decreased and transaction costs and food commodity shortages increased. The prices of wheat and rice increased in flooded areas.

The losses of crops and livestock, the poor functioning capacity of markets, and high inflation have reduced the expected real income of all occupational groups. According to a World Food Programme (WFP) study in 2010, about half of flood-affected households were making less than half as much as usual from their principal sources of liveli-hoods. The flood pushed poor people in deeper into poverty as of those who lost their income by more than 75%, 45% were already below the national poverty line. Sixty per cent of daily wage labourers lost more than 50% of their income. The flood has severely affected 20 million people. Since around a third were poor prior to flood and another third have moved into poverty because of the flood, the flood may have added 6–7 million poor people at the national level.

The farm households need assistance in sowing, while the needs of livestock and non-agriculture households are different for restoration of their livelihood. But the apprehension is that a delay in assistance, and benefiting influential people at the cost of small farmers, may slow the rehabilitation process or even make it less effective. Another apprehension is that the non-agriculture households will be ignored. These households are among the poorest rural households and could be further excluded socially if they are not made an integral part of the rehabilitation process. The preliminary investigation of the flood-affected areas of Pakistan shows that besides selling their assets, poor households are coping with the crisis by (a) borrowing money and (b) shifting their consumption to inferior food items (WFP 2010).

Health Implications

A number of diseases, including gastroenteritis, acute diarrhoea, paralysis, respiratory infections, malaria, and skin infections have affected 6.7 million people in two months. Figure 10.1 shows the trends of diseases after the flood. Diarrhoea is stagnant, while the acute respiratory infections and suspected malaria are increasing in the flood-affected areas. In the north, the incidence of diarrhoea is low and is expected to decline with the change of climate, but it still remains high in the southern areas of Pakistan.

Malaria still remains a threat, especially in Punjab and Sindh provinces. Contaminated water and lack of sanitation are the main causes of malaria and other diseases in flood-affected areas. Health concerns are also rising due to poor nutrition, food security, lack of shelter, and malnutrition. WFP estimates that half of population is not getting acceptable intake according to the global food consumption score (FCS).[3] About 5% of mothers have stopped breastfeeding, and 16% have

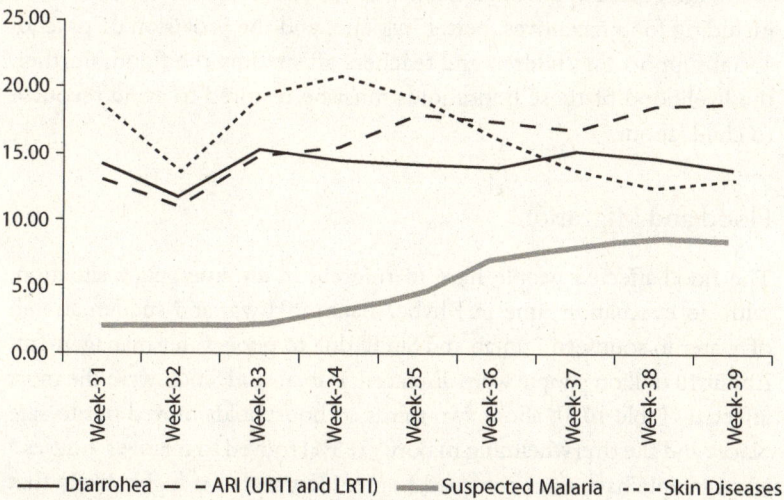

FIGURE 10.1   Trend of Various Diseases in Flood-Affected Areas
Source: WHO (2010a).

[3] FCS was calculated based on the number of days particular food groups were consumed as follows: FCS = 2 (cereal) + 3 (pulses) + 4 (poultry/meat/eggs) + 0.5 (oil) + 4 (milk products) + 1 (vegetables) + 1 (fruit) + 0.5 (sugar/sweets).

reduced breastfeeding. Only 19% of respondents in flood-affected areas are using standard breast milk substitutes (BMS). Increasing numbers of children are expected to develop acute malnutrition combined with infectious diseases. Infectious diseases can be life-threatening in malnourished children (WHO 2010b).

Implications for Education

The flood has damaged school buildings. And the damage to the schools makes them dangerous to children. 461 temporary learning centres have been developed benefiting 39,413 children across the country. However, the performance of these centres is very poor. Based the amount of damages the flood caused, about $36.39 million is required. But only 31.4% of this amount is received (Table 10.4). About $252.3 million is required for the recovery of water, sanitation, and hygiene, and education rehabilitation. However, only $92.2 million is available, with a shortfall of $160.8 million.

An integrated approach is needed to sustain the quality of education, including food incentives, better hygiene, and the provision of psychosocial support for children and teachers affected by the flood. Further, the livelihood of these households must be restored to avoid recourse to child labour.

Flood and Migration

The flood-affected people have to migrate in an emergency situation, with no evacuation time in Khyber Pakhtunkhwa, and sudden stretch of water in southern Punjab and Sindh due to poor water management. About 10 million people were displaced. Punjab and Sindh were the most affected (Table 10.5); about two-thirds of households moved out to safe places and the overwhelming majority (88%) moved to relatives' houses.[4] Most people have since returned home. However, it is highly likely that

---

Cut-offs were applied as follows: (a) Poor food consumption is score between 0.5 and 21. (b) Moderate food consumption is score between 21.5 and 34.5. (c) Adequate food consumption is a score of more than 35.

[4] This figure is based on the 2010 PPHS data from Muzaffargah district.

TABLE 10.4 Required and Available Amount for Floods Emergency Response Plan

Key Sectors	Strategic Results	Required Resources ($ in millions)	Received (in %)
Water, sanitation, and hygiene	Girls, boys, and women have protected and reliable access to sufficient, safe water, and sanitation and facilities	123.82	31.4
Health	Excess mortality among girls, boys, and women in humanitarian crisis is prevented	50.83	32.1
Nutrition	The nutritional status of girls, boys, and women is protected from the effects of humanitarian crisis	27.6	65.1
Education	Girls and boys access safe and secure education and critical information for their own well-being	36.4	31.4
Child protection	Girls and boys rights to protection from violence, abuse, and exploitation are sustained and promoted	12.98	47.8
Total		252.3	92.2

Source: UNICEF (2010).

at least one member of a displaced family would migrate to cities as they have few opportunities locally. It may not have serious implications for the overall level of urbanization. However, if cities like Lahore and Karachi witness an influx, it will put stress on their infrastructures and increase pollution. Unemployment and crimes may increase.

Policy Responses

The government identified six priorities for early recovery, on-farm livelihoods, shelter, community restoration, education, health, infrastructure,

TABLE 10.5   Province-wise Internally Displaced Persons (IDPs) (as of 24 September 2010)

Province	Total Displaced Persons*	Number of Relief Camps**
Balochistan	218,000	17
Khyber Pakhtunkhwa	651,700	825
Punjab	2,666,000	327
Sindh	4,596,000	4,196
North-Eastern Pakistan areas	–	27
All	8,131,700	5,392

Source: *Initial assessment by WFP; **NDMA (2010).

and public utilities. The Watan Card scheme was launched for the reha-bilitation of flood victims. About 90,000 cards were issued with an initial instalment of Rs 20,000 per household. With the assistance of inter-national organizations, a number of steps were taken in various fields, agriculture, camp coordination/management, community restoration, education, shelter, telecommunication, health, food, information man-agement, logistic, nutrition, water, sanitation, hygienic, and protection. The aim of these steps was to promote emergency relief by ensuring greater predictability, accountability, and partnership. Moreover, the government of Pakistan provided free seeds for cultivation in flood-affected areas. The priorities set by the government for the rehabilitation of flood victims, the steps taken for emergency relief, and the provision of seed are steps in right direction. However, the level of commitment, resources, and actual steps taken are not adequate for rehabilitation pro-cess. According to the PPHS 2010 data, almost all respondents consider assistance received as inadequate and are looking for more assistance.

* * *

The analysis carried out in this study leads to the following conclusions: First, the 2010 flood disproportionately affected the poor regions of the country, particularly in south Punjab and Sindh. Second, the flood caused serious damages to crops, infrastructure, and public and private property. The damage to crops and infrastructure severely affected employment, growth, and exports. Third, the 2010 flood directly affected poverty status of households through the loss of household assets and income, deterioration in health status, and the destruction of education, health, and infrastructure facilities. It has probably pushed 6–7 million people into poverty.

The flood-affected people have largely returned to their communities. However, they need support in restoring their damaged houses and livelihoods. Small farmers and landless households in particular should be targeted for rehabilitation.

The policy implications are: (a) there is an urgent need to identify unpopulated areas in severely affected districts where flood flow could be diverted in future so as to protect the populated areas; (b) the construction of new dams and the repair of old dams should be carried out on a regular basis; (c) the forestation process should be implemented at the national level; (d) the sea beaches should be widened, and (e) and flood-prone areas should be converted into wetlands where inhabitation is not allowed in order to prevent the construction of permanent structures in these areas.

References

Azhar, A. 2011. 'An Analysis of Spatial Dimensions of Poverty in the Punjab', MPhil Thesis, Economics Department, Pakistan Institute of Development Economics, Islamabad.

Cheema, I. A. 2010. 'Tracing the Spatial Dimensions of Poverty', Working Paper 2010–02, Oxford Policy Management, UK.

Government of Pakistan. 2007. 'Pakistan Demographic Survey 2007', Federal Bureau of Statistics, Statistics Division, Government of Pakistan, Islamabad.

———. 2010a. 'Pakistan Economic Survey 2009–10', Ministry of Finance, Islamabad.

———. 2010b. 'Pakistan 2008 MOUZA Statistics (settled Areas)', Ministry of Economic Affairs and Statistics/Statistics Division/Agriculture Census Organization.

———. 2009. 'Pakistan Economic Survey 2008–09', Ministry of Finance, Islamabad.

———. 2000. Agriculture Census, Agriculture Census Organization, Statistics Division, Government of Pakistan, Lahore.

———. Various issues. 'Pakistan Integrated Household Survey (PIHS) 1998/99 and 2001/02', Federal Bureau of Statistics, Islamabad.

————. Various issues. 'Pakistan Social and Living Standards Measurement (PSLM) Survey', Federal Bureau of Statistics, Islamabad.

Jamal, H. 2006. 'Does Inequality Matter for Poverty Reduction? Evidence from Pakistan's Poverty Trends' *The Pakistan Development Review* 45 (3): 439–59.

Jamal, H. 2007. *Updating Poverty and Inequality Estimates: 2005 Panorama.* SPDC Research Report No. 69, Social Policy and Development Centre, Karachi.

Jamal, H., A.J. Khan, I.A. Toor, and N. Amir. 2003. 'Mapping the Spatial Deprivation of Pakistan' *The Pakistan Development Review* 42 (2): 91–111.

Nayab, Durr-e-e and G.M. Arif. 2012. Pakistan Panel Household Survey: Sample Size, Attrition, and Socio-demographic Dynamics, 'Poverty and Social Dynamics Paper Series (PSDPS) 1', Pakistan Institute of Development Economics, Islamabad.

NDMA. 2007. National Disaster Risk Management Framework Pakistan.

————. 2010. National Disaster Management Authority. Available at: http://ndma.gov.pk/.

PARC. 2010. 'Assessment of 2010 Flood Impacts in Pakistan: Extent and Coverage of Impacts and Adaptation Strategy', Pakistan Agricultural Research Council, Pakistan.

WFP. 2010. 'Pakistan Flood Impact Assessment', World Food Programme.

WHO. 2010a. Weekly Epidemiological Bulletins, government of Pakistan and WHO. Available at: http://www.whopak.org/idps/index.asp.

————. 'Pakistan Health Cluster no. 19', World Health Organization, 28 September 2010. Available at: http://www.whopak.org/idps/documents/bulletins/Health%20Cluster%20Bulletin%20No%2019-Final.pdf.

UNICEF. 2010. Available at: http://www.unicef.org/pakistan/.

11

G. BHASKAR REDDY

Climate Change Adaptation in the Western Odisha Rural Livelihoods Project

In this chapter, I discuss the ways people in the Indian state of Odisha are adapting to climate change, and the way that the Western Odisha Rural Livelihoods Project (WORLP) has contributed in making livelihoods there more resilient. The economy of Odisha is primarily agrarian. Agriculture contributes nearly 30% to the Net State Domestic Product. About 70% of the total workforce (as per 2001 census) is engaged in agriculture. Over the last two or three decades, there has been stagnation in agriculture in Odisha. Triennium annual compound growth in agriculture production is well below the national average (Satyanarayana et al. 2009). The state has wide disparities in agricultural growth. Districts like Kalahandi and Koraput rank much lower than other districts of the state. Some of the Western Odisha districts are poorest in India, with 70% of their 4 million people living below the poverty line. People in Western Odisha are highly vulnerable to climate change, partly because poverty limits their capacity to deal with shocks and stresses, and partly because they live in an area of high environmental risk. This is a region of India where the mean temperatures are rising, and where the vulnerability profile places it among the highest risk areas in the country (WORLP 1999).

Bolangir and Bargarh districts are a part of the 'West Central Table Land Zone' and have a hot and sub-humid climate.[1] Similarly, Kalahandi and Nuapada districts are a part of the 'Western Undulating Zone' and have hot moist and sub-humid climate.[2] Both agroclimatic zones are located in Eastern Plateau and Hills Zone (Zone Number 7) of India (Behera et al. 2005). People living in this region are likely to be witnessing deteriorating climatic conditions, with increased risks from disease and pests, and with associated implications for human and livestock health.

The Western Odisha Rural Livelihoods Project

Odisha implements around 10 different watershed programmes and projects in the state through the Odisha Watershed Development Mission (OWDM), an autonomous state agency constituted under the Department for Agriculture that plans, implements, and monitors watershed development programmes in the state. The Western Odisha Rural Livelihoods Project (WORLP) is one of these programmes. WORLP is a Government of Odisha initiative and is funded by United Kingdom's Department for International Development (DFID) implemented over a period of 10 years; that is, from 2000 to 2010. The cost of the project is Rs 2,300 million (GBP 32.75 million).

The aim of WORLP is to alleviate poverty and reduce vulnerability to poverty. It works in four of the most disadvantaged districts in Odisha: Bargarh, Balangir, Kalahandi, and Nuapada. It was designed to cover 1,180 villages in 677 watersheds in these 4 districts, where human development indicators are very low. The project initiated a new approach to watershed management, termed 'Watershed Plus' during its design. It provides a range of livelihood support services to the poor.

WORLP was designed using the sustainable livelihoods approach, which provides a conceptual and methodological framework for

---

[1] This zone is situated within 20° 9' and 22° N latitudes and 82° 39' and 85° 15'E longitudes.

[2] This zone is situated within 19° 3' and 21° 55' N latitudes and 82° 20' and 83° 47' E longitudes.

addressing poverty (DFID 1999). It was not designed with any climate change objectives, and no environmental impact was envisaged other than the enhancement of natural resource assets. Nonetheless, the project has increased the asset levels of the poor and very poor, which in turn has ensured that they are better able to cope with anticipated hazards and adapt to a changing environment by building their resilience.

Climate change adaptation in WORLP consists of a range of measures and initiatives that reduce the vulnerability of human and natural systems to climate change. The goal, purpose, and outputs of the project, as described in the project framework, are as follows:

- Ultimate goal: Reduce poverty in rain-fed areas of India.
- Intermediate goal: See to it that by the end of the project year (2010) government agencies and other stakeholders in Koraput, Bolangir, and Kalahandi districts and elsewhere adopted more effective approaches to sustainable rural livelihoods.
- Purpose: Promote sustainable livelihoods, particularly for the poorest, in 4 districts (Bolangir—14 blocks, Nuapara—5 blocks, Bargarh—4 blocks, and Kalahandi—6 blocks) in replicable ways by 2010.

The five project outputs are tabulated as follows, with comments regarding their potential bearing on climate change.

The objectives of WORLP can be seen to link with current national climate change objectives (as illustrated in Figure 11.1).

There are strong links with water conservation and plantation activities. Sustainable agriculture, including crop diversification, also have fairly strong linkages since project stakeholders are part of the low carbon economy—mechanization is virtually non-existent and fertilizer usage is low. The project has created several knowledge bases and if used properly these can be useful in developing a model of climate-friendly practices that are replicable.

The link between the project's approach to reducing vulnerability and adaptation to climate change shows that there are opposing forces which interact and influence livelihoods. There are the positive effects of poverty reduction through project investment, and negative pressures exerted by climate change on an already fragile environment.

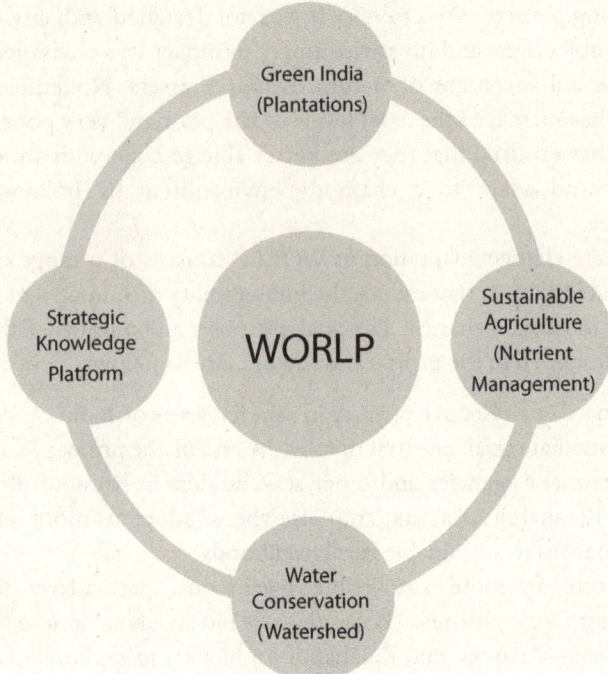

FIGURE 11.1   Linkage of WORLP Activity and National Priorities
Source: Author's compilation.

Institutional Arrangements

In order to analyse the state's response to extreme climate events, it helps to understand the institutional arrangements within the OWDM and the WORLP. It also helps to understand how those institutional arrangements have likely impacts on potential mechanisms for coping with climate change (Figure 11.2).

WORLP Project Structure

At the state level, WORLP is under the aegis of the director of the OWDM. The WORLP institutional arrangements have delivered results. Government of Odisha and India have taken lessons from WORLP and have strengthened the institutional delivery mechanisms.

At the district level, the Project Director (PD) watersheds located in the project districts have independent offices. Project-implementing agencies and watershed development teams implement the project in a specified number of watersheds at the block level. The implementation and governance functions are segregated at each level by the empowered committee at the state level and by the district watershed development committee at the district level.

WORLP has a structure at the district level that supports the implementation of the watershed and watershed plus activities. The district project director manages the watershed activities in a district with the support of assistant project directors. PD's office also has the capacity-building team consisting of four members specializing in livelihoods, micro-enterprise, natural resource management, and monitoring and evaluation.

At the block level, the activities are coordinated by project implementing agencies. The project implementing agencies could either be an NGO or a government staff. A three-member livelihood support team made up of specialists from the agriculture, micro-enterprise, and social development sectors are attached to the project-implementing agency to support the implementation and monitoring of watershed plus activities in the intervention areas. The social development livelihood support team is responsible for gender and community organization activities. The firm frontline contact is made by the watershed development team at the village level with support of community link workers and village volunteers who work closely with the community. The community link workers act as bridge between the project and the community and provide services on agriculture, natural resources management, livestock, and community mobilization activities.

At the watershed level, WORLP has an environment that encourages the participation of women, the poor, and other marginalized groups in watershed activities.

At each level, WORLP has created parallel support structures for capacity building, enabling policy formulation, and facilitating project processes. Thus, the creation of project support units, capacity building teams, and livelihood support teams was an innovation that has helped the project to achieve its purpose. The links and roles of institutions in the project that have a bearing on climate change–related action are

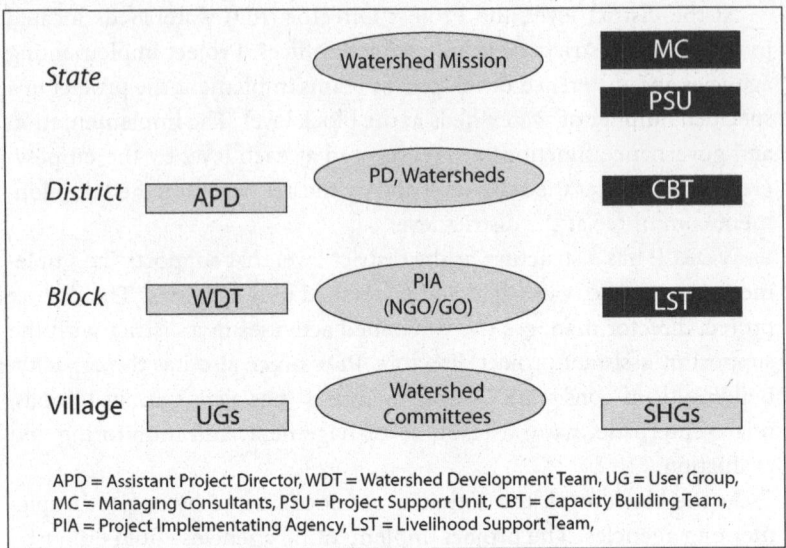

FIGURE 11.2 Institutional Arrangements in WORLP
Source: Author's compilation.

described in Table 11.1. Some of these roles have been performed in the past and some are desired for the future.

Strategic decisions on adaptation and convergence are taken by the director of the OWDM. Most responses to the climate crisis are coordinated by the collector in the district. Project-implementing agencies take operating decisions by taking watershed associations and self-help groups into confidence for adaptation and coping. Some project-implementing agencies also work with district authorities on responding to climate-induced events and other critical events. Capacity-building teams provide strategic coordination for adaptive actions, and livelihood support teams have the same role, but with a more hands-on approach in watershed areas.

In summary, there is an institutional set-up within WORLP, driven by the OWDM, which has allowed a high level of autonomy and flexibility. The structure at every level has maximized opportunities for increasing people's participation. Activities that appear to be very beneficial in terms of increasing people's capacity to adapt to and cope with climate-related stress have been implemented in a quick, effective, and

TABLE 11.1   Institutional Link to Climate Change in WORLP

Input/Activity	Institution Responsible	Possible Linkages	Remarks
Overall linkage and awareness about climate events	OWDM	Adaptation Mitigation Coping	Even though not done consciously, the direction of OWDM has a direct bearing on reduction of climate stress.
District-level planning and convergence	PDs	Adaptation Mitigation Coping	PDs plan activities in consultation with line departments and provide platform for convergence.
Capacity building on aspects of water-harvesting structures	CBT-NRM PIAs WDTs	Adaptation and coping	Soil moisture conservation help in adaptation as well as coping.
Capacity building on aspects of cropping systems	CBT-NRM LSTs and WDTs	Adaptation	Advice on cropping system and moisture management through intercrop.
Capacity Building on aspects of land use, irrigation, plantation	LSTs PIAs WDTs	Adaptation	Land use change and varietal change due to change in moisture.
Animal health care	CLWs PIAs	Response	Better preparedness.
Social capital building	SHGs, CIGs	Response, coping	It has a strong linkage in risk mitigation and coping.

Source: Author's compilation.

participatory way, and through a direct chain of command. This has allowed the project institutions that were established to operate effectively and substantially improve project delivery.

Major climate-induced events in the region include drought and heat waves in summer and flash floods in the rainy season. Invariably, the responses to climatic events are coordinated by the district administration. Odisha has combined revenue and disaster mitigation into a single department and district collectors (the administrative heads of districts) act as nodal officers in the districts. In addition, the Odisha

Disaster Mitigation Authority undertakes several actions for climate events such as droughts, floods, and cyclones. Their role is primarily to develop capacity for preparedness. The Health, Rural Water Supply, and Sanitation Department provide support in checking waterborne diseases. Agriculture and animal husbandry departments provide support in terms of restoring the depleted input supply, and in disease and pest surveillance. Table 11.2 shows how specific institutions should respond to weather events, how communities may be expected to react, and the potential role of the private sector.

Climate Change Adaptation Study

A study documented the ways WORLP area communities coped with and adapted to increased climate-induced vulnerability. It made recommendations for adaptation and mitigation that improves livelihoods. The study identified ways people in the project area are adapting to climate change and proposed ways to make livelihoods more resilient. In summary, the study was intended to (a) understand adaptation, coping, and responses of the project community to climate variability; (b) identify climate resilient technical measures that might be replicated and help in promoting sustainable livelihoods; and (c) identify and recommend socially acceptable adaptation and mitigation options for the project.

The indicators used in the analysis of this study are given in the following list; wherever possible, comparisons are made between ex-post and ex-ante project scenarios:

- Socioeconomic factors and anthropogenic effects on land use change
- Natural resource management interventions and their effect on soil moisture
- Effect on crop production and crop intensification cycles
- Social capital and community resilience for adaptation
- Strategies for coping and community responses to weather events
- Carbon cycle and mitigation efforts
- Macro and micro models using national climate data and local data (soil, rainfall, temperature) for assessing variability in bio-physical factors

TABLE 11.2 Response of Various Institutions in the Event of Climatic Stress

Major Climatic Events	Period	Response of Government Institutions	Response of Community	Response by Private Sector
Drought	Critical drought occurred in years 1964, 1972, 1996	Revenue and Disaster Mitigation Department coordinates the following: Starts labour intensive works and relief centres in most vulnerable locations if area is small. Supplementation in food for work and drinking water for human and cattle consumption. Food for the BPL families Repair of water harvesting structures, canals, ponds Supply of medicine Crop insurance and medium-term credit	Community kitchen Group farming Cutting of food intake and water use Shifting to gathering of edible material from forest for consumption and other materials for exchange of food Postponement of repair, ceremony, etc.	If we consider moneylender to be one institution they provide instant liquidity. Banks and financial institutions are slower in response but they provide limited credit. Market clearing sub-optimal price offered by the traders
Dry spell	Almost every year	Agriculture Department and Water Resources Department start working on the water and crop management. Water Resources Department instructs basin managers for release of waters to canals	Community uses available water in ponds. Change field management and intercultural operations. Conflicts arise for water-sharing.	

(Cont'd)

TABLE 11.2 (Cont'd)

Major Climatic Events	Period	Response of Government Institutions	Response of Community	Response by Private sector
Heat wave	Almost every year	Revenue Department and OSDMA issue advice, School and Mass Education Department advises closure of schools and District Administration issues enabling orders for other offices.	People use locally available bio-mass like Bena (*vertiver*) for cooling, some use wet straw, people avoid work during mid-day. Livestock grazing is restricted.	Some private sectors keep drinking water in public places.
Flash flood	Almost every year	Check dam and contour bunding to prevent sand casting through Soil Conservation Department.	Community also puts bunds—sometime may not be with accurate slope.	
Disease and pest incidence	Almost every year	Agriculture Department advises on pest control measures.	Informed farmers use *neem* oil cake, cow dung with some local herbs as organic pesticides.	Several pesticide farms reach farmers through their distributors.

Source: Author's compilation.

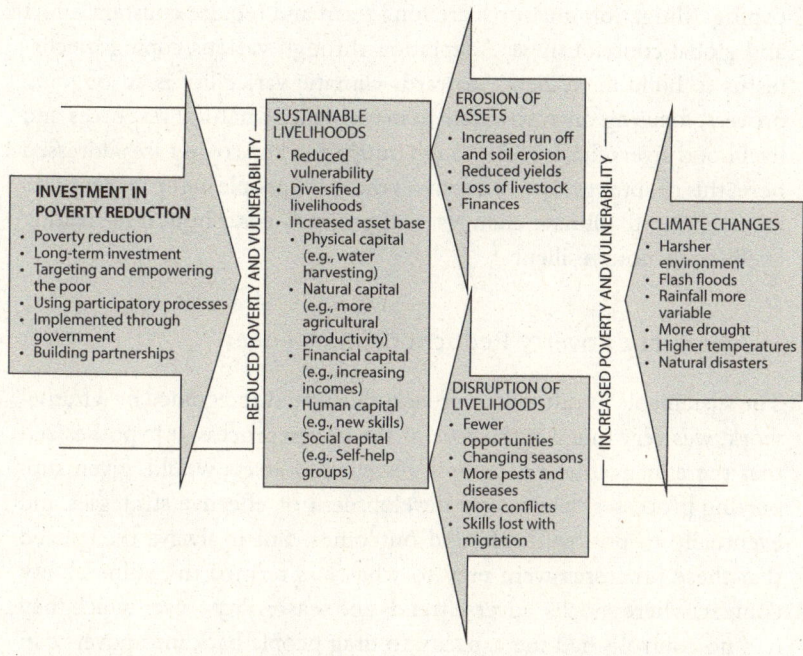

FIGURE 11.3   Relationship between Poverty Education and Climate Change in WORLP
Source: Author's compilation.

Results of the Study and Further Discussions

WORLP lies in an area of India where the mean temperatures are rising, and where the vulnerability profile places it among the highest risk areas in the country. The following climate risks have been identified in the project area:

- High variability of rainfall, leaving people with two peak periods of food stress in the region
- Droughts and dry-spells every two years, with a major drought every five to six years
- Flash floods during the rainy season

There are different ways to address climate change phenomena: (a) through mitigation measures, (b) through adaptation processes, or (c) coping. Mitigation measures are long-term and require constant effort and global consciousness. Adaptation through various coping mechanisms to build in resilience towards climatic variability is an ongoing process, focusing on sustainable management of natural resources and livelihood diversification. Although mitigation and coping are addressed here, this chapter primarily discusses the ways people in the project area are adapting to climate changes, and project's contribution in making livelihoods more resilient.

Vulnerability, Poverty Reduction, and Gender

The sustainable livelihoods approach, illustrated and guided by a framework, was very much at the core of the design process. It hypothesized that the enhancement of people's livelihood assets would, given supporting processes, lead to the development of effective strategies and eventually to positive livelihood outcomes. But it always recognized that these processes were prey to what was termed the vulnerability context, where shocks, adverse trends and seasonality—over which they had no control—had the capacity to drag people back into poverty. In many ways, this model has proven to be a powerful one in the light of more recent climate change evidence, and the sustainable livelihoods approach hypothesis has been to a large extent confirmed.

WORLP districts have a high level of vulnerability because they have a lot of poor people (the population density is often over 300/sq. km, with some 30% scheduled caste/scheduled tribe people) living in a reduced natural environment. There is very weak asset base. Access to natural, financial, and human capital is restricted. High levels of unemployment and low levels of literacy exacerbate the situation.

In the partnership between the communities, the project, and government staff, engaged in participatory micro-planning processes with the full engagement of poor people. This helped to build trust and good relations, identifying the needs and concerns of those most at risk. The approach has created an enabling environment, empowering and informing people, and allowing them to make informed choices for their long-term well-being.

As a result, in the areas where WORLP was implemented, the incidence of poverty reduced during the project time by 30%, meaning that approximately 15,000 households or 72,000 people have moved above the poverty line. Much of this can be attributed to increased levels of financial, human, natural, and social assets brought in under the project, assets which also have built resilience, and improved adaptability to climate change.

Increased community resilience has developed through the project's efforts to build the capacity of individuals, households, and groups that face multiple environmental and other pressures, and in ensuring their increasing control over resources. Farmers have been supported to increase their skills related to crop diversification, vegetable gardens, aquaculture, duckery, goatery, etc. This increase in skills enables people to adapt their livelihoods and build resilience to climate changes and shocks. This has also been supported by increases in health and well-being through health camps, water and sanitation initiatives, the introduction of smokeless *chullahs* (firewood stoves) and other technologies, such as surface treadle pumps.

The increase in skills and opportunities have been evidenced by a decrease in stress-induced migration from 47% of households in 2000 to less than 15% in 2008 (WORLP 2008). It is the poorest of the poor who constitute the distress migrants. Previously they were unable to find work in the rabi season when water is scarce.

Project initiatives appear to have also had positive effect on women as they increased women's capacity to adapt to climate-induced stress and to cope in situations of crisis. This has to a large extent happened through the strengthened resilience brought about through a large number of capable self-help groups, where women are able to share resources and ideas, and thus reduce their inherently high levels of vulnerability to disasters caused by climate change. Migration and the associated stress, which is particularly acute in the case of women, have been very substantially checked by project activities (from almost 50% incidence of migration to under 15%). In addition to these positive effects of increased social capital, some of the effects of enhanced natural capital may be seen as favouring women, such as improved food security, improved health status including child nutrition, and reduced drudgery.

Institutions and Social Capital

The institutional set-up within WORLP, driven by the OWDM, has allowed a high level of autonomy and flexibility. Activities that appear to increase people's capacity to adapt to and cope with climate-related stress have been implemented in a quick, effective, and participatory way, and through a direct chain of command. This has allowed the project institutions, which were designed to operate in a highly participatory mode at all levels, to operate more effectively.

The project has made substantial investments in capacity building of project beneficiaries. The social capital of the community was thereby increased. This is possibly the project's greatest contribution to increasing people's capacity to adapt in crisis. Greater social capital is likely to increase people's resilience and capacity to cope. They will be better informed and able to make more appropriate responses to stress situations. The increased number and strength of self-help groups (some 65,000 members in over 5,000 self-help groups) has increased the stock of social capital within the project, and this has had an immediately reduced people's vulnerability to the negative effects of climate change. Through the groups' exposure to participatory planning processes, people are better able to manage common property resources and are more prepared for crises than those in areas where such groups are non-existent or weak.

Environment and Food Security

There is some evidence of changing trends in the project area's micro-climate over recent decades. There has been up to 10% more rain in the monsoon periods (although it has been more variable), and less outside of it. As a result, the likelihood of prolonged dry spells or drought has declined. The OWDM has undertaken many interventions since 2001, and many watershed projects have completed their project period of five years. The recorded recovery from drought-like conditions during these intervention periods is an indication that the interventions may have played a role in ushering more favourable weather conditions in all four districts, although this may also be a simple coincidence. Nevertheless, these results should be treated as important, and should be further explored.

Natural resource management interventions appear to have successfully increased the adaptive capacity of the community during climate stress, especially in areas where the land and its holding capacity are more marginal. A large number of natural resource management activities are being implemented in the four concerned districts. The activities are typically aimed at managing and checking runoff from different catchments and reducing the sediment load in water bodies. The goal is to increase water resources and make the land more productive.

In Western Odisha, the capacity to adapt to changes in climate depends to a large extent on securing entitlements to natural resources, particularly water. Control over resources affects the strategies available, such as soil and water conservation, investment in resilient agriculture (pest or drought resistant seed, improved farming practices, etc.), and drawing on alternative sources of food and income when the main supplies fail.

Water storage structures and soil and water conservation, developed in partnership with communities through participatory microplanning and the use of local labour, have provided more immediate groundwater recharge, reducing intra-annual fluctuation in the water table and improving hydrological and soil moisture conditions. This has improved resilience to the increasingly variable monsoon rain, prolonged dry spells, and drought. Interventions have also had marked effects on groundwater tables, which have been raised by 2–4 metres.

Water harvesting technologies have also checked runoff and reduced sediment, increasing crop production and the productivity of water resources, which now include fish farming. Through increased water availability, the land-use patterns have changed, permitting a second crop during the rabi season. The gross cropped area has expanded by 16%, and cropping intensity is up by at least 10%.

Increased water availability affected agricultural production and productivity, mainly through greater crop diversification and improved crop yields. Yield increases in the order of 50%–100% have been regularly recorded. Livelihoods have become more robust through diversification into livestock, aquaculture, horticulture, silviculture plantation, and activities such as honeybee keeping and mushroom cultivation. The growing practice of seed exchange and onion storage has also increased returns.

Fewer households now suffer 'lean season' food deficit days, a decrease from 25% before the project to 5% in 2009; thus food security has improved. This has happened as a result of increased coping capacity and increased income. The increased income resulted from an increase in agricultural production and a diversification of livelihood activities. This includes support and training in artisan craftwork, and the establishment and management of small businesses by the very poor, particularly by women and the landless. These marginal groups have increased access to employment and consumption credit.

* * *

Successful interventions and approaches of the project which have reduced vulnerability and helped community to adapt to climatic variability with high potential for replications are summarized in the following paragraphs.

Reducing poverty through livelihoods diversity offers a good platform for climate change adaptation. WORLP has succeeded in reducing poverty, and this is a prerequisite in development of greater climate change adaptability. The dual focus on natural resource management and people's livelihoods provides a strong response to increased vulnerability.

The sustainable livelihoods approach recognized that poor people are prey to increased vulnerability, where shocks, adverse trends, and seasonality have the capacity to drag people back into poverty if permitted to do so. The model has proven to be robust in the face of recent climate change evidence.

Building institutions of the poor is fundamental for reducing vulnerability and enhancing their capacity to adapt. WORLP has put into place institutions, organizational practices, systems, and procedures necessary for communities to be at the centre, and better able to address issues of inclusion and equity.

WORLP operates within the government, and the Government of Odisha has already scaled up the project to non-WORLP districts. National policy has also been influenced through inclusion of a livelihoods focus. This will help build resilience to climate change for millions of the rural poor in India.

WORLP is long-term, large-scale investment, and this has enabled it to achieve its goals in a sustainable way. Advocating new approaches, building capacity, and strengthening processes through existing institutional structures is not easy and requires a big investment in time and resources.

Future climate change may be of a different order. Whilst there is good evidence that project activities have increased resilience, it seems likely that in future things will get worse. Continuous assessment of the adequacy of current strategies needs to be institutionalized.

References

Behera, A.K., U.K. Mishra, B.C. Nayak, K. Das, B. Maharana, and P.C. Acharya. 2005. 'Cropping System Strategy for Western Orissa Rural Livelihoods Project', WORLP working paper number 52, APICOL, Bhubaneswar.

DFID. 1999. *Sustainable Livelihoods Guidance Sheets*. London: DFID.

Satyanarayana, M. et al. 2009. 'Effect of Climate Change in Western Orissa'. WORLP working paper number 69.

WORLP. 1999. *Project Memorandum, Western Orissa Rural livelihoods Project*, project memorandum, Ministry of Rural Development, Government of India.

———. 2008. 'Impact Assessment Report, Western Orissa Rural Livelihoods Project'. Unpublished.

UPLAND POVERTY

12

SHYAM UPADHYAYA

The Role of the Environment in Upland Poverty in Nepal

The upland areas of Nepal constitute 77% of total area of the country and have 52% of the total population. There is a high level of poverty in upland areas. In 2003/04, the incidence of poverty in mountains, hills, and the lower plain areas (Terai) was about 33%, 35%, and 28%, respectively. The environment and poverty are closely linked. The environment is a major cause of upland poverty. The upland poor are highly dependent on natural resources for their livelihood. The quality of environmental resources is poor. The productivity of land and forest is low. The upland poor live in harsh climatic conditions. The loss of human life due to water-induced disasters is higher in upland areas than elsewhere. Climate change has worsened the conditions of upland poor. The rate of the increase in temperature is higher in hills and mountains than in the Terai.

The environment is also a major asset for upland people to alleviate poverty with. There are good opportunities for green economy in upland areas. Snow-capped mountain peaks are major attractions for tourists. Tourism has had a significant effect in the economic development of major trekking routes. Nepal has been a pioneer in adopting alternate energy technologies, such as micro-hydro, biogas, solar energy, and improved cooking stoves, and in innovative forest management practices. These programmes are beginning to make a positive contribution to poverty reduction and environment conservation. Hills and mountains are important sources of environmental services. There is an enormous potential for the generation of hydropower.

The government's efforts to counter the adverse effects of climate change are inadequate. There is a need for more research and more monitoring of the effect of climate change and adaptation measures. Programmes to increase the capacity of upland poor to cope with adverse effects of climate change need to be implemented. Investment in income-generating activities and infrastructure development needs to be increased significantly.

Background

The environment is a major cause of poverty. Poor people often inhabit marginal lands, flood-prone areas, slums, and squatter areas, which are characterized by poor environmental resources. The effects of the environment on poverty are more evident in Nepal where the majority of people still depend on environmental resources for their livelihood. The environment is also an important resource for alleviating poverty. While poor environmental conditions increase poverty, improvements in the environment have reduced poverty. In this chapter, I explore the effect of the natural environment on poverty in the upland areas of Nepal. Nepal is divided into three ecological belts—mountains, hills, and Terai. For administrative purpose, Nepal is divided into five development regions (eastern, central, western, mid-western, and far-western) and 75 districts (see Table 12.1). For the purpose of this chapter, hills and mountains (high hills) are considered the 'upland areas'.

The upland areas of Nepal constitute three quarters (77%) of the total area of the country and have half (52%) of total population. Nepal has an area of 147,181 sq. km. The mountains, hills, and Terai constitute 35%, 42%, and 23% of the total area. As per census 2001, the total population was 23.1 million. The share of mountains, hills, and Terai in total population was 7%, 44%, and 48%, respectively.

The remaining part of the chapter is organized as follows. The second section identifies characteristics of poor. The third section discusses causes of poverty. The fourth section examines the regional dimension of poverty. The fifth section discusses how climate change is

TABLE 12.1   Number of Districts by Ecological and Development Regions

Development Region	Mountain	Hill	Terai	Total
Eastern	3	8	5	16
Central	3	9	7	19
Western	2	11	3	16
Mid-Western	5	7	3	15
Far-Western	3	4	2	9
Total	16	39	20	75

Source: Central Bureau of Statistics.

aggravating environment poverty problem. The sixth section discusses coping mechanisms of the poor. The seventh section discusses government programmes that address climate change. The eighth section explores opportunities for a green economy in the upland areas. The final section provides a few recommendations.

Dimension of Poverty in Nepal

Despite decades of planned development efforts, poverty is still severe and widespread. The latest estimate is that a quarter (25%) of population is living below poverty line.[1] Nepal Living Standard Survey (NLSS) has been the main source of data for poverty measurement. NLSS defines a poverty line income as the income level needed to buy basic calorie requirements (21,144 KCal per person per day in 2003–04) and other essential non-food needs. Poverty lines at current prices for 1995/96 and 2003/04 were computed as NRs 5,088.7 and NRs 7,695.7 per person per year, respectively. According to NLSS, the incidence of poverty was about 42% in 1995/96, which fell to about 31% in 2003–04 (Table 12.2).

Poverty varies greatly among regions (see Table 12.2).[2] In 2003/04, poverty in the rural areas was more than three times that of urban

[1] See NPC (2010).
[2] NLSS regions are defined as follows: Rural western hills include hills and mountains from the Western, Mid-Western, and Far-Western Development regions; rural eastern hills include hills and mountains from the Eastern and Central Development regions; 'rural western Terai' includes Terai belt from the western, mid-western, and far-western development regions; 'rural eastern Terai' includes Terai belt from eastern and central development regions.

TABLE 12.2 Incidence of Poverty in Nepal

Region	1995–96	2003–04
Urban	21.6	9.6
Rural	43.3	34.6
Ecological Belt		
Mountain	57.0	32.6
Hill	40.7	34.5
Terai	40.3	27.6
Development Region		
Eastern	38.9	29.3
Central	32.5	27.1
Western	38.6	27.1
Mid-western	59.9	44.8
Far western	63.9	41.0
NLSS Region		
Kathmandu	4.3	3.3
Other urban	31.6	13.0
Rural Western Hill	55.0	37.4
Rural Eastern Hill	36.1	42.9
Rural Western Terai	46.1	38.1
Rural Eastern Terai	37.2	24.9
Nepal	41.8	30.8

Source: CBS (2005a).

areas. It is also evident from the table that poverty is higher in upland areas than in lowlands. In 2003/04, the incidence of poverty in rural western hills was slightly lower than that of rural western Terai, but the incidence of poverty in rural eastern hills was higher than that of rural eastern Terai (Figure 12.1). Of the Nepal's poor, 7.5% live on mountains, 47.1% on hills, and 45.4% in the Terai (MOF 2010). Between 1995/96 and 2003/04, the mountain region experienced the largest decline in poverty, due to migration and remittance income.

Multidimensional measures of poverty, such as the Human Poverty Index (HPI), indicate higher level of poverty in hills and mountains. HPI was highest in mountains (Figure 12.2) and the values for the hills and

---

'Kathmandu' comprises urban areas in the districts of Kathmandu, Lalitpur, and Bhaktapur. 'Other urban' comprises all other urban areas outside Kathmandu Valley.

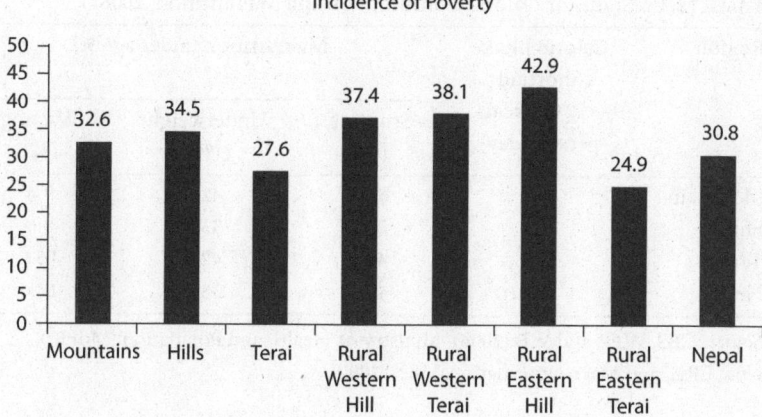

FIGURE 12.1   Regional Dimension of Poverty in Nepal, 2003–04
Source: CBS (2005a).

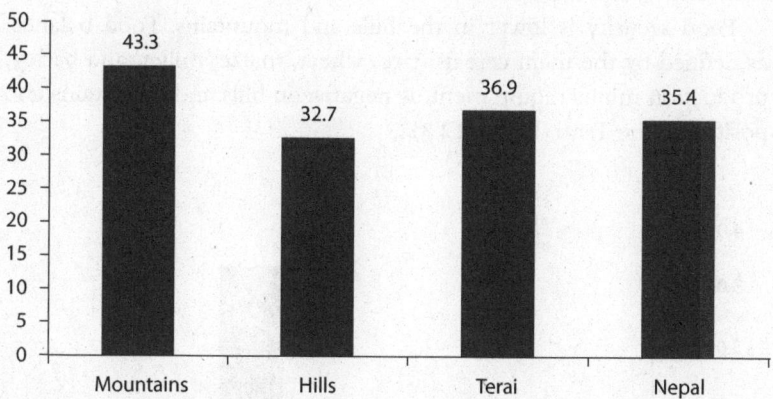

FIGURE 12.2   Human Poverty Index (HPI), 2006
Source: UNDP (2009).

the Terai were almost equal. The Human Development Index, on the other hand, was lowest for mountains (UNDP 2009).

Anthropometric indicators of poverty show a higher level of poverty in upland areas. Stunting is highest in the mountains, followed by hills and Terai (Table 12.3). Underweight was highest in the mountains, followed by the Terai and the hills. Wasting, however, was highest in the

TABLE 12.3   Status of Calorie Consumption and Malnutrition, 2006

Region	Calorie Intake Shortfall (< 2124 kcal/ person/day)	Malnutrition under age 5		
		Stunting (%)	Underweight (%)	Wasting (%)
Mountain	45.2	62.3	42.4	9.4
Hills	41.8	50.3	33.2	8.4
Terai	37.4	46.3	42.3	16.6
Nepal	39.8	49.3	38.6	12.6

Source: CBS, WFP, and WB (2006); Ministry of Health and Population (MoHP), New ERA, and Macro International Inc. (2007).

Terai followed by hills and mountains. About 40% of the population was consuming fewer calories from food than required. The calorie intake shortfall was highest in the mountains (45.2%), followed by the hills (41.8%) and the Terai (37.4%) (Table 12.3).

Food security is lower in the hills and mountains. Food balance, as defined by the main cereals (rice, wheat, maize, millet, and barley) production minus requirement, is negative in hills and mountains and positive in the Terai (Figure 12.3).

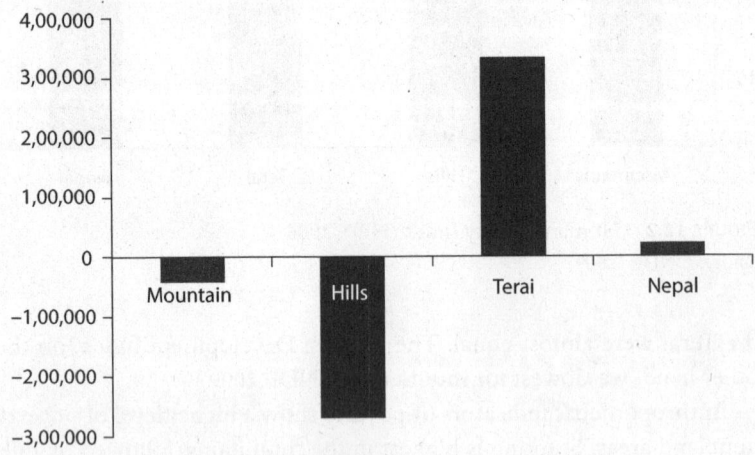

FIGURE 12.3   Food Balance in Nepal, 2007–08
Source: MOAC (2008).

Characteristics of the Poor

The majority of the poor live in rural areas. In 2003/04, 35% of the rural population was living below the poverty line, compared to 10% of the urban population. The proportion of the rural population is highest in mountains. Poverty varies greatly according to caste. Poverty is higher among Dalits and indigenous population. The indigenous people of hills and mountains were the largest social group of poor in 2003/04. Poverty increases with the decline in education level of household heads, the increase of household size, and increase in the number of children. Poverty and lack of agricultural opportunities are closely linked. Table 12.4 presents the incidence of poverty by the sector in which the head of the household is employed. About 78% of the poor are associated with agriculture. About 33% of people are self-employed in agriculture and 54% of agricultural labourers are below poverty line. The proportion of poor people associated with agriculture is higher than the proportion of people directly involved in agriculture.

Farm income constitutes an important source of household income for the poor (Table 12.5). The share of farm income in total household income was highest (59%) in mountains. The importance of farm

TABLE 12.4   Poverty by Employment Sector of the Household Head, 2003–04

Self-Employed	Poverty Head Count Rate	Distribution of the Poor	Distribution of the Population
Self-Employed			
Agriculture	32.9	66.9	62.7
Manufacturing	31.2	4.5	4.4
Trade	11.1	1.6	4.5
Services	14.4	1.5	3.2
Wage Earners			
Agriculture	53.8	10.9	6.2
Professional	2.1	0.2	2.9
Other	28.8	10	10.7
Unemployed	2.9	0	0.2
Non-active	26.9	4.4	5.1
Total	30.8	100	100

Source: CBS (2005).

TABLE 12.5   Share of Household Income from Various Sources, 2003–04

Region	Farm Income	Non-farm Income	Remittances	Other
Ecological Region				
Mountains	59	19	9	13
Hills	44	28	11	17
Terai	49	28	12	11
Consumption Quintile				
Poorest	62	23	8	7
Second	55	25	9	11
Third	56	24	10	10
Fourth	47	25	14	14
Richest	25	38	13	24
Nepal	48	28	11	13

Source: CBS (2005b).

income increases as the households move towards the lower rungs of the economic ladder. The share of farm income in total household income of the poorest 20% of the population was more than twice than that of the richest 20% of population.

The majority of the poor owns smaller landholdings. In general, the incidence of poverty increases with the decline in size of landholdings (Table 12.6).

Causes of Poverty

Several factors have been identified as indicators of poverty. These are: low economic growth, low agricultural productivity, low levels

TABLE 12.6   Poverty Measurement by Land Ownership in Rural Areas of Nepal

Land Holdings	1995–96	2003–04	Change in %
Less than 0.2 ha	47.7	39.3	−18
0.2–1 ha	45.0	38.1	−15
1–2 ha	38.8	27.3	−30
More than 2 ha	38.9	23.8	−39
Total	41.8	30.8	−26

Source: CBS (2005).

of social and economic infrastructure, high population growth, lack of non-agricultural employment opportunities, historical inequities in distribution of social and economic power, the environment, and governance (UNDP 2001). This chapter focuses on the role of environmental factors.

The quantity of agricultural land is a major cause of poverty in upland area. There is less land suitable for agriculture in the hills and mountain than in the Terai. Agricultural land and grasslands constitutes 10% in mountains and 27% in hills as compared to 55% in the Terai. Agricultural land holdings are smaller and fragmented in upland areas. The average size of agricultural land holding is lowest in the hills followed by mountains and the Terai (Table 12.7). About 42% of households in mountains and 46% in hills own less than 0.5 ha of agricultural land.

The quality of agricultural land determines level of poverty. Most agricultural land in hills and mountain are sloped and highly prone to landslides. Soil is stony and less fertile. Soil erosion is high (Tiwary et al. 2002). Irrigation facilities are poor. Nearly 28% of cultivable land in mountains and 26% land in hills had irrigation facilities (Figure 12.4). Agricultural land holdings are highly fragmented. The average number of parcels was 5.46 in mountain, 3.80 in hills, and 3.34 in the Terai. Even in the hills and mountain, the poor have the land that is the most marginal and fragile (UNDP 2001). Consequently, the productivity of land and labour is low in the hills and the mountains.

Forests are important determinants of poverty and well-being in upland areas. Forests are the main source of fodder for livestock in the hills and mountains. Forests also provide bedding materials for livestock. Livestock farming is an integral part of crop farming. The use of chemical fertilizer is very low in the hills and mountains as it needs to be transported from the Terai. Given the poor road infrastructure,

TABLE 12.7 Average Landholding by Region (ha)

Region	1991–92	2000–01
Mountains	0.679	0.733
Hills	0.771	0.655
Terai	1.230	0.944
Nepal	0.950	0.789

Source: CBS (2000, 2012).

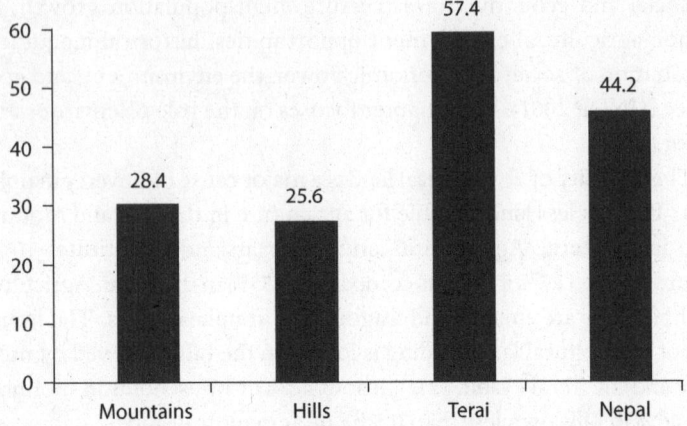

FIGURE 12.4 Irrigated Land as a Percentage of Total Cultivable Land
Source: CBS (2008).

it is expensive and time-consuming to transport fertilizers to hills and mountains. Animal dung and fallen leaves are used for compost, which is the main source of nutrients for crops. It is estimated that 2–6 ha of forestland is needed to support 1 ha of cultivated land in the hills (APROSC and JMA 1995).

Forests are the main source of energy in the upland areas. About 96% of households in the mountains and 72% in hills use fuelwood for cooking (Table 12.8). As many as three quarters of the people in the Karnali

TABLE 12.8 Distribution of Households by Various Sources of Fuel Used for Cooking, 2001

Region	Main Source of Fuel Used for Cooking						
	Wood	Kerosene	LPG	Biogas	Cow Dung	Others	Total
Mountains	95.5	3.2	0.4	0.1	0.7	0.2	100
Hills	72.3	16.0	8.9	1.9	0.1	0.8	100
Terai	55.6	12.8	7.7	1.7	21.5	0.7	100
Urban	33.2	34.1	27.3	1.8	2.5	1.0	100
Rural	72.4	9.8	4.0	1.7	11.5	0.6	100
Nepal	66.2	13.7	7.7	1.7	10.1	0.7	100

Source: CBS (2008).

zone are using resin wood for lighting (Pokharel and Dhital 2006). Hence, the quantity and quality of forests directly affect upland poverty.

About 40% of the total area is covered by forest and shrubs (Table 12.9). The forest cover is lowest in the mountains, followed by the Terai and then the hills. Moreover, the forests in hills and mountains are less productive. Although the forests on the mountains have a good potential for non-timber forest products, the lack of transportation and marketing infrastructure prevent mountain people benefiting from it.

Changes in the management regime of the forests has caused poverty. Prior to the 1950s, Nepal's forests were managed by local people. Nepal nationalized the forests in late 1950s. Nationalization led to loss of ownership of forests by local communities and set the 'tragedy of commons' in motion. In the following decades, Nepal experienced massive deforestation. The rate of deforestation was higher in the hills and the mountains. Deforestation caused a scarcity of fuelwood and fodder, the loss of grazing land, and more time spent by rural households in fetching forest products. Poor households suffered more as richer households were able to cope by planting trees on private land.

With the passage of 1992 Forest Act, Nepal embraced the participatory forest management concept and encouraged local communities to participate. Under community forestry, a group of households formed 'community forest user groups' to manage patches of forests within their vicinity. The community forest user groups prepare management plans for the forest and apply to the district forest office of the government for registration. Once it approves the management plans, the community forest user groups are given rights to forest management. There are 15,051 community forest user groups in Nepal managing about 1,138, 066 hectares of forest (about 21% of the total forest area).

TABLE 12.9   Status of Forest in Nepal

Region	Total Area (sq. km)	Total Forest and Shrub Area (sq. km)	Forest and Shrub Area as a % of Total Area	Forest Area as a % of Total Area
Mountains	51,817	3,959	7.64	4.4
Hills	61,345	40,266	65.64	43.27
Terai	34,019	14,059	41.33	40.99
Nepal	147,181	58,284	39.6	29.05

Source: CBS (2008).

About 90% of the community forest user groups and 85% of the community forests are located in hills and mountains (Table 12.10).

The success of community forestry in regenerating the forest hills and mountains is widely recognized. However, the community forests also have adverse effect on the poor. Community forests put restrictions on the collection of forest products and grazing. Wealthier households are able to cope with restrictions by planting trees or by buying forest products from the market. Many poor people in upland areas derive their livelihood by selling forest products. Landless poor households use forests for grazing. Restrictions put by community forest user groups led to the loss of livelihoods. In some areas which charge membership fees, households are so poor that they are unable to pay. For example, herders and traders from the mid-western mountain district of Humla used to earn their living by rearing sheep and Tibetan mountain goats that were used to transport foodgrains from the lower plains to the upland areas. The herders and traders used forests along the walking trails to feed their animals. After the formation of community forests, the community forest user groups in the lower hills banned herders and traders from using forests along the trekking routes. Such a ban on the use of forests led to a drastic decline in the population of sheep and goats in Humla, causing a loss of livelihood by poor herders and traders (Winrock International, 2003).[3]

TABLE 12.10   Status of Community Forests

Region	Number of Forest Users Groups	Community Forest Area (ha)	Number of Beneficiary Households
Mountains	2,638 (17.5)	244,225 (18.52)	269,222 (15.2)
Hills	10,871 (72.2)	876,443 (66.4)	1,155,795 (65.6)
Terai	1,542 (10.24)	197,337 (14.9)	336,562 (19.1)
Nepal	15,051 (100)	1,318,006 (1000	1,761,579 (100)

Source: MIS, Community Forestry Division, Department of Forest (as of 4 October 2010).

[3] Winrock International (2003) writes: 'In 1998, 400 people died in Humla due to famine and a diarrhea epidemic. Although a variety of events contributed to this tragedy, excluding Humlis from traditionally used land through community forestry certainly contributed to their food insecurity.'

The improper development of infrastructure projects based on natural resources (hydropower projects) has removed the livelihoods of some local people and pushed them into poverty (Upadhyaya 2002). Adequate attention was not given to the resettlement of people displaced by hydropower projects and national parks. There is distinct correlation between climatic conditions and level of poverty in upland areas. Climatic conditions are harsh at higher altitude of mountain districts. These areas are subject to natural hazards. Natural disasters lead to losses of various sorts. The loss of human lives caused by water-induced disasters is higher in upland areas (Figure 12.5).

Mountain districts receive less than average annual precipitation. Precipitation increases with altitude from south to north, up to an altitude of 3,000 metres and then starts declining (ANZDEC 2002). The hills and mountains of mid-western and far-western development regions receive less rainfall than the hills and mountains of the eastern and central development regions.[4] Monsoon rainfall also starts later in the western regions than in the eastern regions. The incidence of

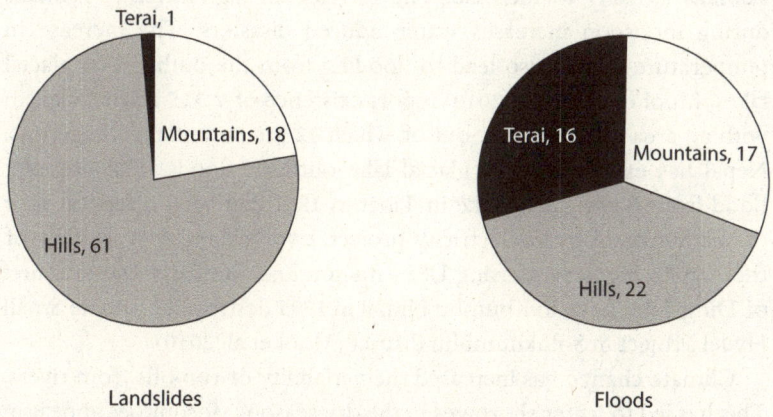

FIGURE 12.5 Number of Deaths Caused by Landslides and Floods in 2009
Source: DWIDP (2010).

---

[4] However, the northwestern mountain and hills receive more winter (December to March) precipitation than other regions. About 80% of rainfall in Nepal occurs during monsoon (June to September). Winter precipitation accounts for about 3%–5% of total annual precipitation.

poverty is highest in the hills and mountains of mid-western and far-western development regions. Such correlations are expected given the dependence of poor people on agriculture.

Effects of Climate Change

Climate change is having an effect on the environment. Between 1975 and 2005, mean temperature increased at the rate of 0.04°C/year (Baidya et al. 2007), resulting in warmer days and nights. The increase in temperature was higher in the hills and mountain. Monsoon rainfall increased slightly between 1971 and 2005, but given the large year-to-year variations, the increase in rainfall was insignificant (Baidya et al. 2007).

Climate change is expected to have a negative effect on agriculture, water resources, biodiversity, and health. The increase in temperature would lead to more water stress in the hills and mountains. The Ministry of Population and Environment predicts that an increase in temperature up to 4°C would have adverse impact on production of maize (MOPE 2004). Baidya et al. (2008) predict that the number of high-intensity rainfalls is likely to increase. The increase in high-intensity rainfalls during monsoon increases water-induced disasters. The increase in temperature would also lead to flooding from the outburst of glacial lakes. Mool et al. (2001; 2010) report existence of 2,315 glacial lakes in with an area of 75 sq. km, out of which 12 are potentially dangerous. Nepal has experienced 25 glacial lake outburst floods. The outburst flood from Baqu glacial lake in Tibet in 1981 damaged diversion weir of the Sunkoshi hydroelectricity project, two bridges, and sections of the Arniko highway, causing US$3 million loss. Similarly, the outburst of Ding Tsho Lake in Khumbu Himal in 1995 destroyed Namche Small Hydel Project in Solukhumbhu district (Mool et al. 2010).

Climate change has increased the variability of run-offs from rivers. This has led to water shortages in the dry season. Mosquitoes appear in higher altitude areas, posing risks to poor people.

Coping Mechanisms of the Poor

Migration has been the main coping mechanism for the poor in the recent years. NLSS data indicates that about 32% of households were receiving remittances in 2003 / 04 (CBS 2005a). About 29% of households from the poorest 20% population received remittances from migration. The proportion of people migrating for work was highest in the rural western mountains and hills. About 45% of males over 15 years of age from rural western hills migrated for work in 2003 / 04. For the poorest, India remains the most popular destination for migration, followed by other rural and urban parts of Nepal.[5]

Poor people also adopt a variety of other mechanisms to cope with poverty and food insecurity in the short term. They reduce their food intake and switch to less preferred food items. They take loans from moneylenders at high interest rates. They consume wild foods, such as mushrooms, yams, etc. Poor people also resort to distress sale of livestock, land, and other valuable to cope with severe crisis (Adhikari 2008; Tiwary et al. 2002).

Government Programmes to Address Climate Change in Upland Areas

Nepal began to take an active interest in environment management in the mid-1980s. The main achievements so far have been the development of policies, institutions, and legislation for environment management. However, the implementation of laws and regulations is weak, and they brought so far only few tangible results for the lives of the poor people. The policy documents include National Conservation Strategy (1988), the Nepal Environment Policy and Action Plan (1993), and the Sustainable Development Agenda (2003). Laws and regulations include the Environment Protection Act (1996) and Environment Protection Regulations (1997). Development projects are required to make an environment impact assessment.

Lately, climate change has received increased attention from policymakers and researchers. In 1992, Nepal became the signatory of the United Nations Framework Convention on Climate Change (UNFCCC). Nepal ratified the Kyoto Protocol of the UNFCCC in 2005. Nepal submitted an Initial National Communication Report of the UNFCCC in 2004. The new Development Plan (2009/10–2012/13) has devoted a separate chapter for environment management and climate change.[6]

---

[5] See CBS (2006) for an analysis of migration and poverty in Nepal.

However, the focus has been mainly on the analysis of trends and the likely effects of climate change. The Sustainable Development Agenda for Nepal (2003) and the Initial National Communication Report to the UNFCCC provide some analysis of trends and likely consequences of climate change (MOPE 2004). Nepal is responsible for only 0.025% of annual global greenhouse gas emissions. Nepal's response to climate change involves two-pronged strategy—increase capacity to benefit from the new opportunities created by Clean Development Mechanism and Carbon trade, and increase the capacity of people to adapt to effects of climate change.

Nepal is aware of the opportunities created by the Clean Development Mechanism and other international carbon finance mechanisms. Nepal is also preparing to benefit from Reducing Emission from Deforestation and Forest Degradation. In 2008, the Ministry of Forest and Soil Conservation submitted a Readiness Plan Idea Note to the World Bank. The World Bank provided US$20,000 to the Ministry of Forest and Soil Conservation from its Forest Carbon Partnership Facility to prepare a Readiness Plan. In April 2010, Nepal submitted a Readiness Preparation Proposal to Forest Carbon Partnership Facility.

The government has initiated some adaptation works. In the 1990s, Nepal, with the help of donors, established early warning systems in 19 villages downstream of Tsho Rolpa glacial lake. About 3 metres of water was drained from Tsho Rolpa, reducing risks of glacial lakes outburst floods by about 20%. The Government of Nepal finalized and approved a National Adaptation Programme of Action in 2010. The programme has identified priority adaptation action programmes. A national climate change policy and a National Strategy on Climate Risk Prevention and Mitigation are under preparation.

Opportunities for a Greener Economy

Environment not only causes poverty in upland areas, it is also a major asset of upland people for alleviating poverty. Nepal's development plans and policies have clearly recognized the value of environment in poverty alleviation (APROSC and JMA 1995). Soil and climatic

---

[6] In earlier plan documents, the chapter heading on environment used to be 'Environment Management'.

conditions in the hills are suitable for cultivating high-value crops. Mountain regions are suitable for growing temperate fruits and for rearing yak and sheep.

The innovation of specific management concept of natural resources such as leasehold forestry is making contribution to poverty alleviation. Under leasehold forestry, patches of degraded forestland are leased to groups of poor households. Leasehold forest users groups are allowed to grow fodder, non-timber forest products, medicinal plants, and practice agroforests. Almost all leasehold forest user groups and leasehold forest areas are located in the hills and mountains. About 23,534 ha of degraded forestland is leased to 5,206 leasehold forest groups, which is benefiting 44,197 families. Studies indicate that leasehold forestry programme is making positive impact on poverty reduction and forest regeneration (FAO and DOF 2009).

Responding to the criticism of neglecting poor, community forestry programmes are paying more attention to poor households. The Ministry of Forest and Soil Conservation (MOFSC) issued a guideline for community forestry development in 2009 that community forest user groups are required to allocate 35% of their income on programmes benefiting poor and disadvantaged groups (MOFSC 2009). Some community forest user groups are leasing parts of degraded forestland to poor household members for income generation. Leasehold forestry is practiced in some community forests. A recent impact study of community forests in 7 hill districts found that the percentage of households living in poverty fell from 65% in 2003 to 28% in 2008.[7] The average household income increased by 61%. About 25% of that increase was attributed to income generation activities related to community forestry programme (LFP 2009).

Hills and mountains are important sources of environmental services, such as biodiversity, carbon sequestration, hydrological services, and ecotourism. Snow-capped mountain peaks are a major attraction for tourists.[8] A total of 500,277 tourists visited in 2008. Of these, 20% visited for trekking (MOF 2010). Nepal has a policy of sharing royalties

[7] The study districts are Dhankuta, Terathum, Sankhuwasabha, Bhojpur, Baglung, Parbat, and Myagdi.

[8] See Millennium Ecosystem Assessment (2005) for a discussion of various ecosystem services.

from tourism with the districts in the trekking routes. Mountain districts in major trekking routes, such as Solukhumbhu, Manag, and Mustang have benefited from tourism and have fared better in development performance.

Forests and wildlife are other attractions for tourists. Nepal has 9 national parks, of which 5 are located in mountains, 2 in hills, and 2 in the Terai. Most national parks have declared surrounding areas to be buffer zones. A total of 291,040 tourists visited protected areas in 2007/08. In the same year, the protected areas generated about NRs 117,898,991 of revenue. By law, national parks are required to invest 30%–50% of income in buffer zones. With proper targeting, such investments could make a substantial impact on poverty alleviation.

Forest conservation in upland watersheds provide hydrological services that benefit communities. If appropriate policies were put in place, the upland areas would be able to secure payments for such environmental services from the beneficiaries. Some pilot efforts are being carried out. For example, the government of Makawanpur district has started paying royalties to the upland communities of the Kulekhani watershed. They provide environmental services that reduce sedimentation in the downstream hydropower reservoir and increases power production (Upadhyaya 2005; 2007).

The hills and mountains have the potential to generate hydropower. All existing hydropower plants are located in hilly districts. The development of hydropower in a socially and environmentally responsible way generates employment for local poor people. Hydropower projects pay royalties to the government, which could be used to support poverty alleviation programmes.

Nepal has been a pioneer in adopting alternate energy technologies such as micro-hydro, biogas, solar energy, and improved cooking stoves. The gradient of rivers in the hills and mountains is very suitable for micro-hydro development with limited water. Studies have shown that micro-hydro have made positive contribution towards poverty alleviation and the achievement of the Millennium Development Goals. More than 220,000 biogas plants have been installed, half of which are located in the hills and mountains. The biogas programme has generated employment for more than 13,000 persons. Biogas programmes make positive contribution to human health as they encourage people to construct improved toilets.[9] Similarly, more than 200,000 'improved cooking stoves' have been installed in the hills and mountains. Improved cooking stoves saves time spent by poor rural women in fuelwood collection, and contributes to health by reducing indoor air pollution.[10] Many rural poor get employment in installing and repairing improved cooking stoves.

The use of alternate energy saves carbon, which is sold in the international carbon market. Nepal has registered two biogas projects of 19,396 plants with the Clean Development Mechanism. Nepal is receiving carbon payments of about US$607,000 for two projects from the Community Development Carbon Fund of the World Bank. Another Clean Development Mechanism project of micro-hydro plants has been prepared. Several other projects related to biogas, improved cooking stoves, improved water mills, and solar energy are under preparation.

Recommendations

Further research is needed on the following:

- The effects of climate change and adaptation measures on people, especially the poor.
- Economic valuation of the environmental resources of the upland areas, including the design of institutions and policies that enable poor local people to benefit from ecosystem services.
- The development of mechanisms for the equitable distribution of carbon and other ecosystem services payments. Ensure that such payments benefit poor people of the hills and mountains.

More investment in infrastructure is needed in the upland areas. New roads can reduce poverty (CBS 2006). Roads improve the access of poor to social services. More investment is also needed in the commercialization of environment-friendly agriculture. The policies of the Government of Nepal have promoted the cultivation of horticultural crops in sloped lands. However, Nepal should increase investment in

---

[9] About 63%–69% of toilets are connected with biogas plants. See www.bsp-nepal.org.

[10] Improved cooking stoves saves 10%–30% of energy compared to traditional stoves.

agricultural research and extension and infrastructure development significantly to put policy in practice. Water conservation technologies should be developed and adopted. Crop varieties that thrive in adverse environment such as drought should be developed.

References

Adhikari, Jagannath. 2008. *Food Crisis in Karnali: A Historical and Politico-economic Perspective*. Kathmandu: Martin Chautari.

ANZDEC Limited. 2002. *Nepal Agricultural Sector Performance Review*. ADB TA No. 3536 NEP, Final Report, ANZDEC Limited, New Zealand in association with CMS Limited, Nepal.

APROSC/Nepal and JMA/USA. 1995. *Nepal Agriculture Perspective Plan*. Kathmandu: Agriculture Projects Services Centre and John Mellor Associates, Inc.

Baidya, Saraju K., Ramesh K. Regmi, and Madan L. Shrestha. 2007. 'Climate Profile, Observed Climate Change and Climate Variability in Nepal'. Final Draft, Department of Hydrology and Meteorology, Kathmandu, Nepal.

Baidya, Saraju K., Madan L. Shrestha, and Muhammad Munir Sheikh. 2008. 'Trends in daily climatic extremes of temperature and precipitation in Nepal', *Journal of Hydrology and Meteorology* 5(1).

CBS. 2000. Statistical Pocket Book of Nepal, 2000. Government of Nepal, National Planning Commission Secretariat, Central Bureau of Statistics, Nepal.

———. 2005a. *Poverty Trends in Nepal (1995–96 and 2003–04)*. Government of Nepal, National Planning Commission, Central Bureau of Statistics.

———. 2005b. Nepal Living Standard Survey, 2003–04. Volume II. Government of Nepal, National Planning Commission, Central Bureau of Statistics, Nepal.

———. 2006. *Resilience Amidst Conflict: An Assessment of Poverty in Nepal, 1995-96 and 2003-04*. Government of Nepal, National Planning Commission, Central Bureau of Statistics.

———. 2012. Statistical Pocket Book of Nepal, 2012. Government of Nepal, National Planning Commission Secretariat, Central Bureau of Statistics, Nepal.

CBS, WFP, and WB. 2006. 'Small Area Estimation of Poverty, Calorie Intake, and Malnutrition in Nepal.' Central Bureau of Statistics (CBS), World Food Programme, and World Bank, Nepal.

———. 2008. *Environment Statistics of Nepal 2008*. Government of Nepal, National Planning Commission, Central Bureau of Statistics.

DWIDP. 2010. *Annual Disaster Review*. Government of Nepal, Ministry of Irrigation, Department of Water Induced Disaster Prevention (DWIDP), Kathmandu, Nepal.

FAO and DOF. 2009. *Effectiveness of Leasehold Forestry to Poverty Reduction. Food and Agriculture Organization of the United Nations (FAO) and Department of Forests (DOF)*, FAO/NEP/3102 Working Document, Kathmandu, Nepal.

LFP. 2009. *Community Forestry for Poverty Alleviation: How UK AID Has Increased Household Income in Nepal's Middle Hills*. Livelihoods and Forestry Programme (LFP), 2009.

Millennium Ecosystem Assessment. 2005. *Ecosystems and Human Well-Being: Synthesis*. Washington, D.C.: Island Press.

Ministry of Health and Population (MoHP), New ERA, and Macro International Inc. 2007. Nepal Demographic and Health Survey, 2006. Kathmandu, Nepal: Ministry of Health and Population, New ERA, Macro International, Inc.

MOAC. 2008. *Statistical Information on Nepalese Agriculture, 2007/08*. Government of Nepal, Ministry of Agriculture and Cooperatives (MOAC), Kathmandu, Nepal.

MOF. 2010. *Economic Survey, 2009/10*. Government of Nepal, Ministry of Finance (MOF), Nepal.

MOFSC. 2009. *Guidelines for Community Forests Development Program (in Nepali)*. Ministry of Forest and Soil Conservation (MOFSC), Department of Forest, Community Forest Division.

Mool, P. K., Rajendra Shrestha, and Jack D. Ives. 2010. *Glacial Lakes and Associated Floods in the Hindu Kush-Himalayas*. Information Sheet # 2/10, ICIMOD, Kathmandu, Nepal.

Mool, P.K., Wangda, D., Bajrachary, S.R., Kunzang, K., Gurung, D.R., Joshi, S.P. 2001. 'Inventory of Glaciers, Glacier Lakes, and Glacial Lake Outburst Floods, Monitoring and Early Warning Systems in the Hindu Kush-Himalayan Region, Nepal, Kathmandu, ICIMOD.

MOPE. 2004. *Initial National Communication to the Conference of the Parties of the United Nations Framework Convention on Climate Change*. Ministry of Population and Environment (MOPE), Kathmandu, Nepal.

NPC. 2010. *Approach Paper to the Three-Year Plan (2010/11–2012/13)*. Government of Nepal, National Planning Commission (NPC), Kathmandu, Nepal.

Pokharel, Govind R. and Ram P. Dhital. 2006. *Report on Assessment of Renewable Energy Intervention Possibilities in Karnali Districts*. A report submitted to SNV/Nepal, Lalitpur, Nepal.

Shardul A., Vivin R. Maarten, V. A., Peter, L. Joel, S and John, R. 2003. *Development and Climate Change In Nepal: Focus on Water Resources and Hydropower*. OECD.

Tiwary, Manish, Ganapati Ojha, Shyam Upadhyaya, Krishna Hari Maharjan, Ameena Shrestha, and Barbara Huddleston. 2002. *Profiles of Vulnerable*

Livelihood Groups in Nepal. Food and Agriculture Organization of the United Nations, Rome.

UNDP. 2001. *Nepal Human Development Report 2001: Poverty Reduction and Governance.* Kathmandu: United Nations Development Program (UNDP).

———. 2009. Nepal Human Development Report 2009: *State Transformation and Human Development.* Kathmandu: United Nations Development Program.

Upadhyaya, Shyam K. 2002. 'Hydropower Development in Nepal: Issues of Equity and Environmental Justice', Equitable Hydro Working Paper 1, Winrock International, Nepal.

———. 2005. 'Payments for Environmental Services: Sharing Hydropower Benefits with Upland Communities'. RUPES Working Paper 1, Kathmandu, Nepal: Winrock International.

———. 2007. 'Characteristics of Environmental Service Providers in Kulekhani Watershed, Nepal: Implications for the Development of PES Mechanism'. Insight: Notes from the Field, RECOFTC, Bangkok, Thailand.

Winrock International. 2002. *Emerging Issues in Community Forestry in Nepal.* Nepal: Winrock International.

13

MIN BIKRAM MALLA THAKURI

Modernizing the Cooking Fuel of the Poor in Upland Nepal

Indoor air pollution from burning solid fuels for cooking is a major environmental health problem in Nepal, predominantly affecting children and women. The problem is more severe in upland areas as the households need more energy for cooking as well as for space heating. High transportation costs, poor supply, and poor purchasing power are main hindering factors for adopting clean fuel and technologies. Past experiences suggest that there is a need to introduce locally accept-able technologies, increasing access to credit, and social marketing to encourage use of clean fuels and technologies to mitigate the indoor air pollution (IAP) problem. Such interventions contribute to improve health, women empowerment, and environmental protection.

Heavy reliance on solid biomass fuel to meet cooking energy need is a big environment health problem in Nepal. In Nepal, about 85% of households still depend on solid biomass fuels for cooking energy (CBS 2004). Solid biomass fuels such as wood, animal dung, and crop residues, which are considered the most polluting fuels, are typically burnt in open fires or poorly functioning stoves and more often with inadequate ventilation, creating a dangerous cocktail of hundreds of pollutants to which women and young children are exposed on a daily basis. There is abundant evidence supporting negative health impact of IAP, such as acute respiratory infections, chronic obstructive pulmonary disease, and lung cancer in women (Smith 1999; Ezzati and Kammen 2002). Air pollution from solid biomass fuel burning in kitchen is responsible for annual premature death of 8,700 people (3.2% of total premature death) 225,558 Disability-Adjusted Life Years[1] and 2.7% of the national burden of diseases in Nepal (WHO, environmental burden of disease updated estimates for 2004). Besides the health impact, the heavy use of solid fuel has been contributing to external economic cost such as deforestation, green house gas emission, illiteracy, and drudgery. Cooking and heating fires using solid fuels are a major global emission source of Black Carbon and other aerosol species (Bond et al. 2004).

Energy access and poverty are very much interlinked having forward and backward linkages. Due to poverty, people are unable to switch to clean fuel. Similarly, in the absence of proper energy, people are restricted for economic development. Solid biomass fuels are considered the most polluting fuels, lie at the bottom of the energy ladder, and are used mostly by the very poor people. Due to health problems generated from heavy exposure to IAP, significant amount of productive time and money are spent. The first energy priority of people living in poverty is their household energy needs. Poor spend up to a third of their income on energy, primarily for cooking. Women, in particular, devote considerable time collecting, processing, and using traditional fuel for cooking. In India, 2 to 7 hours each day are devoted in collection of fuel for cooking (quoted in *World Energy Outlook* 2002); alternatively this could be spent on childcare, education, socializing, or income generation.

The problem of IAP and access to energy is more severe in upland areas as they need more energy as the households need it for cooking as well as for space heating. Most of the households are still using traditional stoves. A recent study shows that about 76.5% households from mountain region compared to 57.0% in Nepal are dependent on traditional cooking stoves with combustion efficiency less than 20.0% (based on 2006 data, Practical Action 2009). Due to high transportation costs, poor supply, and generally poor purchasing power

---

[1] DALY is a measure of overall disease burden, expressed as the number of years lost due to ill-health, disability, or early death.

of households they are unable to use clean fuel and technology, so they are compelled to use solid biomass fuel to meet their cooking energy need. Even use of very smoky fuels like dung cake is increasing in upland areas due to diminishing fuelwood availability. Due to heavy (deficit) wood use and long gestation period to grow tree in high hills and mountain regions, availability of wood is decreasing at an alarming rate. Likewise, there is negative impact of climate change on fuelwood availability. According to available data, average annual mean temperatures have been increasing in Nepal by 0.06°C between 1977 and 2000 and these increases are more pronounced at higher altitudes and in winter (quoted from Oxfam 2009). Increased forest fires in hill and mountain ecological zones due to long spell of no precipitation in the winter results to scarcity in the fuelwood. Additionally, decline in forest annual regeneration due to change in water cycle causing higher deforestation due to deficit in supply to meet the yearly increasing demands. Likewise, increasing crop failure has increased the migration of men leading to additional burden to women for energy management.

Project Intervention

Project Rational, Introduced Technology, and Impact Study

Current energy use and availability trend in upland areas indicates that use of solid fuel will continue to dominate for the next several years. Considering this fact, Practical Action (a development charity) introduced a suitable intervention package for reducing solid biomass fuel use and improving indoor air quality. The intervention package includes installation of smoke hoods, stove improvement, ventilation improvement, and awareness on better quality of solid fuel use and other behavioural changes.

The smoke hood made of GI sheet is built against the wall with an improved tripod stove beneath it constructed with a mud base. The smoke hood has a provision of a chimney to vent the smokes from the kitchen and it has been designed for better drafting of smoke. Apart from that the traditional inefficient stoves are improved by building a protecting base around the back and two sides of the tripod. A wide area at the front is left exposed for fuel feeding and to allow the users to see the fire. Likewise, a bar is set across the front of the stove, to allow air to pass beneath it to improve combustion. Special needs of the households from high hill areas were considered where room heating is one of the prime requirements besides cooking while designing the smoke hood. Moreover, by incorporating a grill rod inside the smoke hood, provision was made for smoking and agrobased products.

To check the viability of investment in such technology and project, a research was carried out in the financial and technical support of South Asian Network for Development and Environmental Economics. This chapter is an output of the research.

Project Location and Study Area

In the first phase (2005–07), the project was implemented in Rasuwa district in the financial support of Department for International Development, World Health Organization and trust funds from United Kingdom. Rasuwa district lies in the northern part of Central Nepal, about 80 miles from Kathmandu. In 2001, there were 8,696 households with a population of 44,731 (CBS 2002). The main ethnic group (about 84%) of the district is Tamang. Most of the households (91.3%) are totally dependent on biomass energy for cooking and room heating and most of them use inefficient traditional stoves.

The second phase (2008–10) of the project was implemented in 10 villages of Gorkha and Dhading districts with the financial support of Partnership for Clean Indoor Air (PCIA/USEPA) and trust funds from the UK. The districts lie in the central part of Nepal. There are 62,579 households with a population of 338,658 in Dhading and 58,923 households with a population of 288,134 in Gorkha (CBS 2007). Among them 93% in Dhading and 82% in Gorkha are totally dependent on solid fuel for cooking (CBS 2003). In Gorkha, the project was implemented in Bapak, Simjung, and Hansapur Village Development Committees (VDCs), and in Dhading, it was in Darkha, Satyadevi, Jharlang, Jyamrung, Katunje, and Bhumesthan. There were 2,685 households in project villages in Gorkha where intervention was in 500 (18.6%) households. In Dhading, there were 7,121 households in the project area, where intervention was in 500 (7.0%) households.

This study is based on primary data collected from household surveys and indoor air quality monitoring in Rasuwa district for 2006. For the purpose of the study we administered household surveys to 400 households (80 with and 320 without intervention).

Scaling-Up Approach

Holistic market development approach was adopted under the project for up-scaling of smoke hoods (see Figure 13.1).

Demand Creation: To create demand, social marketing activities were carried out on a large scale. Home-to-home visits were carried out in targeted project areas to create awareness against negative health and environmental impacts from traditional stove use and its solutions. Additionally, focus group discussions and video shows were held at different locations. Advertisement and interviews with key stakeholders on IAP problems and its solutions were broadcasted through local radios. The project activities and learning were disseminated to a large audience through local radio, dissemination workshops, and publications. Exchange visits were carried out to make the villagers familiar about the technology.

Establishing Sustainable Supply Chain of Quality Smoke Hoods: Efforts were made to establish strong and sustainable supply chain of the

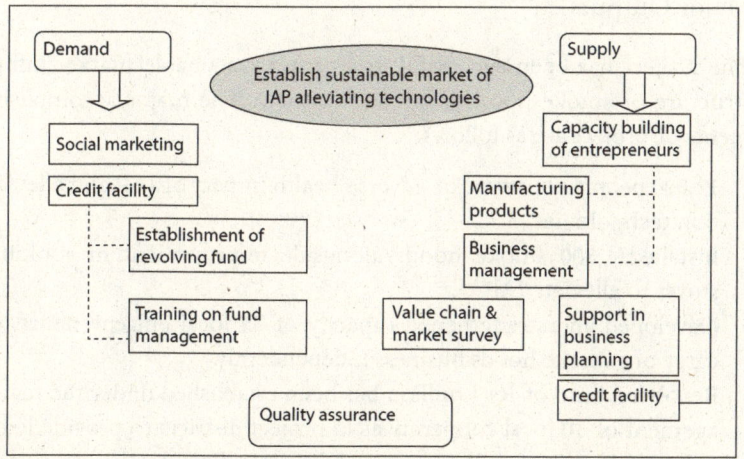

FIGURE 13.1   Framework for Establishing Sustainable Market of Smoke Hoods
Source: Practical Action.

smoke hood business. To ensure supply, a strong base was created by developing capacities of local manufacturers for fabrication and installation of smoke hoods as well as to run the smoke hoods supply business. Capacity-building trainings were imparted on smoke hoods manufacturing and installation, and business management to local entrepreneurs. Additionally, a value chain study of smoke hoods and baseline surveys were carried out to support smoke hoods entrepreneurs to develop their business plan. Likewise, efforts have been made to establish self-functioning and sustainable mechanism for smooth supply of raw materials. A quality control team has been formed in each project villages. Likewise, issuing warrantee card and service after sale mechanisms were introduced to ensure quality.

Financing Mechanism: Instead of subsidy, soft loan was provided through local cooperatives to install smoke hoods. The project provided seed money as grant to 10 local cooperatives to run revolving funds. Likewise, the project imparted capacity-building trainings to local cooperatives to manage revolving fund. A potential customer needed to make an upfront payment of about 25% of total cost to install a smoke hood. Once they get loan, the customer had to repay loan in two years on monthly instalment basis.

Major Outputs

The project has been successful in creating sustainable market infrastructure of smoke hoods in project districts. The major accomplishments of project are as follows:

- 12,000 people are aware of adverse health impact of IAP and alleviation technologies.
- Installed 1,800 smoke hoods alongside improvement in cooking stoves to alleviate IAP.
- Developed and strengthened capacity of 35 local entrepreneurs to carry out smoke hoods business independently.
- Revolving fund of Rs 4 million has been established under the management of 10 local cooperatives in project districts to provide loan to buy indoor smoke alleviating technologies. Enhanced institutional capacity of those cooperatives in cooperative management and to manage the funds.

Impact of the Interventions—The Results

Benefits of Intervention

Indoor Air Quality Improvement

To test indoor air quality, levels of two major pollutants, viz. particulate matter (PM) and carbon monoxide (CO) were measured. The monitoring results show that the 24-hour average PM_{10} level is 763 $\mu g/m^3$ in households without intervention, which is about 15 times higher than the World Health Organization–recommended safe level of 50 $\mu g/m^3$. In the sample households with intervention, the 24-hour average PM_{10} level is 255 $\mu g/m^3$, which is 66% less than for the control group (Table 13.1).

The World Health Organization recommends an 8-hour average CO level should be below 9 ppm. Our findings indicate that the 24-hour average CO level is 9.39 ppm in households with traditional stoves compared to 2.26 ppm (that is, 76% less) in households with smoke hoods. The results show that the difference in the levels of pollution (PM_{10} and CO) in the intervention and control groups is statistically significant (Table 13.1).

A range of factors are assessed that might influence IAP levels, known as confounding variables, in order to analyse their potential effects on CO. Results indicate that coefficient of intervention is negative and significant indicating that interventions are effective in reducing the IAP level significantly. More specifically, average reduction of CO concentration due to intervention is 6.74 ppm (Table 13.2). Likewise, the size of the kitchen significantly reduces the IAP level—the larger the kitchen area the lower is IAP level.

Health Benefits Leading to a Reduction in Treatment Cost and Savings in Days Lost Due to Illness

The occurrence of respiratory illnesses is significantly less among the cooks and children (Table 13.3) in the intervention groups compared to control groups. The probability of reduction in respiratory illness in women cooks and children below 5 years after the intervention is significantly high (see Table 13.4).

TABLE 13.1 Characteristics of Intervention and Control Households

Description	Unit	Without Intervention	With Intervention	t-stat
PM_{10} level—24 hrs average	($\mu g/m^3$)	764	255	4.78***
CO level—24 hrs average	(ppm)	9.39	2.26	6.91***
Annual fuel consumption	(kg/year)	2,886	2,174	7.19***
Annual trip for fuel collection	(hours)	96	73	7.17***
Average fuel collection time per *bhari*	(minutes)	6.41	6.33	0.473
Annual fuel collection time (in hours)	hours/year	617	454	6.23***
Daily cooking hours	hours/day	3.32	3.09	1.70*
Carbon dioxide (CO_2) emission	(kg/year/HH)	4329	3,261	7.19***
Frequency of illness due to IAP	episodes/year	3.3	2.5	4.35***
Days lost due to IAP-generated health problems due to illness (days/year)	days/year	9.55	3.84	4.82***
Days lost of economically active population due to illness (days/year)	days/year	2.00	0.74	2.39***
Days lost of children below 15 years illness (days/year)	days/year	5.63	1.94	3.53***
Days lost to caretakers				

Source: Household Survey (2006) carried out under SANDEE research grant.
Note: *** Significant at 1% level, ** significant at 5% level, and * significant at 10% level.

TABLE 13.2   OLS and IV Regression Results (Dep. Var.: CO Level)

Variables	OLS	
	Coefficient	t-stat
Intervention	−6.74	−5.35***
Rain dummy	−0.65	−0.51
Average temperature	0.32	2.14**
Size of kitchen	−0.11	−2.20**
Number of windows in the kitchen	0.26	0.50
Total family size	0.26	1.02
Hours used for heating purposes	1.93	2.78***
Foods other than regular food prepared	4.88	2.23**
Number of cooking sessions	1.34	2.44**
Use of polluting fuel for lighting	0.04	0.03
Smoking dummy	3.32	3.41***
(Constant)	−3.25	−0.82
R-square	0.337	
Adjusted R-square	0.299	
Number of observations	203	
F-value	8.083***	

Source: Household Survey (2006) carried out under SANDEE research grant.
Note: (a) Dependent Variable: CO level—24 hrs average; (b) *** significant at 1% level; ** significant at 5% level; * significant at 10% level.

The result suggests that intervention contributes to a reduction in treatment costs by about Rs 987/year per household (Table 13.5, IV estimates). The government provides medical check-ups and medicines at subsidized rates through public health facilities. On average the cost of subsidized medicines and health check-ups comes to Rs 375/household/year. If we factor the marginal saving due to intervention, this would come to Rs 1,362/year per household. Likewise, there were savings in sick days after intervention due to fewer occurrences of diseases.

As Table 13.6 shows, the saving in annual sick days for people in economically active age is approximately 10 days/household due to intervention, which is equivalent to Rs 1,000/year (or Rs 500/year at economic price[2]).

[2] Economic price includes direct, indirect, and hidden costs like opportunity cost. For the time saving, we assume that only 50% of the saved time would be used productively so it is less than the financial price. The average daily wage rate in the study area is Rs 100/day.

TABLE 13.3 Symptoms of Illness in Main Cook (Woman) and Children below 5 Years (over 12-month period)

Symptoms	Without Intervention		With Intervention		t-stat
	%	SD	%	SD	
Women Cook					
Cough most days, at least 3 months, for 2 more years	24.1	0.43	15.0	0.36	1.745*
Phlegm most days, at least 3 months, for more than 2 years	41.6	0.49	15.0	0.36	4.521***
Episodes of both cough and phlegm continue for 3 weeks	60.9	0.49	12.5	0.33	8.389***
Wheezing	20.3	0.40	7.5	0.27	2.700***
Sore/watering eyes most of the days	28.8	0.45	5.0	0.36	4.552***
Headaches for most of the days	30.0	0.46	7.5	0.27	4.210***
Children below 5 years					
Cough during last two weeks	81.0	0.39	20.4	0.41	9.663***
Coughs and colds of children over last 12-month period	86.9	0.34	64.8	0.48	3.670***
Burn or scalds over last 12-month period	5.2	0.25	0.0	0.00	1.528
Pneumonia over last 12-month period	6.5	0.25	5.6	0.23	0.254

Source: Household Survey (2006) carried out under SANDEE research grant.

Note: *** significant at 1% level; ** significant at 5% level; * significant at 10% level.

TABLE 13.4   Probability of Reduction in Illness in Women Cooks and
Children Below 5 years (after Intervention)

Symptoms	Probability of reduction in illness after intervention (marginal effect)	z-statistics
Symptoms in women cooks		
Chronic cough	−0.279	−4.31***
Chronic phlegm (phlegm for more than 3 months)	−0.302	−4.66***
Cough and phlegm symptom regularly for 3 weeks	−0.503	−7.24***
Wheezing	−0.104	−2.14**
Sore/watering eyes	−0.237	−4.16***
Symptoms in children below 5 years		
Cough	−0.607	−7.55***
Breathing rapidly during coughing	−0.592	−7.20***

Source: Household Survey (2006) carried out under SANDEE research grant.
Note: (a) The results were derived from separate Probit Regression Analyses; (b)
*** significant at 1% level; ** significant at 5% level; * significant at 10% level.

Fuelwood Saving and Its Associated Benefits

All the households use fuelwood for cooking in the surveyed area. Only
a few households use clean fuels (biogas, LPG, etc.) along with fuelwood (fuel mix).

Fuel saving: The analysis shows that intervention results in a significant saving in fuelwood consumption. Average fuelwood saving due to
the intervention is 1,150 kg/year per household (3.148 kg / 365 days
[Table 13.7]).

Time saving in fuel collection: The households do not purchase fuelwood but collect from nearby forests. In the sample, the quantity of fuel
wood collected per person per trip is 30 kg. The average time per trip
comes to 6.41 hrs. Results indicate that 31 workings days (the equivalent
of Rs 1,550 at economic price) are saved per household annually with
installation of improved stove with smoke hood. As mostly women are
involved in fuelwood collection, time saving has been contributing to

TABLE 13.5 OLS, IV, and Tobit Results (Dep. Var.: log of treatment cost)

	OLS		IV-Estimates		Tobit Regression	
	Coef.	t-stat	Coef.	t-stat	Coef.	t
Intervention	-1.824	-5.61***	-2.986	-2.37**	-2.160	-5.57***
Smoking by a household member (Dummy)	-0.003	-0.01	-0.014	-0.05	-0.085	-0.28
Distance from health facilities (in hours)	0.822	4.74***	0.999	3.87***	0.848	4.14***
Distance from motorable road head (in hours)	0.136	1.69*	0.156	1.79*	0.129	1.36
Total family size	-0.004	-0.06	-0.014	-0.19	-0.005	-0.07
Log of income (Rs '000/year)	0.834	4.68***	1.000	3.95***	0.944	4.50***
Number of children below 5 years	0.128	0.94	0.213	1.35	0.199	1.25
Number of adults above 60 years	-0.426	-1.92*	-0.521	-2.05**	-0.431	-1.66*
Chronic illness (Dummy)	2.367	2.72***	2.771	2.82***	2.757	2.73***
(Constant)	-0.314	-0.42	-0.877	-0.89	-0.960	-1.08
R-square	0.1422		0.0856	Log likelihood	-874.114	–
Adjusted R-square	0.1224		0.0641	Sigma	2.708849	
F	7.18***		3.99***	Pseudo R2	0.0302	–
Number of observations	400		400	Number of observation	400	

Source: Household Survey (2006) carried out under SANDEE research grant.

Note: *** significant at 1% level; ** significant at 5% level; * significant at 10% level.

TABLE 13.6 Marginal Effects: Negative Binomial Estimates (Dep. Var.: Days (Lost Due to Illness)

	Regression	
	dy/dx	z
Intervention	−10.491	−9.86***
Smoking by a household member (dummy)	0.314	0.24
Distance from health facilities (in hours)	1.707	1.95*
Distance from motorable road head (in hours)	−0.440	−1.07
Total family size	−0.217	−0.58
Log of income (Rs '000/year)	2.399	2.63***
Number of children below 5 years	0.767	1.12
Number of adults above 60 years	−0.539	−0.51
Chronic illness (dummy)	7.045	1.04
Log likelihood	−1,418.6568	
Ln alpha	−0.1492762	
Alpha	0.8613312	
Pseudo R^2	0.0215	
Number of observations	400	

Source: Household Survey (2006) carried out under SANDEE research grant.
Note: *** significant at 1% level; ** significant at 5% level; * significant at 10% level.

empowerment of women as they have been able to use saved time for their personal and childcare, and attending community meetings.

Time Saving in Cooking: Improvement in stove combustion efficiency and changes in cooking practices lead to significant savings in cooking time. The analysis suggests that intervention saves 14 minutes/day (Table 13.1) of cooking time. If converted into monetary terms, saving is equivalent to Rs 525/household at economic price per year.

Finally, due to significant reduction in use of fuelwood at 1,150 kg/year, it is estimated that there would be 1,700 kg/household/year less of CO_2 emission which contributes to an improvement in global environment. If one assumes economic value of one tonne of CO_2 avoided to be US$6.00,[3] the saving in fuelwood use results in a saving of Rs 724/household/year in terms of a reduction in level of CO_2 emission. If savings are aggregated for all 1,800 households with

---

[3] In this study, the exchange rate between the US dollar and Nepalese currency was taken as US$1.00 = Rs 70.00.

TABLE 13.7   Determinants of Fuelwood Consumption—OLS and IV
Estimates

	OLS		IV Estimates	
	Coeff.	*t*-stat	Coef.	*t*-stat
Intervention	−3.148	10.39***	−4.815	−3.82***
Food other than regular food prepared (dummy)	6.808	11.92***	6.497	9.69***
Total family size	0.511	8.47***	0.540	7.63***
Income (Rs '000/year)	−0.103	−0.66	0.058	0.27
Use of other fuel (dummy)	−2.325	−2.06**	−1.657	−1.24
Rain (dummy)	−0.285	−1.16	−0.694	−1.65*
Stove used for heating purpose (dummy)	−0.023	−0.13	0.142	0.62
Number of cooking sessions	1.743	13.25***	1.776	11.99***
Fuel collection time	0.049	0.58	0.005	0.05
(Constant)	−0.768	−0.81	−0.954	−0.89
R-square	0.6045		0.5162	
Adjusted R-square	0.5954		0.5048	
F	66.24***		45.52***	
Number of observations	400		394	

Source: Household Survey (2006) carried out under SANDEE research grant.
Note: (a) Dependent Variable: Total use of fuel a day (in kg); (b) *** significant at
1% level; ** significant at 5% level; * significant at 10% level.

intervention, the project has been contributing to offset 3,060 tonnes
of CO_2 annually.

Cost of Intervention

The initial investment cost for intervention per household is Rs 5,000
with maintenance of Rs 100/year (see Table 13.8). This cost is estimated
as net costs based on the costs of smoke hoods plus stove modification minus cost of traditional stove. Similarly, programme costs are
calculated based on Practical Action Nepal's direct programme cost in
Rasuwa (1st phase) in order to calculate cost to society. The total programme cost was approximately Rs 4.76 million (1.12 million for seed
money, 0.79 million for grants, and 2.85 million for other programme
costs) during the three years of the project period (see Table 13.8).

TABLE 13.8 Summary of Cost and Benefits

Headings	Perspectives	
	Household (in Rs)	Societal (in Rs)
Costs		
Cost of a smoke hood	5,000	(5000 + 150) × 640
Annual maintenance cost (Rs/year)	100	100 × 640
Programme cost (excluding support for smoke hoods)	–	2,850,870
Annual Benefits (Rs/Year)		
Annual treatment cost saving	987	(987 + 375) × 640
Annual day loss saving due to illness saving	1,900 (19 days)	950 × 640
Fuel collection time saving	4,000 (40 days)	2,000 × 640
Cooking hour saving	1,050 (10.5 days)	525 × 640
Carbon dioxide (CO_2) emission saving	-	962 × 640

Source: Household Survey (2006) carried out under SANDEE research grant.

Cost–Benefit Analysis

A cost–benefit analysis has been carried out to assess viability of investment for intervention. For a household, total investment includes price of intervention which is Rs 5,000 with a maintenance of Rs 100/household per year (see Table 13.8). The annual financial benefit of intervention is Rs 987/household from treatment costs and Rs 1,900/household (19 days) from healthcare-related time savings. Similarly, there is a Rs 5,050/household (or 50.5 days) saving from indirect time savings (that is, time savings in cooking and fuelwood collection). Thus, the total annual financial savings comes to Rs 7,937/household/year (see Table 13.8).

A cost–benefit analysis from household perspective suggests that investment for smoke hood is highly viable on economic grounds with estimated Economic Internal Rate of Return (EIRR) being 156%, which is 13 times higher than cut-off discount rate (12%). If one considers only health benefits of intervention, the Financial Internal Rate

TABLE 13.9   Cost–Benefit Analysis—the Results

Scenarios	IRR	B/C Ratio
From Household Perspective		
With treatment cost (cash) saving only	12.06%	1.00
With health benefits only	55.05%	2.93
Base results (with total benefits)	156.73%	8.06
From Societal Perspective		
Base results	71.39%	4.70
Without CO_2 saving benefits	57.46%	3.92

Source: Household Survey (2006) carried out under SANDEE research grant.

of Return (FIRR) comes to 55%. If one considers only monetary cost saving, the IRR goes down to 12% (see Table 13.9).[4]

In order to check the viability of the IAP alleviation programme from a societal perspective, we undertake an economic cost–benefit analysis. The analysis from a societal perspective shows that investment in scaling-up programme on indoor smoke alleviating technologies is economically viable with an IRR of 71% and B/C ratio of 4.7 at 3% discount rate (Table 13.9). Moreover, even in absence of financial benefits from CO_2 savings, programme seems viable with an IRR of 57%.

Contribution to Millennium Development Goals and Global Environment

Although the scale of intervention is small, it is evident from results that if implementation of such an initiative is carried out on a large scale it can contribute to achieving the Nepal government's commitments to Millennium Development Goals (MDGs) targets. There is strong empirical evidence that such interventions reduce child mortality rates, improve maternal health, reduce the time and transportation burdens on women and young children, and lessen the pressure on fragile eco-systems. As the intervention is for a short period, only the immediate acute health effects are considered. We had to ignore chronic diseases resulting from long-term exposure.

[4] The benefits include treatment cost saving, and day loss saving on health-care and fuel collection.

With the smoke hoods technology there is significant improvement of indoor air quality leading to health improvement and contributing to achieving MDG goal 4 ('reduce child mortality') and goal 5 ('improve maternal health'). As women cook and children spend most of their time inside the kitchen, they are more exposed to IAP. There is huge possibility of reducing the occurrence of acute respiratory infections, chronic obstructive pulmonary disease, lung cancer, pneumonia, still-birth, perinatal mortality, and low birth weight by improving indoor air quality. Getting rid of open fires in the kitchen has helped to prevent children from being burned or scalded. Likewise, improvements in the combustion efficiency of stoves has reduced women's labour burden and associated health risks.

Improved stove programmes also contribute to achieving MDGs 1, 2, and 3. In the project described in the previous paragraphs, the reduction in the drudgery of fuel collection and cooking time has given women free time for productive endeavours, education, and childcare. With less time consumed in collecting fuel and with improved health, children have more time available for school and homework. Additionally, with the time saving of parents, they have more time to care for their children resulting in improved education of the children. Savings in health costs and time after intervention has been helping achieve MDG 1, 'eradicate extreme poverty and hunger'. Likewise, the project has developed local entrepreneurs and opened up opportunities for them to generate income. Finally, it is also contributing to MDG 7, 'ensure environmental sustainability', as it has been contributing to reducing fuelwood consumption. This leads to less pressure on forests and lower greenhouse gas emissions.

Lessons Learned and Implications for Government's Programmes and Policies

The project experience suggests that the local solutions can pave the way for global solutions—there is need to exploit these win-win possibilities by working on household energy management and introducing clean and efficient technologies. Few initiatives are in progress but looking at the need, the scale of interventions are very small. To meet the demand there is need of aggressive intervention requiring huge investment (need of external support). There is need of joint effort of government, non-governmental, and business organization partnership to tackle this problem. A holistic approach of micro-financing, innovative social marketing, local capacity/institutional building, and linking it with income-generating activities to scaling up of stoves seems very successful.

Women's participation in household decision-making was lacking in the project area. IAP alleviation does not primarily affect adult males. But efforts to increase the demand for improved stoves through awareness campaigns should be targeted at both men and women. In this way, they can jointly make informed decisions concerning IAP reduction. Social marketing can change people's preferences and investment decisions. Awareness materials in local languages and staff who know the local languages were found very effective in creating awareness.

The Government of Nepal has endorsed the National Indoor Air Quality Standards and Guidelines (NIAQSG 2009), an initiative of the Practical Action Nepal Office. NIAQSG 2009 aims to improve public health by maintaining indoor air quality, mainly through stove and ventilation improvement. Although on a small scale, the project made significant contribution to the development in the region, as it came up with new scaling-up models and information (knowledge materials), which are vital for other projects also. Additionally, it is believed that this type of intervention contributes to fulfilling the Government of Nepal's commitment to achieve MDGs. Similarly, such initiatives help to implement the Rural Energy Policy 2006 and achieve household energy-related targets set by the government in its Three-Year Interim Plan (2007–10).

The national improved cook stove programme run by Alternative Energy Promotion Centre/Energy Sector Assistance Programme has been able to disseminate more than 350,000 stoves between 1999 and May 2010. Although lots of efforts are in progress, the scale of the interventions is small compared to the need. In addition, the subsidy-focused supply-driven approach is having difficulty generating enough demand. There is the problem of sustainability and there is the dependency syndrome. Problems include inappropriate dissemination practices, ignorance of people's felt needs and aspirations in terms of intervention, the passive participation of end users, poor operations, and maintenance, and a lack of technical supervision and follow-up from the implementing agency. The success of the project suggests there is a need to work on micro-financing, innovative social marketing, gender problems, the increase of income bases, and making it demand-led. The project implemented by the Practical Action (Nepal Office) that such innovative scaling-up models can be successful. There is a need to scale up such models to the whole country. Sustainable markets for improved stoves need to be established in various parts of the country.

In 2001, about 88.2% households were dependent on traditional biomass fuel stoves. The number had decreased to 80.9% by 2006. Although there are improvements, growth is not satisfactory. To introduce efficient and clean stoves in all Nepalese households there is a need for aggressive intervention. Practical Action (Nepal Office) estimates that by 2026 about 54% of people in the country will have access to commercial energy technology. The other 46% of households (2.7 million) need improved biomass technology to solve the IAP. For this, a huge investment (219 million euro) must be spent to introduce improved stoves, smoke hoods, gasifiers, and biogas in households (Practical Action 2009) (Figure 13.2).

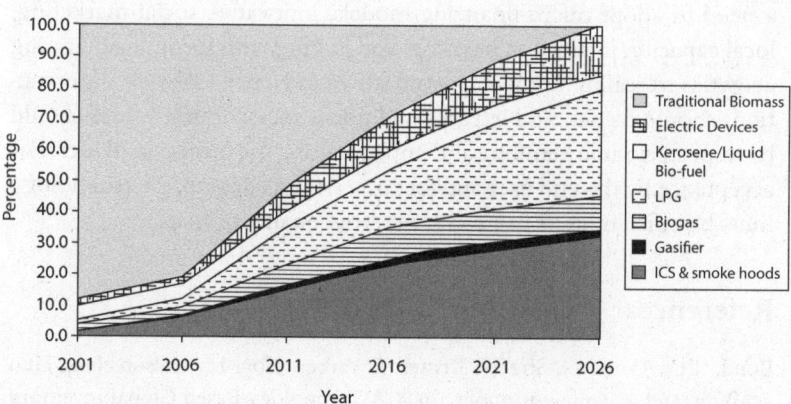

FIGURE 13.2 Types of Cooking Devices in Use in Nepal (Past Trend and Future Projection)
Source: Practical Action (2009).

Conclusions and Recommendations

The problem of IAP is grave in upland rural Nepal. This is due to a combination of poor ventilation the heavy use of solid fuel when cooking with traditional, inefficient stoves. As women cook and with their small children nearby, the children end up suffering from respiratory health problems. The intervention package introduced by Practical Action has proved to be effective in upland areas. The intervention has reduced IAP levels by 66.6% and fuel use by 24.7%. It has improved respiratory health, saved time, and improved the global environment (by reducing deforestation and green house gas emission). It has reduced the drudgery of women. The cost–benefit analysis suggests that it is viable to invest in this type of intervention and its scaling up programme. Yet, adoption of these interventions is limited. There are three reasons why scaling up is not taking place: (a) an information gap (households not aware of the benefits), (b) a lack of credit facilities, and (c) the absence of a regular supply of intervention technologies (because there is no established market). It is imperative for policymakers to deal with these challenges if the problem of IAP is to be seriously addressed. This cannot be done through private sector or public sector alone. There is a need for a public–private partnership to overcome the problem. With success of the project implemented by Practical Action, it is evident there is a need to adopt micro-financing models, innovative social marketing, local capacity/institution building, and linking with income-generating activities to scaling-up of improved stoves in Nepal. Likewise, interventions should be demand-led and traditional sociocultural values should be respected while planning and implementing the project activities. For acceptance by the end user and for successful scaling up, the technology must be efficient in its use and serve strict quality principles.

References

Bond, T.C., David G. Streets, Kristen F. Yarber, Sibyl M. Nelson, Jung-Hun Woo, and Zbigniew Klimont. 2004 'A Technology-Based Global Inventory of Black and Organic Carbon Emissions from Combustion.' *Journal of Geophysical Research* 109 (D14203). doi: 10.1029/2003JD003697.

CBS. 2002. 'Population Census 2001', Central Bureau of Statistics, National Planning Commission Secretariat, Government of Nepal, Kathmandu, Nepal.

CBS. 2003. 'District-Level Indicators of Nepal for Monitoring Overall Development', Central Bureau of Statistics, National Planning Commission Secretariat, Government of Nepal, Kathmandu, Nepal.

———. 2004. 'Nepal Living Standards Survey,' Central Bureau of Statistics, National Planning Commission Secretariat, Government of Nepal, Kathmandu, Nepal.

Ezzati, M. and D. M. Kammen. 2002. 'Household Energy, Indoor Air Pollution, and Public Health in Developing Countries', Issue Brief, 02-26, Resources for the Future, Washington, D.C.

OECD/IEA. 2002. *World Energy Outlook 2002.* Report by OECD/IEA.

Oxfam. 2009. *Climate Change, Poverty and Adaptation in Nepal.* Nepal: Oxfam International Nepal Office.

Practical Action. 2009. *Study to Determine Outline Plans for Eliminating Energy Poverty in Nepal.* Nepal: Practical Action Nepal Office.

Smith, K. R. 1999. 'Indoor Air Pollution', Pollution Management in Focus, Discussion Note Number 4, The World Bank, Washington D.C.

WHO. 2006. *Fuel for Life, Household Energy and Health.* Geneva: World Health Organization.

———. 2007. *Indoor Air Pollution: National Burden of Disease Estimates (2004 revised estimates).* Geneva: World Health Organization.

SLUMLAND POVERTY

14

BANASHREE BANERJEE

Slum Poverty in Asia

Characteristics, Policy Responses, New Challenges, and Opportunities

Urban development and climate change increase environmental risks and vulnerabilities of slums in Asian cities. On the one hand, wealth production of cities increasingly excludes poor from access to land and housing; on the other hand, it has also been used to improve the housing conditions of slum dwellers. Innovative approaches of using the market to benefit the poor and to integrate slums with the rest of the city show the way for effective adaptation to climate change. Climate change effects threaten slums with more frequent disasters and greater damage, but there is an opportunity to take forward adaptation strategies in a way that they benefit the slum poor. The commitment of countries and cities to climate change mitigation would lead to better facilities for the poor. In this chapter, I look into the new challenges and opportunities in cities of South Asia and Southeast Asia and explore the potential to bring about a strategic shift in the way slum poverty is addressed.

Urbanization and Slums

The Asian economic miracle is driven by cities. The Asian economic miracle is driving city growth and transformation. Most of the economic growth that constitutes the Asian economic miracle has taken place in the cities. The poor have benefited from this growth—income poverty has declined. In India for example, urban poverty levels declined from 32.6% in 1993–94 to 25.7% in 2004/05 (Hashim 2009). Yet, better incomes have not been synonymous with a better quality of life. In spite of declining income poverty, the number of people living in informal settlements has increased. In 2001, there were about 332 million slum dwellers in Asian cities; in 2010 this figure increased to 505 million (UNESCAP & UN-Habitat 2010).

Economic activity and urban development have been accompanied by a commensurate growth in slums and an increase in the population at risk. The new reality of Asian cities shows worsening access to land and housing for a growing population in the face of space requirements for infrastructure, business establishments, luxury housing, and leisure activities. In Asian metros, 'slum poverty', which relates to deprivations and risks of living in slums, is not limited to those who fall within the official definition of 'poor' (Barrett and Beardmore 2002).

The growing vulnerability of the slum poor to environmental risks is caused not only by competition for land, but also by residual effects of environmental problems. Some of these are floods caused by indiscriminate landfills, living and working near contaminated rivers and lakes, proximity to untreated garbage and industrial waste, and exposure to greenhouse gas emissions from vehicles. In Manila, for instance, 20% of slum dwellers, or 108,000 people, live in danger zones (Cities Alliance 2008). Added to this is the increasing frequency and intensity of extreme weather events like floods, sea surges, land slides, and cyclones that threaten lives, health, and livelihoods and cause loss of assets of slum dwellers who occupy hazardous areas and are least able to cope.

In this chapter, I argue that measures to improve living conditions of people in urban slums have to be seen in a different perspective to address the new environmental vulnerabilities of slum dwellers. Since the 1970s, the government, NGOs, and international agencies have implemented slum improvement programmes in cities throughout South Asia and Southeast Asia. Some good practices and valuable lessons have emerged from the long years of engagement in initiatives such as the Kampung Improvement Programme of Indonesia. One of the lessons is that by focusing on provision of in-slum infrastructure slum upgrading programmes most often fail to address environmental risks, such as flooding, pollution, and unsafe and overcrowded hous-ing—all of which slum dwellers are increasingly exposed to because of climate change and urban development pressures.

Slums and Slum Poverty in South Asia and Southeast Asia

Slums and Slum Poverty

Slums in South Asia and Southeast Asia consist of a variety of settle-ments, such as inner city dilapidated housing, squatter settlements, shanty towns, illegal subdivisions, and villages within cities. They vary in size from a few huts to thousands of dwellings. This variety makes comparisons across the region difficult. The operational definition of slums adopted by UN-Habitat is useful for comparing slum situations as it uses measurable indicators at the household level . Four of the five indicators measure physical expressions of slum conditions: lack of water, lack of sanitation, overcrowding, and non-durable housing struc-tures. These indicators—known as shelter deprivations—focus atten-tion on the circumstances that surround slum life, depicting deficiencies and casting poverty as an attribute of the environments in which slum dwellers live. The fifth indicator—security of tenure—has to do with legality, which is not as easy to measure or monitor, as the status of slum dwellers often depends on de facto or de jure rights—or the lack of them (UN-Habitat 2006).

A working definition of 'slum poverty' in its simplest form is: pov-erty which is experienced as a consequence of living in slums. In other words, the determinants of slum poverty consist of varying combina-tions and intensities of poor housing quality, unsafe water and waste disposal, poor site conditions, and insecure tenure. In addition, there is the burden of the environmental problems of the city, such as pol-lution of the air, water, and land, and natural and man-made disasters (Figure 14.1).

Slum poverty is experienced differently in different situations. Evidence across Asian shows that not all slum dwellers are poor, and not all of the urban poor people live in slums. Studies in India indicate that 50% slum households are below the poverty line based on income. Ten per cent are just above it and 40% of are well above the poverty line

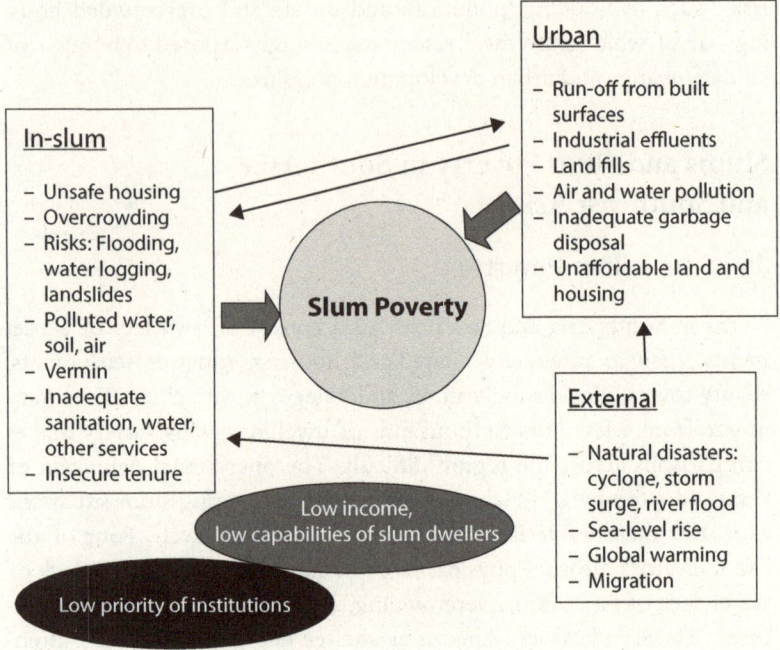

FIGURE 14.1   Determinants of Slum Poverty
Source: Developed by the author.

(Barrett and Beardmore 2002). Thus, the number of people living in slums cannot be taken as a proxy for urban poor population. Figure 14.2 shows the relationship between slum poverty and urban poverty.

Effect of Slums and Slum Poverty

Living in slums brings with it various kinds of vulnerabilities and insecurities, which detract from economic prosperity. At the same time, the central location of slums is a poverty-reduction strategy of the poor, even though the quality of life is low. Easy and inexpensive access to workplaces is a locational advantage of most slums. In the Indian city of Bhopal, a survey of slum dwellers found that more than 60% lived within 1 km of their workplaces to which they would walk, and another 20% were close enough to be able to use bicycles (Manit 2009).

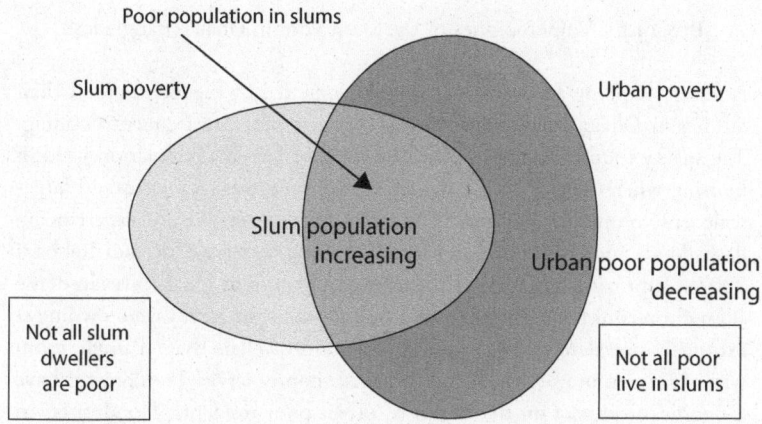

Poor population in slums

Slum poverty

Urban poverty

Slum population increasing

Urban poor population decreasing

Not all slum dwellers are poor

Not all poor live in slums

FIGURE 14.2   Relationship between Slum Poverty and Urban Poverty
Source: Developed by the author.

The main negative effect of living in slums is on people's health, even though there is hardly any slum-level disaggregated epidemiological data to support this for the cities in South and Southeast Asia (Satterthwaite 2007). Slum populations face greater health hazards and disease burdens than non-slum populations. The causes are overcrowding, dampness, poor sanitation, lack of access to safe drinking water, water logging, and environmental pollution. In the absence of adequate municipal services, slum dwellers have to incur higher expenditure for services, especially water. The long time spent procuring water from public standpipes is another concern, particularly for women (Satterthwaite 2007).

Slum dwellers face loss of assets, injury, or mortality from periodic hazards such as fires, flash floods, cyclones, and landslides which are exacerbated by extreme and uncertain weather conditions caused by climate change (refer to Box 14.1 for Dhaka). This, together with insecure tenure, discourages investment in housing and perpetuates vulnerabilities due to inadequate shelter. Informal tenure may also make households ineligible for water and electricity connections. This is compounded by social and institutional exclusion and low Human Development Index (HDI) (Satterthwaite 2007). Available data on access to basic services and HDI in slums of Delhi compare poorly with other low-income settlements, such as resettlement colonies and public

Box 14.1   Vulnerabilities of the Slum Poor in Dhaka, Bangladesh

A recent mapping and census of slums conducted by the Centre for Urban Studies in Dhaka showed that nearly 60% are prone to frequent flooding. The survey found that more than one-third of Dhaka's population lived in housing where almost all the structures were too weak to withstand large-scale environmental disasters. Slums in Dhaka are already experiencing flash floods and higher levels of standing flood waters (Alam and Rabbani 2007). Approximately 80% of the slum population in Dhaka lives in dense slum clusters of between 500 and 1,500 persons per acre. Overcrowding is extremely prevalent; more than 90% of slum dwellers share a single room with three or more people. Floods in dense, poorly serviced settlements have a significant impact on the health of urban poor residents. Floodwaters in slums mix with raw sewage and breed waterborne diseases, such as diarrhoea, typhoid, and scabies. Water supplies also become contaminated during floods as pipes in slum areas get damaged.

Source: Case Study: Dhaka's extreme vulnerability to climate change in UN-Habitat 2008.

housing. Morbidity and hospitalization rates are higher in slums. Also higher is the prevalence of acute illnesses among women and children (NCAER 2002).

Challenges for Reducing Slum Poverty

Large-Scale and Rapid Growth of Slums in Risk Areas

There is a large and growing number of people living in slums in cities of South Asia and Southeast Asia. Cities such as Mumbai, Karachi, Dhaka, and Manila have more than half their populations living in informal settlements (UNESCAP 2010). The Asia region is vulnerable to impending sea-level rise, with two-thirds of its population and most of its cities in the endangered low-elevation coastal zone (McGranahan, Balk, and Anderson 2007). South Asia was identified by the IPCC Fourth Assessment Report as one of the most vulnerable regions in the world. The region also has risk of flooding from the Himalyan glacier melt (Tanner and Mitchell 2008). South Asia's slum dwellers constitute 27% of the global total. That proportion is expected to grow as impoverished rural people migrate to the cities after the predicted increase in drought and riverine floods lowers crop yeilds (Tanner and Mitchell 2008). There is a steadily increasing movement of labour from agriculture to urban informal economic activities such as rickshaw pulling, unskilled construction work, and petty commerce. Two-thirds of the migration is to the three largest cities of Dhaka, Khulna, and Chittagong (Herrmann and Svarin 2009).

The region has pioneered many best practices and good policies, which, however, have not reached sufficient scale or checked the proliferation of slums in risk areas. The Orangi project in Karachi, Pakistan is considered as an international best practice with significant gains for the poor and the city, but the project has not been able to scale up to have a national impact in three decades. India has implemented a number of programmes, innovative schemes, and projects for slum improvement since the 1970s but the impact has not been sufficiently felt (UN-Habitat 2006). The new policy emphasis in India then is on scaling up to city-wide slum upgrading and sustaining it through administrative, legal, institutional, and financial reforms. Two multi-city national programmes, Jawaharlal Nehru National Urban Renewal Mission (JNNURM) and Rajiv Awas Yojana (RAY) represent this policy thrust and also the growing importance of the urban sector. The low priority given to urban issues in national policy is often cited as a reason for the neglect of slums. For instance, Bangladesh's development campaigns through the Bangladesh Rural Advancement Corporation and its Grameen Bank have focused on alleviating rural poverty, with negligible impact in urban areas to which the rural poor continue to migrate.

Thailand has been successful in slowing slum growth significantly. A strong political commitment by its leadership, accompanied by a tradition of strategic planning and monitoring for the last 30 years, have contributed to this. Many of the sub-region's countries also have an active civil society that, with the support of the Asian Coalition of Housing Rights (ACHR), has influenced policy and urban development in favour of the poor (UN-Habitat 2006).

Urban Planning and Regulations Bypass the Poor

Historically, urban planning and regulatory frameworks have not responded to the poverty dimension of Asian cities. The poor build and live outside the purview of zoning and building regulations. Government schemes for improving settlements of the poor are seen as exceptions that are not mainstreamed into formal procedures. Apart from the risk element, non-compliance with regulations bars families from access to institutional financing. The informal status of the slums prevents local authorities from taking a stand. Thus, unsafe housing continues (UN-Habitat 2008).

There have been mounting pressures to make their cities more competitive or respond to the demand for high- and middle-income housing and commercial interests. City authorities have been accused of slipping into policies and measures that exclude the poor. Some of the worst types of evictions and demolitions have been experienced in the last two decades in cities such as Delhi, Mumbai, and Dhaka (COHRE 2008).

It is recognized that the city planning and regulatory frameworks need to be altered. The process of change has begun with countries such as India, the Philippines, and Thailand. They have been making efforts to use urban regulations in an inclusionary manner to deliver land and housing to the poor within a market framework. But still the environmental dimension is not significantly taken care of because of fragmented and small-scale implementation.

Limited View of Slum Improvement

The deeply entrenched assumption of international agencies and national and local governments that the living conditions of slum dwellers can be improved at a low cost mainly through in-slum interventions is in itself a challenge to overcome. First, in situ upgrading does nothing to change the inequitable land distribution of cities or the high density of slums. Regularization paves the way for further densification (Banerjee 2006a). For example, the slums in Delhi accommodate 30% of the population on 5% of total city land (DDA 2007). Second, in-situ upgrading does nothing to protect settlements from disasters such as fires and floods, which occur because of the precariousness of their location and the low quality of the housing (Banerji 2005). If the full cost of negative environmental externalities associated with slums are taken into account, the costs of slum upgrading programmes will be either the same or greater than the cost of constructing new public housing for the same number of households (UN-Habitat 2003). This view is supported by empirical research in three Indian cities on long-term effect of slum upgrading (Banerjee 2006a). The research points to the need for interventions beyond the slum level in order for there to be meaningful environmental improvement.

Inadequate Information Base on Slums

The information base on slums and urban poverty possessed by most Asian cities is inadequate for interventions. Many cities do not include informal land occupations in maps and statistics. Peri-urban areas are invariably left out since they are outside the cities' jurisdiction. But the settlements that are excluded are often the poorest and most environmentally deficient (Banerjee 2006b). There has been a change in the last few years with both governments and civil society organizations in some countries; for example, Thailand, Cambodia, Pakistan, and India. The RAY programme recently launched in India encourages the participation of local communities for mapping slums. Funds are earmarked for this exercise as part of the assistance to municipalities for the preparation of their Slum Free City Plan. Similarly, mapping and surveying are important for slum upgrading and redevelopment projects of the Community Organizations Development Institute (CODI) in Thailand. The National Slum Dwellers Federation and Society for Promotion of Area Resource Centres (SPARC) have been using participatory slum mapping and enumeration in Mumbai as a tool for preventing evictions, establishing rights based on evidence, and planning housing improvement (Burra 2005).

UN-Habitat in 2003 concluded that one-fifth of the Asian slum population lacked durable housing. Similar data about overcrowding in slums is lacking. Instead, a positive correlation between overcrowding and the high incidence of slums is taken as a proxy for overcrowding in slums. This data gap was found to be particularly significant for cities such as Yangon in Myanmar, Dhaka and Rajshahi in Bangladesh, and Karachi, Faisalabad and Islamabad in Pakistan where around 40% of the urban population are known to live in overcrowded dwellings (UN-Habitat 2008).

Institutional Limitations

Most Asian countries have subscribed to the decentralization agenda, but local governments are often not strong enough to address new challenges. First, the place of municipal government is eroded by special-purpose vehicles, parastatals, and public–private partnerships. These institutions draw their power from higher levels of government and from special laws. They undertake infrastructure work, such as expressways, metros, riverfront development, etc. Second, there are specialized organizations for service delivery, particularly in metro cities. They have their own mandates, which sometimes overlap with municipalities but often without coordination with them. The severe flooding in Dhaka in 1998 and 2004 was attributed more to institutional failure than to natural causes (Alam and Rabbani 2007).

City governments often work with budgetary limitations and legal impediments for slum areas. Sometimes, city governments are constrained by legislations that prevent spending public resources in settlements where residents do not pay property tax. Colombo is an example (Devas and Batley 2004). Legislations also prevent public resources from being spent on slums that are not officially recognized . This is what happens in India. There are also technical difficulties of retrofitting services in settlements in difficult areas (Banerjee 2006a). Finally, local institutions lack the staff skills, management systems, and attitudes and practices necessary in order to meet the needs of the slum poor (Devas and Batley 2004; Banerjee 2006b).

Typically, there is a separation of functional domains between urban and environmental in most countries. Urban institutions seldom concern themselves with issues of climate change, even though the resilience to withstand climate change as well as adapt to its impacts lies in the way cities are built and managed. Setting up elaborate coordination mechanisms is often seen as a way out, but most of these arrangements are yet to be tested fully.

Makati City in Manila set up the Makati City Disaster Coordination Council (MCDCC) as the apex body for planning disaster risk management. It also set up the Makati City Environmental Protection Council (MCEPC) as the apex body for planning environment and climate change management. Both organizations include representatives of all the relevant departments of the national and city governments. They are intended to facilitate coordinated planning and ensure that crosscutting problems are fully dealt with (World Bank 2008).

Opportunities for Slum Dwellers in the Climate Change Mitigation Agenda

Making Use of Existing Opportunities

Although urbanization and climate change increase the environmental problems in slums, they also provide opportunities for improving living conditions of slum poor and increase their economic opportunities. In the last few years, most governments in South Asia and Southeast Asia have initiated policy measures to combat slum poverty. Some cities have taken bold and innovative measures to channel their economic development and land-based resources towards better and safer living environments for the poor.

Opportunities for the Slum Poor in Climate Resilience Measures

In keeping with international climate change protocols and conventions, Asian countries are implementing mitigation measures. Such measures present growth potentials for sectors such as public transport, non-motorized transport, green building technologies, waste recycling for energy production, urban forestry, and urban agriculture. The resulting business and employment opportunities for the poor are considerable. In India, the National Mission for Sustainable Habitat is one of the policy initiatives that is supposed to guide cities towards climate change mitigation and adaptation. However, the Mission document is not explicit about slums (Government of India 2010).

Inclusive National Policies and Programmes

National governments are giving policy support for improving slums and providing land and housing through a combination of public and private organizations. When scaled up, the implementation of these policies can be effective in climate change adaptation. The example of the Philippines is worth mentioning for its comprehensive national policy (Box 14.2).

Thailand has moved forward with practical strategies over a three-decade period of institution building. The Baan Mankong (BMK)

Box 14.2   National Policy towards Slums and Low-Income
Housing in the Philippines

The Urban Development and Housing Act of 1992 of the Philippines government is a comprehensive policy document which provides for a range of housing and slum upgrading options for the urban poor including the following:

– Provision of socialized housing and basic services.
– Balanced housing development in which private developers make available 20% of the subdivision area or 20% of the project cost for slum improvement or new housing for the poor.
– Liberalized housing loans and land survey and registration at minimal cost for households in slum upgrading and resettlement projects.
– Urban renewal and slum upgrading.
– Relocation and settlement of persons living in danger areas such as esteros, railroad tracks, garbage dumps, and public places such as sidewalks, roads, parks, and playgrounds.
– Community Mortgage Programme (CMP), which assists organized slum communities to collectively purchase land and improve their neighbourhood and homes.
– Allocation of government land for socialized housing and CMP.
– Incentives such as exemption from paying certain taxes to public and private sector organizations providing land and housing for the poor.

Source: Republic of the Philippines (1992) Urban Development and Housing Act, Republic Act No. 7279.

programme of CODI provides financial and technical support to local stakeholder groups to (a) prepare city-wide plans for slums, (b) prioritize slum upgrading projects (vis-à-vis new city development) for phased implementation, and (c) channel infrastructure subsidies directly to slum communities. The problems of environmental risk (especially flooding) and disaster management are among the deciding factors for settlements to be upgraded in situ or relocated. BMK together with the National Housing Authority's Baan Eua-Arthorn (BEA), a community-housing programme, enables lower income households to have home-ownership in new communities (UN-Habitat and UNESCAP 2008).

In India, slums have long been on the policy agenda, but it is only in the last few years, with the introduction of the JNNURM and RAY programmes, that substantial funds have been allocated for slum upgrading and redevelopment and for related financial and institutional reforms.

Inclusive Urban Planning and Development

I expect the present effort by national governments and international agencies to expand urban planning to include the poor and the environment to bear fruit. Increasingly, government agencies and donor programmes include the environments of the poor in urban and slum upgrading programmes. For example, while the Pasig River project in Manila will result in a cleaner river, it will also lead to a larger holding capacity for flood mitigation, especially in the areas where the poor live. And it will provide 10,000 squatter families with relocation housing. These families are now living in deprived living conditions. Another 80,000 families will benefit from secure tenure and improved infrastructure in existing neighbourhoods. Finally, around 185,000 households will benefit from sanitation services, and most of them are for the poorer communities (ADB PID 2008–13). The Hyderabad Green Belt Project and the Hyderabad Environment Programme (1994–2006) have transformed the Indian city of Hyderabad into a green city with cleaner lakes. This has contributed to its image as a global city. The projects had several pro-poor elements, which have been continued by Hyderabad Metropolitan Development Authority. The projects involved women from slums maintaining plant nurseries in city parks, lakesides, and in open spaces in slums, including rooftops. The usufruct rights to biomass products such as fruit and fodder have been established for local community groups. Lake restoration has reduced flooding in the surrounding slums and traditional housing areas (Banerjee 2004).

Tapping into the Prosperity of Cities

Asian cities are increasingly adopting slum redevelopment, the renewal of blighted areas, and new housing as opportunities to improve the living conditions of the poor. This is different from the earlier practice of regularizing informal settlements and providing them with basic services. The Chinese example stands out for its large scale of affordable housing meant to check the growth of slums. The use of equity grants to poor households living in substandard housing and incen-

Box 14.3   Transferable Development Rights as an Incentive for Slum
Housing in Mumbai

The Slum Rehabilitation Scheme (SRS) is being implemented in Mumbai
by the Slum Rehabilitation Authority (SRA) since 1995 to provide formal
housing free of cost to slum dwellers on the land occupied by them, or on
relocation sites agreed by them. The SRS makes it profitable for the private
sector to build housing for slum dwellers' cooperative housing societies by
providing an incentive Floor Space Index (FSI). This can be used on the
plot within the permissible FSI in the area after housing all the co-operative
members and converted to TDR for building in other parts of the city or
trading in the market. High land values and the present low FSI regulation ensure profits for developers and landowners even after providing slum
dwellers with rehabilitation tenements free of cost (SRA 1997). Private sector participation in SRS is a budget-neutral way to fulfil the political agenda
of providing free houses for 800,000 slum families of Mumbai (Burra 2005).
In the last 15 years, SRS has resulted in about 350,000 slum families getting
access to formal housing and another 100,000 in transit camps. Even so,
progress has not been as rapid as anticipated because of land market fluctuations and hazy land records.

Source: Banerjee (2012).

tives to private developers is making this possible. In Mumbai, India,
the well-known city planning instrument of transferable development
rights (TDR) is used as an incentive for private developers to produce
housing for slum dwellers (Box 14.3).

Such initiatives, which respond to the local-land market conditions,
provide significant opportunities for climate change adaptation through
overcoming the disadvantages of slum living. The challenge is to scale
up such redevelopment approaches within more inclusive urban development frameworks. It is also relevant to integrate pro-poor adaptation
to climate change with general city planning activities.

Preparing for Disaster Management

Due to the increase in occurrence and intensity of environmental
disasters, all countries in the region have initiated disaster management

programmes. Community-based disaster risk-management programmes are improving the capacity of local people to respond to
disasters in Tokyo and Jakarta. The main operations in Singapore follow a four-pronged system: warning, protection, rescue, and the 3Cs
(command, control, and communication) (World Bank 2008). India has
set up the Disaster Management Authority at the national level, and several state governments have set up warning systems. However, at city
level, institutional responsibilities are not well defined, limiting action
to include the poor at the local level (Revi 2008). Satellite-based warning
systems and disaster mapping has improved vulnerability assessment
and risk response in Asia. At the same time addressing in a practical
way, the differential vulnerabilities of population groups within cities is
a serious challenge (Revi 2008).

* * *

Revisiting the Urban Development and Climate Change Framework

Until recently, the typical approach of the governments of Asia to the
problem of climate change has been to focus on national plans for reducing contributions to global warming by technical means. Many such
plans are implemented in the urban areas, and this development more
generally will also result in benefits to the poor in the form of mass
transportation, or in job opportunities in new sectors, such as green
building and alternate energy. In addition to taking steps to reduce the
negative effects of climate change in cities—such as flooding—through
more resilient infrastructure and disaster preparedness programmes
also help the urban poor.

However, a pro-poor urban development would need to do more by
specifically targeting population groups living in slum areas: Efforts to
improve the living conditions of the slum poor and to make them less
vulnerable to the negative effects of climate change should be carried out
within the framework of urban development and transformation on one
hand, and mitigation and adaptation strategies related to climate change
on the other. The framework should be sensitive to living and livelihood
links of the poor with the city. Cities need to find solutions for accommo-
dating more poor people, and for making their current settlement areas
more secure and resilient against climate change risks. Moving out the

poor to alternate locations, which are safe from environmental hazards, is often not a good solution, as such places mostly do not provide sufficient income opportunities and access to social services.

Spatial planning for the slum poor would require more inclusive urban land use. It would also require environmental and transportation planning. Specifically, it requires the actual implementation of plans which are written down in the name of poverty reduction but are often then not followed through. This is only achievable through a change in approach of city governments towards working in true partnership with slum dwellers, private sector players, civil society, and public institutions (ADB 2008). In other words, a strategic shift would be required, one from providing basic services to slums to addressing slum poverty as part of an inclusive and equitable urban planning and development agenda. This new strategy would also require much more than eliminating slums. It requires a concerted effort to protect populations at risk from environmental hazards. It requires ensuring adequate and affordable service delivery. It requires housing and energy conservation.

Levers for Action and Starting Points at City Level

The layers for action and starting points may be different in different cities, but there is a need to overcome existing challenges and build on good practices for addressing slum poverty within the reality of each city. One of the first actions would be to understand slum poverty and associated environmental risks through mapping and surveys as a base for planning and as an advocacy tool. Considering that environmental risks are not uniform, it would be important to prioritize regions, cities, and slums. In South Asia and Southeast Asia, priority cities would essentially consist of densely populated cities threatened by sea-level rise. At the top of the list would be South Asian cities that are facing the additional threats of glacier melt, heavy downpours, and flash floods. Within cities, the most vulnerable areas are those densely populated areas that are susceptible to environmental disasters, such as flooding, landslides, and pollution. Since slum poverty involves both urban development and climate change, it would be possible to get funding on both grounds. In addition, the interest of city governments in attracting private resources for housing for the poor through making appropriate regulations and incentives is likely to sustain, especially in cities of high economic growth. Even so, it may be necessary to commit substantial public resources to urban development, for instance, to improving citywide drainage. The present institutional arrangements would need to be tested and made more robust, in terms of new responsibilities of individual institutions for disaster management, risk mitigation, and shelter improvement in slums and their integration with city systems.

Environmental Risk Management in Slums

This chapter, therefore, argues for a strategy for risk management in slums within the framework of inclusive urban planning. The three main elements of risk management can lead to improvement of living conditions of the slum poor and minimize environmental risks, with or without climate change (Box 14.4).

Box 14.4	Environmental Risk Management in Slums
1. Local disaster management	Build capacity of city institution, slum community, and civil society to deal with fire, flash floods, landslides, etc. Create basic infrastructure. Set up disaster management fund.
2. Risk mitigation	Ensure access to basic infrastructure with city linkages. Flood control, ground stabilization, drainage, garbage collection Improve self-built housing: advocacy, low cost building material, credit, tenure regularization Adapt settlement layout for access to fire tenders, ambulance Undertake community-based redevelopment Access poverty reduction and climate change adaption funds
3. Relocation to safer sites, where mitigation not possible	Acquisition of land at suitable sites, use of government land Land reservation by private developers, PPPs In consultation with slum community

Source: Developed by the author.

References

Alam, Mozaharul and Md. Golam Rabbani. 2007. 'Vulnerabilities and Responses to Climate Change for Dhaka'. *Environment and Urbanization* 19: 81.

Asian Development Bank. 2008. *Managing Asian Cities*. Manila: ADB.

ADB PID. 2008–13. ADB–Pasig River Environmental Management and Rehabilitation Sector Development Program Loan (Investment Loan), Philippines 2008–2013. Available at: www.adb.org.

Banerjee, Banashree. 2004. 'Giving City Open Space Back to Citizens in Hyderabad'. UNDP–HUDCO International Workshop on Urban Renewal, 17–19 February 2004, Manesar.

———. 2006a. 'Impact of Tenure and Infrastructure Programmes on Housing Conditions in Squatter Settlements in Indian Cities'. In *Indian Cities in Transition*, edited by A. Shaw. New Delhi, India: Orient Longmans.

———. 2006b. 'Giving Voice to the Poor in Municipal Planning: Learning from the Andhra Pradesh Urban Services for the Poor', pp. 213–35. In *Urban Governance and Management: Indian Initiatives*, edited by P.S.N. Rao. New Delhi: IIPA.

———. 2012. 'From Informal Settlements to Prime Real Estate in Indian Cities'. (Forthcoming) In *Trialog*.

Banerji, Manjistha. 2005. 'Provision of Basic Services in the Slums and Resettlement Colonies of Delhi in Ensuring Public Accountability Through Community Action'. New Delhi: Institute of Social Studies Trust.

Barrett, Alison and Richard Beardmore. 2002. 'Understanding the Poor in Cities and Formulating Appropriate Anti-Poverty Actions'. World Bank Institute, discussion paper for South Asia Urban and City Management Course, Goa, India

Burra, Sundar. 2005. 'Towards a Pro-poor Framework for Slum Upgrading in Mumbai, India'. *Environment and Urbanization* 17 (1, April).

Cities Alliance. 2008. *Slum Upgrading Up Close: Experience of Six Cities*. Washington: Cities Alliance.

COHRE. 2008. 'Successes and Strategies: Responses to Forced Evictions,' Centre on Housing Rights and Evictions, Geneva, Switzerland.

Delhi Development Authority (DDA). 2007. *Delhi Master Plan 2021*. New Delhi: Rupa Publishers.

Devas, Nick and Richard Batley. 2004. 'Urban Governance and Poverty: Lessons from a Study of Ten Cities, Regional Seminar and Learning Event on Local Government and Pro-poor Service Delivery'. 10–12 February 2004, ADB Headquarters, Manila, Philippines.

Government of India. 2010. *National Mission on Sustainable Habitat*. GoI, Ministry of Urban Development.

Hashim, S. R. 2009. *Economic Development and Urban Poverty*. India Urban Poverty Report 2009, New Delhi, Oxford University Press.

Herrmann, Michael and David Svarin. 2009. 'Environmental Pressures and Rural-Urban Migration: The Case of Bangladesh'. UNCTAD. Available at: http://mpra.ub.uni-muenchen.de/12879/ MPRA Paper No. 12879.

Maulana Azad National Institute of Technology (MANIT). 2009. 'Survey of Slums in TT Nagar area of Bhopal'. Madhya Pradesh Urban Services for the Poor (MPUSP) Project (Unpublished)

McGranahan, Gordon, Deborah Balk, and Bridget Anderson. 2007. 'The Rising Tide: Assessing the Risk of Climate Change in Low Elevation Coastal Zones', *Environment and Urbanisation* 19(1).

National Council of Applied Economic Research (NCAER). 2002. *The Burden of Ill Health among the Poor: The Cases of Slums and Resettlement Colonies in Delhi and Chennai*. New Delhi: NCAER

Revi, A. 2008. 'Climate Change Risk: An Adaptation and Mitigation Agenda for Indian Cities'. *Environment and Urbanisation* 20 (1).

Satterthwaite, David. 2007. 'In Pursuit of a Healthy Urban Environment in Low and Middle Income Nations'. In *Scaling up Environmental Challenges*, edited by Peter Marcotullio and Gordon McGranahan. UK: Earthscan.

Government of Maharashtra. 1997. *Guidelines for Slum Rehabilitation Scheme*. GoM, Slum Redevelopment Authority.

Tanner, Thomas and Tom Mitchell. 2008. 'Entrenchment or Enhancement: Could Climate Change Adaptation Help or Reduce Chronic Poverty?' *IDS Bulletin* 39 (4, September).

UN ESCAP and UN Habitat. 2010. 'The State of Asian Cities 2010/2011', UN HABITAT, Nairobi.

UN-Habitat. 2003. 'The Challenge of Slums: Global Report on Human Settlements 2003.' UK, Earthscan.

———. 2006. *State of the World's Cities 2006/2007*. UK: Earthscan.

———. 2008. *State of the World's Cities 2008/2009*. UK: Earthscan.

UN-Habitat and UNESCAP. 2008. 'Housing the Poor in Asian Cities: Quick Guides for Policy Makers. No. 3 Land: A Crucial Element in Housing the Poor', Bangkok, UN-Habitat, Nairobi.

World Bank. 2008. *Climate Resilient Cities: A Primer on Reducing Vulnerabilities to Climate Change Impacts and Strengthening Disaster Risk Management in East Asian Cities*. World Bank, Global Facility for Disaster Reduction and Recovery, Washington.

15

DILRUBA BANU

Slum Poverty in Bangladesh

Environment and Climate Changes as Factors

E nvironmental causes are intensifying the process of urbanization in Bangladesh through unanimously increasing the number of poor in the slums. The poor contribute to increased economic growth in the city; nevertheless, they lack basic urban services. Along with other socioeconomic poverty factors, urban slum dwellers are continuously fighting against the climate change challenges. High temperature, heavy rainfall, prolonged waterlogging, salinity, cyclone, drought, and other extreme climate events exacerbate their poor living conditions in ways that ultimately affect the health. Due to their gender role, women support the survival of the households during climate change adversities. Adaptation is being considered as an urban poverty strategy in policymaking, comprehensive planning, and related researches. It allows the slum poor to cope with climate change better. Adaptation should be based on slum poor's priorities, needs, knowledge, and capacities. Regional mitigation and adaptation for rich are needed to be sufficiently inclusive which importantly increases the capacity of the poor.

Urban Poverty: Livelihoods of the Slum Poor

Poverty in Bangladesh originates in a number of socioeconomic and environmental factors. Poverty is evident in all the cities of Bangladesh. It is estimated that in the cities of Bangladesh, 43% of the residents live below the poverty line and out of those 23% of the residents are extremely poor. Around 35% of the population of the six major cities in Bangladesh live in slums. These six cities cover only 4% of the land area of the country. Slums have limited or no access to services. Slums are often located in urban sites that are prone to natural disasters, such as flooding. Residents are exposed to health hazards. Loss of health reduces their savings and productivity.

The number of city dwellers in Bangladesh is increasing continuously. Poor people in rural areas lack earning opportunities mainly due to loss of cultivable land. City development contributes to increased economic growth by creating job opportunities, facilitating commercial activities, and driving industrial development. Economic opportunities in urban areas attract large numbers of migrants from rural areas. New migrants and second-generation migrants are living in the slums. They lack housing and basic urban services. Most of the slum households are made of bamboo, straw, and plastic sheets. Only a few have temporary weak structure of low-quality wood, tin, and even bricks. The population density in the slums ranges from 700 to 4,210 per acre. A minimum of 4 and a maximum of 10 people share a room, which is highly congested and unhealthy (Akash and Singha 2003, cited in Khan 2010). Utility services are inadequate in the slums; only a single pipeline of water is available at limited points. Latrines are mostly uncovered and hanging. This contaminates open water bodies and pipe water through its leakage. A lack of basic amenities, such as safe drinking water, proper housing, drainage, and excreta disposal services makes slum population vulnerable to infections. These further compromise the nutritional requirements of those living in slums.

Rapid urbanization places great pressure on a city's physical and social infrastructure. Overstretched city administrations find it increasingly difficult to provide adequate housing, transportation, waste and sanitation, education, health, and other essential services. The slum poor suffer the consequences of inadequately managed urbanization in the form of poor health, lack of safety, and other problems. Existing public services are often inaccessible to them. They find themselves unable to protect their families against the consequences of unemployment, ill health, eviction, crime, or other shocks that strip them of their assets, destroy their livelihoods, and keep them trapped in poverty.

Over the past decade, there has been a rapid decline in income-based poverty in Bangladesh. Social indicators have also improved. Nevertheless, Bangladesh is still one of the world's poorest nations where half of the urban population lives below the poverty line. Measuring urban poverty is a highly complex activity. The national measures needed for policy purposes often ignore the diversity of experiences and characteristics of the slum poor. Age, gender, educational background, livelihood, ethnicity, religion, and a host of other factors vary within and between groups and individuals. Policy measures that seek to address the needs of the urban poor must be sensitive to this diversity. The slum poor rely heavily on cash income to secure their basic needs. Income-based poverty measures tend to underestimate urban poverty in comparison with those that look at consumption or take into account other dimensions of poverty, such as access to basic services. Trends in other measures of poverty also indicate that the level and distribution of consumption among the poor has also been reduced. The improvements occurred at similar rates for both urban and rural areas (Narayan et al. 2007).

Impacts of Climate Change on Slum Poor

In the context of environmental policy, the term 'climate change'[1] refers to changes in modern climate, including the rise in average surface temperature known as global warming. Vulnerability to the negative

---

[1] Climate change is a significant and lasting change in the statistical distribution of weather patterns over periods ranging from decades to millions of years. It may be a change in average weather conditions or the distribution of events around that average (e.g., more or fewer extreme weather events). Climate change may be limited to a specific region or may occur across the whole Earth. The most general definition of climate change is a change in the statistical properties of the climate system when considered over long periods of time, regardless of cause (source: Wikipedia).

effects of climate change varies with geographical location, seasonality, and exposure of population and infrastructure. Other factors include economic and social conditions, natural resource capital, political and institutional mechanisms, equity of resource distribution, gender, and coping and adaptive capacity (Khan 2010).

Climate change compounds problems of environmental degradation and has led to serious deterioration of ecosystems, adding yet another dimension to poverty. Bangladesh is considered highly vulnerable to climate change and climate variability. If the sea level rises, as some have predicted, 55% of the population could be inundated. Rising sea levels will make the southern coastal areas, especially the islands, uninhabitable. The southern populations will be forced to migrate to cities. Climate change will affect infrastructure, including water systems, housing and settlements, transportation networks, utilities, and industry. Salination will limit traditional types of agriculture and reduce the amount of drinking water. The Sundarban mangroves will be affected, reducing cyclonic tidal surge buffering.

In Bangladesh, the most vulnerable cities are Dhaka and Khulna, both of which have witnessed extreme environmental problems, such as floods, in recent years. The sectors most affected by floods in Bangladesh's cities are energy, transport, construction, industry, trade, commerce, and utility services. Reducing productivity during and after major flooding is increasing the vulnerability of the urban poor. The adverse effects of climate change on rural areas cause increased migration to the cities in search of non-agricultural employment. This migration increases pressure on scarce housing, water, sanitation, and energy services.

High rainfall intensity, waterlogging, salinity, cyclones, drought, and other climate events add difficulties in the livelihoods of the slum poor. In slum households, a major portion of household income is spent on food, followed by expenditure on non-food items and house rent. Many of the poor depend on loans for medical treatment and other emergencies. Extreme weather disrupts the slum dwellers' work and income. Some occupations are affected by weather, such as rickshaw pulling, wage labour, and construction work. In heavy rain or floods, the informal sectors are especially affected. Frequent absences from formal work cause less earning and sometimes threaten jobs. Due to engagement in laborious jobs, poor people feel tired during their work in high temperatures; as a consequence, they lose income. Smaller earnings mean more pressure to manage food for their families. Malnutrition in young children has long-term negative effects on physical and cognitive development. The major causes of childhood malnutrition among the slum population are inappropriate child-feeding practices, infections, improper food security and childcare, poor availability, and inadequate use of healthcare services.

The most direct effects of climate change on human health occur through extreme events such as floods and cyclones that cause deaths. Climate change affects the distribution of climate-sensitive diseases, such as malaria. Its prevalence increases in the sort of warmer, wetter climate that is expected with climate change. Other diseases, such as dysentery, diarrhoea, dengue, and hypertension are associated with heat stress. Asthma and skin diseases increase during the summer. These diseases constrain even the economic activities of the poor. The conditions associated with climate change (e.g., temperature, rainfall, and salinity) and the effects of these conditions on water supplies, sanitation, and food production favour the spread of such diseases (Huq and Ayers 2008).

Addressing Gender Concerns

Poor women living in the slums are particularly vulnerable to the adversity of climate change. In Bangladesh, women are more vulnerable to chronic poverty in general, due to gender inequalities in various social, economic, and political institutions. Climate change is likely to exacerbate this situation. The death rate for women was almost five times higher than for men when cyclones and floods hit Bangladesh. This is because men were able to communicate with each other when they met in public spaces, but information often did not reach the household. And since many women were not allowed to leave their homes unaccompanied by a male relative, many waited for their male relatives to arrive (Huq and Ayers 2008).

Urban floods coupled with drainage congestion is emerging as one of the major concerns these days. The slum dwellers are the most affected by urban drainage congestion. In prolonged waterlogging, women face severe skin diseases and gynaecological problems due to repeated use of polluted water for sanitation. Slum-dwelling women make their living mostly by finding self-employment as temporary housemaids. Due to their gender role, women cannot avoid responding to the household's critical situation. Keeping children and belongings in inundated in house makes them unable to join in income earning outside the slum. Delay or absence at the job often is translated into a loss of employment, with counterproductive results on food security. Many slum dwelling women are self-employed as food producers and vendors. They mostly target rickshaw-pullers and day-labourers as customers. They face enormous hardship during floods due to lack of the purchasing capacity of the urban poor. Children suffer from acute malnutrition though mothers try to feed them with whatever they have, being themselves half-fed or even starving (Neelormi 2010).

In addition, women are the main users and carriers of water for the household. As the availability and quality of water declines and resources become scarcer, women suffer increasing workloads to collect non-saline water to sustain their families. Extreme temperatures also disrupt the water supply. Frequent disruption of the electricity supply causes lesser water supply because water-lifting pumps cannot work, though people need water more in higher temperatures. In hot weather, women collect water after walking long distances and waiting in queues.

Women have limited access to land in Bangladesh. They inherit land from their parents or acquire mostly homestead land through marriage. Ownership of crop fields is very limited for them. Women often lose land, and hence security, with divorce. Climate change variability reduces the fertility of land and also proportion of land that is fertile at all. Climate change adaptation discourse needs to consider gender concerns in particular.

Urban Contribution to Enhance Climate Change Risks

Job opportunities are concentrated in urban areas, requiring many people to commute long distances. Traffic, transportation, fuel consumption, and air pollutions contribute to global warming and climate change (Habitat 2008; IPCC 2007). Climate change effects correlate with people's demand for energy. It increases energy use for water supply such as in pumping, cooling, desalination, recycling, and water distribution.

The major challenges of the slum poor are food insecurity, poor energy supplies, poor infrastructure and transportation, and poor sanitation services. Due to insufficient services, the poor pollute the local environments by illegally dumping waste and discharging wastewater (Moral 2008, cited in GTZ Bangladesh 2010).

With the increase of unplanned and socially and environmentally degraded industries, Bangladesh is posed with a new challenge. The industrial areas of Bangladesh are situated in the midst of densely populated regions. There are many hazardous and potentially dangerous polluting industries situated in the cities. In Dhaka, in the Tejgaon area, food-processing industries are situated along with chemical and heavy metal-processing industries. In Tongi, a pharmaceutical company is situated near a pesticide-producing company. Considering the severity of the environmental threats to the slum dwellers, industrial waste management and waste-water treatment need particular attention.

The major challenges will be getting security of tenure for the slum poor. This will ensure access to services and infrastructure. Climate-induced hazards tend to increase in scale in the absence of infrastructure. The possibility for the government to acquire capacity to meet this high demand of infrastructure is questionable. In the present situation, the urban poor continue to live on the most vulnerable land. In most cases, the land is illegally occupied; the structures are built informally with cheap material. Construction does not follow any standard and building regulations.

Several NGOs and donor-funded projects have worked to develop infrastructure and services, including sanitary latrines, hand tubewells, paved pathways, drains, and streetlights. Although the achievements are limited, but learning from such works, there should be an emphasis on community initiatives that adapt cost-effective locally based infrastructure development.

Economic growth is threatened by the effects of severe poverty, which is worsened by climatic vulnerability. Particular attention is needed for the development of coping strategies that address poverty related to climate change. Special emphasis should be placed on the problems faced by the poor urban population. This is needed to protect the poor against climate change effects and ensure the social and economic stability of the country. The broad range of effects that could be produced by climate change on slum poverty is overwhelming. It is important to clearly understand these effects where climate change is becoming obvious. Foremost effects are apparent, but the critical part is yet to come. As Bangladesh is thought to be making progress in poverty reduction, in both the income and social dimensions, environmental poverty needs to be addressed. The relevant responses to climate change are already being adopted by policymakers, development practitioners, and donor agencies. Comprehensive planning and related research may enable the slum poor to cope with climate change better. The region's development is insufficiently inclusive, and is threatened by climate change and other environmental risks and natural hazards. Adaptation by the rich is just as important as by the poor because adaptation by rich increases the capacity of the poor as well.

Government Responses to Slum Livelihoods

The Government of Bangladesh has undertaken the Second Urban Governance and Infrastructure Improvement (Sector) Project (UGIIP 2) with a loan from the Asian Development Bank, a grant from KfW, and technical cooperation from GIZ. The project is implemented over a period of six years, until 2014. GIZ provides technical support for the capacity development in the scope of UGIIP 2. The primary objective of the project is to promote sustainable human development, economic growth, and poverty reduction by improving urban governance, developing urban infrastructure and services, enhancing municipal management, and strengthening the capacity to deliver municipal services (especially to the poor) in 35 targeted 'municipalities' (*pourashavas*)[2] of Bangladesh. The Local Government Engineering Department (LGED) acts as the executing agency of the project, while the participating pourashavas implement the project components. To achieve the objective, the project assists the selected pourashava to

- increase the capacity of the pourashavas to implement, operate, manage, and maintain basic urban services;

[2] UNESCAP on Bangladesh: 'Local government in urban and rural areas is entrusted to bodies elected by the people. Such bodies are called Municipalities or Pourashavas (numbering 138) in urban areas and Union Parishads or Union Councils (numbering 4,451) in rural areas.' Available at: http://www.unescap.org/huset/lgstudy/country/bangladesh/bangladesh.html.

- improve urban governance by implementing a set of programmes;
- increase the accountability of the pourashavas to their residents, especially the poor and women; and
- provide improved physical infrastructure and urban services.

While UGIIP 2 supports the improvement of urban governance and infrastructure, it adopts a performance-based allocation of investment funds as an incentive mechanism for governance reform. Performance criteria are defined in six areas of urban governance, including 'integration of the urban poor'. Investment funds are used to improve transportation, drainage, solid waste management, water supply, sanitation, municipal facilities, and basic services in municipal slums. The project design is based on the lessons from the ongoing Urban Governance and Infrastructure Improvement (Sector) Project (UGIIP).

All 35 pourashavas formulated their Pourashava Development Plan (PDP) in a participatory manner, including by using a visioning exercise, a situation assessment, priority investments, and activities for governance improvement. Each PDP includes a Poverty Reduction Action Plan (PRAP) that identifies and formulates specific actions for poverty reduction in the pourashava. A Slum Improvement Committee (SIC) has been established in each target slum to execute the PRAP. There are a few committees formed under the project in pourashava, such as the Town Level Coordination Committees and the Ward Level Coordination Committees, which have representation of low-income groups and women to ensure their participation in decision-making processes of pourashava management. To ensure an adequate budget for implementing the PRAP, a minimum of 5% of the investment funds allocated to each pourashava has been earmarked for basic services in urban slums. SIC has been given training on the operation and maintenance of the infrastructure identified in PRAP. Outside the slums, community-based organizations have been formed to manage community infrastructure. They focus on low-income groups. Representatives of the poor include the chairperson of SIC, who is selected by the poor themselves. The selection procedure has been specified in the guidelines for PDP development.

Under the project, pourashavas are expected to invest in basic services to urban slums. The aim is to improve the living conditions of the slum dwellers. The components include improvements in roads, drains, footpaths, water supply, sanitation, solid-waste management, and lighting. Specific components are identified in the PRAP. The investment projects are supposed to carry out the Initial Environmental Examination (IEE) for sustainable environment management in the pourashava.

Under UGIIP 2 pourashavas, the urban poor have prioritized infrastructure development–related activities in their PRAP through which they think can respond to the climate change challenges. Among the services provided by the pourashava, the slum dwellers like to have installation of deep tubewell for pure drinking water and sanitary latrines. Another pourashava service that is a priority for the poor is connecting the slums to pipeline water. To avoid waterlogging, the poor want narrow drains that can be covered with slabs. The slabs can be used as footpaths for safe walking. The poor have insisted on involvement in alternative income generation so they may reduce natural resources dependency. They have initiated community-based management of the door-to-door collection of solid kitchen waste.

UGIIP 2 has commenced community adaptation to climate change through participatory planning by pourashava citizens including the slum poor. Community-based adaptation to climate change is a community-led process, based on a community's priorities, needs, knowledge, and capacities, which empowers people to plan for and cope with climate change (Reid et al. 2009). Adaptation in a built environment emphasizes exploring innovative measures affordable for the urban poor. Bangladesh has experience on community-based disaster management that needs to be disseminated. The built environment of the urban areas can be designed and improved in a way that includes the urban poor in the city-level development process. These possibilities can include the manner of investing in resilient infrastructure: improving drainage, disaster-safe housing, increased access to services (health, water and sanitation, security of tenure in informal settlements, etc.) (Khan 2008).

Climate change adaptation depends on country-specific capacity for economic, social, and human development, which is closely related to income level, inequity, urban poor development capacity, illiteracy rate, and area disparity. Adaptive capacity is also influenced by the financial capability of the government (ADB 2009). Sector development programmes have drawn the attention of the policymakers, development practitioners, and donor agencies. There is a great need to increase the capacity of communities, local governments, and the national government to adapt to climate change. Governance is grossly neglected in adaptation. Regular monitoring and evaluation need to be ensured.

* * *

The poor tend to be concentrated in environmentally marginalized areas, such as slums, dry land, coastal, upland, and flood-affected wetland areas. The poor are left behind in the growth process. They search for marginal livelihood and affordable living space. Poverty and climate change are closely related. The urban poor are disproportionately affected by a badly managed urban environment. Due to climate change, the slum poor face environmental risks that require management. The poor migrate to the cities as a way of adapting to climate change. They bring change to alternative income generation and consumption pattern due to lack of cultivable land in town on which they used to work. The poor breathe differently in the city because of their vulnerability. Better poverty measurement methods for urban areas are needed. Such methods would take account of the complex nature of the urban poor. Community-based, demand-responsive approaches derive sustainable benefits from water and sanitation facilities. The effect of climate change on public health is mostly neglected by the development discourse, but health expenditure is increasing day by day. The ability to use natural resources in a sustainable manner should be increased. Urban populations need to be educated about adaptation to climate change. The education could be about protection, improvement, and effective environmental management practices within slum communities.

Both women and men have to look forward to, survive, cope with, and recover from climate adversity. In this broad context, a gender-sensitive adaptation needs to be addressed for sustainable development. The gender perspective should receive major attention in both adaptation and mitigation of climate change issues. Youth should get attention in climate issue as the change agent for the future. Young people should be discussed at all levels.

It is now essential to develop urban adaptation strategies that lower the risks from climate change and to take advantage of the opportunities climate change affords. In addition, sustainable adaptation is an investment in mitigating potential disasters in the future. Climate change adaptation policies should consider risks at different scales—local, national, regional, and global. Climate change adaptation discourses should be expanded by listening to the priorities of slum poor. At the local level, actions need inclusion of effective urban planning that insists on including the urban poor in decision-making. Efforts should be taken to work on improving effective participation in planning processes for the urban poor in challenging climate, in general, and active engagement in the maintenance of community facilities, in particular.

In response to these challenges, 'action research' is needed to test tools for community adaptation, knowledge generation, and capacity development. People involved in projects should share lessons learnt from project activities with local, national, regional, and international stakeholders. They should elicit support from these stakeholders for climate change adaptation in urban areas. Project-based activities in the urban areas should promote local administration and community, especially the involvement of the poor in planning and budgeting, implementation, and monitoring and evaluation. Such involvement would have a positive effect on the capacity of slum poor to face their challenges. Experience-based inventory of adaptation challenges is required for the slum poor. Subsequently, successful adaptation and lessons learned need to be scaled up.

Finally, in line with increasing international attention to climate change, donors are increasing their focus on climate change in Bangladesh. They now provide direct support for programmes that reduce vulnerability to climate variability and climate change. Bangladesh has developed some capacity for dealing with the effects of climate change at the national level. Policy response options have been activated to deal with reducing vulnerability to environmental variability in general, and more recently, to climate change in particular. Furthermore, the Bangladesh government has undertaken an initiative to establish a separate Department of Climate under the Ministry of Environment and Forests to deal with the climate issues and respond to climate-related challenges in the future.

References

Ahsan S.M.M., A. Jachnow, and M. Walsham. 2010. 'Ensuring Socially Inclusive Urban Development—An International Perspective on Planning in Bangladesh', paper presented in World Town Planning Day 2010, GTZ Bangladesh, Dhaka.

Asian Development Bank (ADB). 2009. *The Economics of Climate Change in Southeast Asia: A Regional Review*. Mandaluyong City, Philippines: Asian Development Bank.

Chowdhury, N.A. 2008. 'Men, Women and the Environment—Gender Issues in Climate Change', *Climate Study Series*, Unnayan Onneshan, Dhaka.

Febi, D. Climate Change Urban Adaptation Strategy, Briefing paper, Institute for Essential Services Reform (IESR).

GTZ Bangladesh. 2010. *Bridging the Urban Divide in Bangladesh*. Expert Report for the Joint Conversation of the Local Government Division, Ministry of Local Government, Rural Development and Cooperatives and the Local Consultative Group Urban Sector, GTZ Bangladesh, Dhaka.

Huq, S. and J. Ayers. 2008. 'Climate Change Impacts and Responses in Bangladesh', Note for Policy Department Economic and Scientific, European Parliament.

IPCC (Intergovernmental Panel on Climate Change). 2007. IPCC Fourth Assessment Report. Working Group III Report 'Mitigation of Climate Change.'

Khan, A.N.M. Maruf. 2010. 'Impact of Climate Change on the Livelihood of the Urban Poor: A Case of Dhaka City', unpublished masters thesis, North South University, Bangladesh.

Khan, H. 2008. 'Challenges for Sustainable Development: Rapid Urbanization, Poverty and Capabilities in Bangladesh', unpublished.

Narayan, A., N. Yoshida, and H. Zaman. 2007. 'Trends and Patterns of Poverty in Bangladesh in Recent Years' (draft), background paper for Bangladesh Poverty Assessment, South Asia Region, World Bank.

Neelormi, S. 2010. 'Addressing Gender Concerns in Adaptation Discourse: Leadership Awaits Bangladesh', keynote paper presented in a National Dialogue, organized by Gender CC and Center for Global Change, Dhaka.

Reid, H., et al. 2009. 'Community-based Adaptation to Climate Change: An Overview', In *Participatory Learning and Action 60*, International Institute for Environment and Development, UK.

UN-Habitat. 2008. 'State of the World's Cities 2008/2009—Harmonious Cities'.

16

ANUSHREE SINHA

The Influence of the Environment on Poor and Migrant Women in India's Slums

The migration information culled out from Census 2001 shows that over 30% of the population or 307 million were migrants. Moreover, the incidence of migration has increased compared to the consistent decline during 1961–91. The usual migration is to go to economically developed regions from more backward regions or states. Moreover, the latest available data on migration as drawn from the 64th Round of the NSS (2007–08)[1] covered 125,578 households with 79,091 in rural areas and 46,487 in urban areas. The report based on these data titled *Employment & Unemployment and Migration Particulars* states that nearly 29% of the sample was migrants. Both rural and urban areas were important as migrant destinations—35% of the population in urban areas was migrants and 26% of the rural population was migrants, so comparatively urban areas have more migrants. Economic motives remain the main reason for migration among male interstate migrants. But a majority of female migrants had not

[1] Raw data of the Census 2001 and the 64th Round NSSO processed at NCAER.

migrated for work and had cited marriage as the main reason for the change in residence.

The population of cities in India is growing faster than the population of the countryside. This is mainly because of migration from the country. The urban slums are growing in India. Much of the growth there also comes from people moving from the country to the cities. Since most of those who migrate are poor, they end up in the slums. People move to the cities for jobs because of marriage, and to escape disasters. Of the people moving to the cities, there are more women than men and we find that most urban women workers are migrants. Women suffer more from slum conditions because they spend more time there. The chapter is based on various data comparisons between 1995 and 1996 and 2008–09 to see if women in urban slums have improved their living conditions over the years.

Slum Poverty in India

Urbanization in India is increasing, albeit at a much lower rate than in many other Asian countries. The percentage of population living in Indian cities increased substantially but most of this increase is among people living in poverty and in slums. The per capita monthly poverty line for India in 2004–05 is Rs 536.8 for the urban areas and Rs 356.30 for rural areas; 25.9% of the city's population are under this poverty line (ADB 2011). The India poverty line is similar to the international severe poverty line of 1.25 per day per capital income/expenditure. Based on this poverty line, in 2010 an estimated 28.9% of the 368.6 million urban people in India lived under the 1.25 international poverty line, up from 36.2% in 2005. Using the $2 international poverty line, 57.6% of India's urban population was severe or moderately poor, down from 65.8% in 2005.[2]

Most of these poor people, and also lower middle-class people, are living in congested city areas with non-durable structures, on insecure tenure blocks, and in houses with inadequate water and sanitation provision and having lack of proper waste collection. Such areas are called slums. Currently in India there are 49,000 slum areas in the urban regions. These slum areas today inhabit about 96 million people, up

---

[2] World Bank PovCalNet, updated in March 2012.

from 62 million in 2001 (TPCO estimates). The people in slum areas comprise about 36% of Indian city population, compared with more than the 32% worldwide.[3]

India's slums are divided into notified (legal) and non-notified (illegal) sorts. Non-notified slums have little access to government-provided basic services. As a result, situation in those areas is worse for the poor than in notified slums. The majority of India's slums are non-notified. Also, conditions of urban slums have deteriorated in the last decade. With rising incidence on hygiene-related diseases among the poor, the percentage of people not receiving medical treatment (when they are sick, having high fever, or other ailments such as diarrhea, etc.) has also increased in the urban areas. Medical facilities in neighbourhoods have deteriorated. Waiting times have grown longer.

The slum poor in India are particularly exposed to environmentally risky conditions. According to NSSO Report (2007–08), 24% of the slums are located along *nallahs*[4] (arm of sea, stream, or watercourse, a steep narrow valley) and drains, and around 12% along railway tracks. Many poor people in the slum areas migrate further within the city due to environmental and climate change–related disasters. A study of India's Ghaghara floodplain found a mixture of movements: permanent moves, when areas are so severely hit by floods so as to cause loss of crops and houses, and periodic movements, when people migrate mostly to higher ground for shelter and temporary jobs.

Female and Male Migration to Urban Slums

With faster decline in the urban birth rate (1.4% for urban areas versus 1.7% in rural areas), migration is a major reason for the population growth in the cities and also the increasing slum poverty. The proportion of migrants in the population in the urban areas was with 35% far

[3] Data are from the 64th Round NSSO survey that covered a sample of 125,578 households (79,091 in rural areas and 46,487 in urban areas). Hence data reflect information from more than 572,254 persons (374,294 in rural areas and 197,960 in urban areas).

[4] 'A Nullah or Nulla (Hindi, also Nallah in Punjabi) is an arm of the sea, stream, or watercourse, a steep narrow valley' (http://en.wikipedia.org/wiki/Nullah).

higher than the migration rate in the rural areas (26%). These migrants are mostly coming from rural areas, and there is little gender difference on the source of migration. Nearly 60% of urban male migrants and 59% of urban female migrants had migrated from rural areas. Many of those migrants end up in slums. In 2007/2008, nearly 29% of the persons in slum areas were estimated to be migrants.

Migration rates of women and men are different depending on the geographical region the migration happens in. However, in most states the patters of substantially higher female migration applies (Table 16.1).

The NSSO statistics show that the share of women migrants is higher than that of men. This is true for both urban and rural migration incidents. The migration rate in urban areas was 25.9% for men and 45.6% for women. Within rural migration, we find that female migration is much higher compared to male migration[5] (see Table 16.2).

Due to the higher migration rate, the growth of female population in the cities is also higher as that of men. Of all the women living in Indian cities, 45.6% are migrants. The number for men was only 25.9% (Table 16.1). In result it is estimated very soon the share of women in total urban population is overtaking that of men. This is an interesting observation particularly if compared to cities in the People's Republic of China and many other countries in Asia, where men form the majority of migrants.

Nearly 80% of the male out-migrants from the rural areas and 71% of the male out-migrants from the urban areas have cited employment as the reason for them to migrate. Reasons for migration of women are mostly marriage, followed by search for employment and by escaping natural disaster (Figure 16.1). The NSSO report states that the most prominent reason for female migration in both the rural and urban areas was marriage as 91% of rural female migrants and 61% of the urban female migrants had migrated as a result of marriage. Marriage accounted for nearly 84% of female outmigration nationally. Economic activities were cited for migration by 80% of male migrants but only 20% by female migrants.

[5] In rural areas, the percentage of female with migrant background is substantially higher (48%) than for male (5%). This sounds surprising given the traditional orientation of India.

TABLE 16.1 Migration Share of Men and Women of India (by Indian states, 2007–08)

Sl. No.	State	Total (Unit: 100,000)	Share Male (%)	Share Female (%)
1	Himachal Pradesh	16.08	37.45	62.55
2	Punjab	23.55	27.98	72.02
3	Chandigarh	0.36	38.79	61.21
4	Uttaranchal	13.85	44.42	55.58
5	Haryana	36.87	14.65	85.35
6	Delhi	3.03	10.53	89.47
7	Rajasthan	93.23	30.21	69.79
8	Uttar Pradesh	236.37	38.23	61.77
9	Bihar	63.48	63.95	36.05
10	Sikkim	0.44	46.37	53.63
11	Nagaland	0.65	45.98	54.02
12	Manipur	0.69	70.36	29.64
13	Mizoram	0.39	55.78	44.22
14	Tripura	1.19	53.91	46.09
15	Meghalaya	0.6	64.55	35.45
16	Assam	11.35	49.65	50.35
17	West Bengal	91.01	27.6	72.4
18	Jharkhand	10.71	66.61	33.39
19	Odisha	38.55	50.05	49.95
20	Chhattisgarh	15.76	32.47	67.53
21	Madhya Pradesh	49.86	23.2	76.8
22	Gujarat	53.12	24.05	75.95
23	Daman & Diu	0.07	45.76	54.24
24	DNH*	0.06	32.3	67.7
25	Maharashtra	124.72	28.23	71.77
26	Andhra Pradesh	90.21	36.49	63.51
27	Karnataka	46.63	35.45	64.55
28	Goa	0.58	54.57	45.43
29	Lakshadweep	0.08	65.9	34.1
30	Kerala	77.7	41.84	58.16
31	Tamil Nadu	55	49.84	50.16
32	Pondicherry	0.43	76.88	23.12
33	ANI**	0.42	45.26	54.74
34	Others	6.97	35.27	64.73
	Total	1,164.01	36.13	63.87

Source: NSSO 64th Round data analysis.
Note: *Dadra and Nagar Haveli; **Andaman and Nicober Islands.

TABLE **16.2**   Migration Rate (per 1,000 Persons) 2007–08 (All India)

Category of Persons	Rural	Urban	Rural + Urban
Male	54	259	109
Female	477	456	472
All	261	354	285

Source: Report NSSO 64th Round.

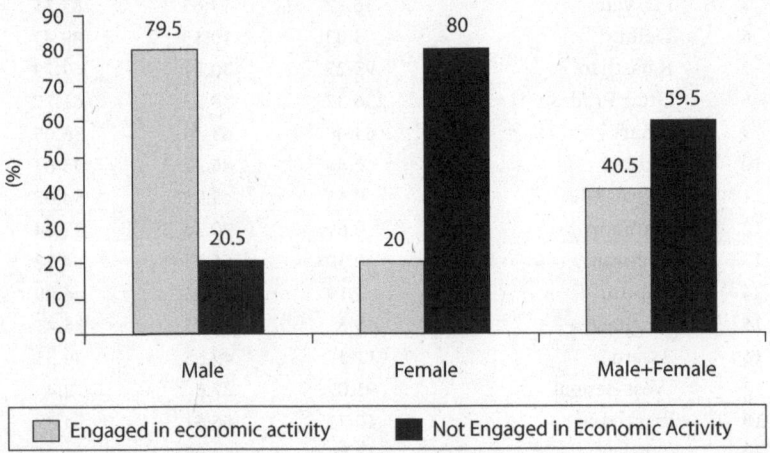

FIGURE **16.1**   Reason for Migration by Gender Differences (2007–08)
Source: Report of the NSSS 64th Round.

But, when we analyse the NSSO data for migrants on their present engagement in economic activity—the results are strikingly different for men and women. Moreover, the findings are counterintuitive and hence very revealing. These analyses show that women migrants are highly involved in economic activities, contrary to general perception, as shown in Table 16.3. Most states have higher shares of women migrants involved in economic activities compared to their male counterparts. This finding is all the more striking as women do not migrate as much for carrying out economic activities, but due to marriage. However, once they have migrated they seem to take the responsibility of earning by taking up economic activities at large.

TABLE 16.3   State and Gender-wise Share of Migrants Actually Engaged in
Economic Activities (2007–08)

Sl. No.	State	Migrants Engaged in Economic Activities	Female Migrants Engaged in Economic Activities	Male Migrants Engaged in Economic Activities
		(Unit = '000)	(%)	(%)
1	Himachal Pradesh	1,295.78	74.64	25.36
2	Punjab	1,692.95	31.77	68.23
3	Chandigarh	191.33	16.06	83.94
4	Uttaranchal	1,321.64	52.55	47.45
5	Haryana	1,996.66	57.62	42.38
6	Delhi	2,460.22	5.46	94.54
7	Rajasthan	6,798.85	74.22	25.78
8	Uttar Pradesh (Eastern)	4,594.21	84.07	15.93
9	Bihar	2,973.92	78.07	21.93
10	Sikkim	95.17	50.38	49.62
11	Nagaland	54.47	33.11	66.89
12	Manipur	5.19	19.81	80.19
13	Mizoram	74.81	39.86	60.14
14	Tripura	121.74	30.09	69.91
15	Meghalaya	50.93	30.69	69.31
16	Assam	823.75	50.70	49.30
17	West Bengal	4,570.50	45.42	54.58
18	Jharkhand	1,599.38	80.39	19.61
19	Odisha	3,144.73	71.40	28.60
20	Chhattisgarh	4,427.07	79.37	20.63
21	Madhya Pradesh	6,959.00	84.02	15.98
22	Gujarat	5,816.43	56.82	43.18
23	Daman & Diu	32.38	9.58	90.42
24	DNH	29.84	16.43	83.57
25	Maharashtra (Mumbai)	4,381.33	22.94	77.06
26	Andhra Pradesh (Hyderabad)	2,795.70	63.11	36.89
27	Karnataka	6,958.30	67.80	32.20
28	Goa	174.50	27.95	72.05
29	Lakshadweep	7.88	13.81	86.19

(Cont'd)

TABLE 16.3   (Cont'd)

SL. No.	State	Migrants Engaged in Economic Activities	Female Migrants Engaged in Economic Activities	Male Migrants Engaged in Economic Activities
		(Unit = '000)	(%)	(%)
30	Kerala	3,289.36	42.14	57.86
31	Tamil Nadu	6,871.95	63.30	36.70
32	Pondicherry	81.31	39.63	60.37
33	ANI	80.89	14.46	85.54
34	Maharashtra (Other)	12,570.16	69.89	30.11
35	Andhra Pradesh (Other)	9,548.01	70.99	29.01
36	Uttar Pradesh (Other)	4,609.07	51.31	48.69
37	Others	207.09	44.69	55.31
	Total	102,706.50	63.22	36.78

Source: Report of the NSSO 64th Round.

As we continue examining the causes of migration, we do not find natural disaster cited as a major reason while we analyse the latest migration round of the NSSO (64th Round Survey). But it is important to note that a few respondents have actually given this as a reason for migrating out. Certain Indian states have faced migration of the poor due to distress, such as that caused by natural disasters (see Figure 16.2). However, again, this is mostly a reason cited by men and not by women. But some of these migrations due to natural disaster are more permanent, as when areas are so severely hit by floods as to cause loss of crops and houses, it is not easy to come back and resettle in these areas in the short term. But other migration is periodic or circular, as when people in cyclical disaster-prone areas (e.g., from flood areas) migrate mostly to higher ground for shelter and temporary jobs. Also, due to the low skill level of most of the poor migrants, they prefer temporary jobs so that they can return home during harvest season (Kayastha and Yadava 1985). It is well accepted that weather patterns and climate variability affect human survival mostly in agrarian context and in obtaining reasonable livelihoods. And the desire to survive and have improved livelihood motivates migration to areas perceived as more developed and less prone to natural disasters. However, such

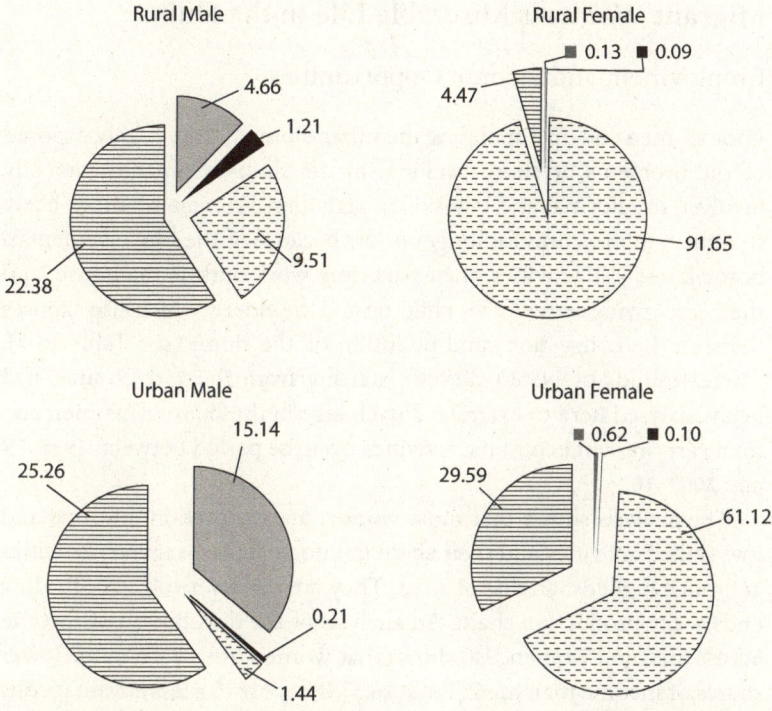

FIGURE 16.2   Reason for Leaving the Last Usual Place of Residence (2007–08)
Source: Report of the NSSO 64th Round.

migrants who migrate from disaster-prone areas are generally poor and low-skilled.

As we examine the gender differential in migration, we find that women migrate mostly due to social reasons. But the ones who migrate and those who end up in urban slums get highly involved in performing not only family duties but also economic activities to support family income. Nationally, the share of female migrants involved in economic activities is 63.2% compared to 36.8% for men. Many states have even higher shares of women migrants involved in economic activities compared to their male counterparts. On the other side, in metropolitan areas (such as Delhi, Mumbai, and Chandigarh) women have a lower share in economic activity. This is has major implications on the job market and on government support for employment policies which still seems to be very much male-dominated.

Migrant Women's Miserable Life in the Slums

Employment and Income Opportunities

Poor women end up populating the urban slums and are highly exposed to the problems of slum dwelling. In the slums, women are mostly involved in informal and low-skilled activities. Women are more likely to remain in the slums for longer hours because of their involvement in home-based job activities, their part-time work outside the house, and their care-giving activities for children and the elderly which also exposes them to the congestions and pollution of the slums (see Table 16.4). Three Rounds of NSSO surveys, starting from the 55th Round, had been analysed here to examine any change in the share of women and men carrying out economic activities over the period between 1998–99 and 2009–10.

The analysis shows that most women are involved in informal and low-skilled activities and their share in informal (non-regular) activities are much higher than that of men. They are mostly involved in the low end of any production chain. An analysis of the distribution of income across men and women also shows that women often earn much lower shares of income than men (Table 16.5). They are in a less advantageous situation and have lower access to the means that are instrumental to improving livelihood options—such as education and technical skills. Hence women tend to be predominantly in the informal economy (Sinha et al. 2003). They are largely employed at the bottom of the livelihood chain and work in very difficult conditions (Khosla 2008).

Access to Amenities and Its Gender Dimensions

As we examine the condition of slum amenities we find that there has been overall improvement in drainage facility in general for both rural and urban areas. It is found that in the cities open and unhygienic (kutcha) drainage has increased substantially though there also has been some expansion in underground (pucca) drainage between 1993 and 2009. However, even this could not cope with population increase in the cities (Figure 16.3). Most of urban slums face hygiene problems due to open drainage, either kutcha, pucca, or due to no drainage even now.

TABLE 16.4   Activities Carried Out by Males and Females across Three NSSO Rounds

Status (Principal + Subsidiary)	66th Round (2009–10)			61st round (2004–05)			55th round (1998–99)		
	Male	Female	Total	Male	Female	Total	Male	Female	Total
OAW	20.09	3.85	12.24	21.07	4.78	13.13	19.31	4.25	11.97
Employer	0.78	0.13	0.46	0.93	0.16	0.56	0.64	0.12	0.39
Worked as helper in HH	6.38	8.14	7.23	7.89	12.65	10.21	7.14	10.29	8.68
Worked as regular employee	9.67	2.29	6.1	9.41	2.39	5.99	9.05	1.86	5.54
Worked as casual labour in public works	0.36	0.47	0.42	0.08	0.04	0.06	0.13	0.05	0.09
Worked as casual labour in other types of work	17.17	7.81	12.64	15.31	8.65	12.06	16.52	9.62	13.16
Didn't work but seeking work	1.22	0.61	0.93	1.22	0.75	0.99	1.35	0.44	0.91
Attended educational institute	28.95	24.05	26.58	26.39	22.02	24.26	25.39	19.83	22.68
Attended domestic duties	0.29	25.53	12.5	0.2	19.72	9.71	0.25	22.61	11.15
Attended domestic duties and engaged in collection of fuels	0.14	12.32	6.03	0.15	11.46	5.66	0.12	10.08	4.98
Retires, pensioner, etc.	1.6	0.93	1.28	1.22	0.68	0.96	0.87	0.41	0.65
Not able to work due to disability	1.3	1.07	1.19	1	0.71	0.86	0.77	0.61	0.69
Others (including begging, prostitution)	3.21	3.79	3.49	4.63	5.6	5.1	7.43	8.78	8.09
Children below 5 years	8.82	9.01	8.91	10.5	10.39	10.45	11.03	11.03	11.03
Total	100	100	100	100	100	100	100	100	100

Source: NSSO 55th, 61st, and 66th rounds.

TABLE 16.5   Share of Gender-wise Wage Earnings by Aggregated Sectors (Year: 2004–05) (Rs Lakh)

Sector	2004–05			2009–10		
	Male	Female	Total	Male	Female	Total
	Percentage share (%)					
Agriculture	75.58	24.42	21.08	76.49	23.51	17.76
Mining & Quarrying	98.98	1.02	1.91	94.58	5.42	2.54
Agroprocessing	84.20	15.80	1.52	84.57	15.43	1.46
Manufacturing	88.39	11.61	10.06	88.65	11.35	11.37
Readymade Garments	71.95	28.05	0.55	74.11	25.89	0.51
Capital Goods	92.24	7.76	1.28	96.84	3.16	2.59
Construction	94.47	5.53	6.50	92.13	7.87	8.49
Other Services	92.49	7.51	50.99	85.16	14.84	49.22
Public Administration	90.74	9.26	6.13	88.85	11.15	6.05
Total	88.42	11.58	100.00	85.31	14.69	100.00

Source: NSSO 61st and 66th Round Employment Unemployment Data and NAS.

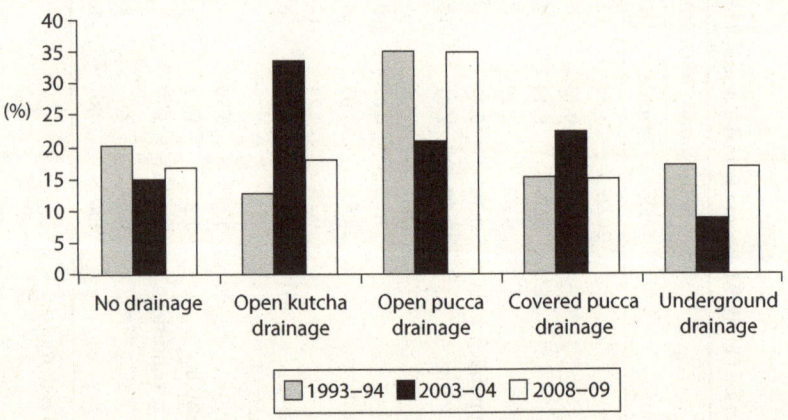

FIGURE 16.3   Changes in Drainage Structure in Urban India
Sources: NSSO 50th, 60th and 65th round.

Again, though sanitary conditions in the slums in terms of toilet facility during 2008–09 showed an improvement since 2002, a lot still needs to be done. Figure 16.3 shows that out of total drainage facilities, the share of open kutcha (un-cemented) drainage has increased substantially and share of underground drainage actually decreased in 2003–04, but just recovered back to the older condition similar to 1993–94 in 2008–09.

Toilets with septic tanks (or similar facility) were available in 68% notified and 47% non-notified slums (up from 66% and 35%, respectively in 2002). The latest information from the NSSO (2008–09) reveals that around 10% of the notified and 20% of non-notified slums still do not have any toilet facility at all. Further, the NSSO report states that around 10% notified and 23% non-notified slums did not have any drainage facility as against 15% for notified and 44% for non-notified slums in 2002 (NSSO, 2008–09), revealing slow improvement (Figure 16.4).

When women and men as well as children get exposed to such poor (open) sanitation facilities, they naturally are at high risk of facing health hazards. Another interesting condition that we examine is the access to health facilities. We find that despite rising incidence of hygiene-related diseases amongst the poor, the percentage of people taking treatment has not increased in urban areas, pointing to the worsening of poor people's access to health facilities in the slums, and especially the informal settlements.

Women bear the brunt of the sub-human living conditions and the weak state of municipal services in India's slums (Moser and Peake 1987;

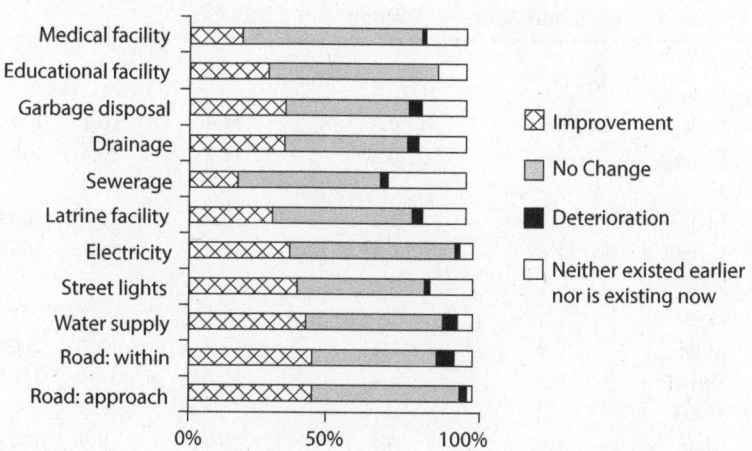

FIGURE 16.4   Conditions of Slums by Various Indicators (2008–09)
Source: Report of the NSSO 65th Round.

Amis 2001). They must fetch water from great distances, maintain cleanliness, take care of their families' nutrition, and run the household on a meagre budget. Girls and women are more susceptible to the adverse health outcomes associated with inadequate housing conditions and the unhealthy slum environment mainly because they stay longer time in the congested slum areas, and they can cope less adequately as men as they need more privacy for their sanitation and toilet.

Impact on Women's Health

The slum environment causes health problems and those who live in the slums as dwellers are most prone to suffer from them. The main reason for the lack of health treatment is the cost. Data suggest that this is more relevant for women than for men. The reason for not seeking treatment due to financial reasons is as high as 26% for women compared to 20% for men (Table 16.6). Another reason is the declining quality and appearance

TABLE 16.6   Percentage Distribution of Persons Not Taking Treatment by Reasons

	No Medical Facility Available in Neighbourhoods	No Treatment Sought Due to Long Waiting	No Treatment Sought Due to Financial Reasons	Others	Total
Rural					
1995–96					
Male	8.5	0.8	25.6	10.1	100.0
Female	9.6	0.2	23.7	10.4	100.0
2003–04					
Male	14.0	1.2	30.5	16.1	100.0
Female	11.6	0.8	31.7	16.7	100.0
Urban					
1995–96					
Male	0.9	1.1	17.7	10.7	100.0
Female	0.7	1.0	22.0	14.3	100.0
2003–04					
Male	1.0	0.7	20.3	13.9	100.0
Female	1.6	2.8	25.7	14.6	100.0

Source: Report of the NSSO 52nd and 60th Round.

of medical facilities in the slum neighbourhoods, resulting in longer waiting time which is again more often faced by women than by men.

The combination of no medical treatment and higher health risks of women in poorer environments make the situation for women precarious. Unit-level NSSO data analyses show that since 1993–94, the share of women not taking any medical treatment has risen sharply from 8.8% to 11.3% compared to that of men which was 8.1% compared to 10.6% in one decade. The situation is also worsened more for urban women than for urban men (Table 16.7).

TABLE 16.7 Percentage Distribution of Persons Not Taking Any Treatment

Population	52nd Round (1995–96)		60th Round (2003–04)	
	Rural	Urban	Rural	Urban
Male	15.81	8.14	17.41	10.57
Female	18.28	8.81	17.71	11.31

Sources: NSSO 52nd and 60th round.

Since women take care of all family members, improving their health and work conditions would have positive externalities, within and outside households. For example, it is reasonable to think that clean water would benefit women as they work with water more. This would have multiplier benefits to the society as a whole, as women are the immediate role models for children and the main caregivers for the elderly and the sick people.

Policy Considerations

The chapter has shown that there is increasing feminization of migration and urbanization in India's slums. Most women initially migrate due to marriage, but once they reach the destination they start working mostly in low-end and low-paid informal production and services activities.

Women are also more exposed to the unhealthy slum conditions for longer period of time compared to men due to their roles in the households and the local economy. They also have less access to health services, implying that governments should place more health services in slum areas and focus them more on possible diseases for women, which are related to the environmental conditions in the slums. Poor drainage facilities provide the biggest concern for the slum women. Overall, the drainage system in the slums has not improved much for the poor, as the statistics show increased per capita figures without disaggregating by slum and richer habitat areas.

Women take care of all family members, so improving the welfare of women in terms of health and work conditions would have positive externalities both within and outside households. It has been seen that intervention to provide clean water has higher positive impact on women. This is so as they collect water and also work with water more. So, it is important to identify direct interventions that would positive impact women's condition of living as women also support the family by taking care of the sick and the children. A healthy woman is an asset that builds an entire society and hence the economy that rests on the function of the society. We need to obtain more data to understand the phenomenon of migration by gender and also to understand the conditions of slum dwellings. Challenges continue to exist with regard to using more location-disaggregated data on municipal services comparing availability of sanitation facilities in slum areas of Indian cities so as to compare these conditions with those in better living areas. Such data need to be always disaggregated by gender and should also comprise information on the environment-migration-health linkages in their differential impact for women and men. More comprehensive data on migration, slum conditions, link of slum population to migration, etc., would help inform policymakers to plan for improved community adaptation strategies to reduce distress and poverty. Also, the need for more uniform development across regions needs to be taken up as a major policy to reduce distress migration as well as to reduce stress on slums that breed so many negative externalities (unhygienic conditions of living, health problems, and stress), which impact women more adversely.

References

ADB. 2011. *Understanding Poverty in India*. November, ADB Publishing.

Amis, P. 2001. 'Rethinking UK Aid in Urban India: Reflections on An Impact Study of Slum Improvement Projects', *Journal of Environment and Urbanization* 13(1, April).

Dutta, Pranati. 2006. 'Urbanisation in India', in proceeding European Population Conference, United Kingdom.

Harry X. Wu, and Li Zhou. 1996. 'Rural-to-Urban Migration in China', *Asian-Pacific Economic Literature* 10(2): 54–67.

Khosla, Renu. 2008. *Addressing Gender Concerns in India's Urban Renewal Mission.* UNDP.

Kundu, A. 1994. 'Pattern of Urbanisation with Special Reference to Small and Medium Towns in India'. In *Sectoral Issues in the Indian Economy*, edited by G. K. Chadha. New Delhi: Har-Anand Publication.

Kayastha, S.L., and R.P. Yadava. 1985. 'Flood Induced Population Migration in India: A Case Study of Ghaghara Zone', pp. 79–88. In *Population, Redistribution and Development in South Asia*, edited by K.M. Elahi, L.A. Kosinski. Dordrecht: D. Reider Publishing.

Moser, C.O.N. and L. Peake. 1987. *Women, Human Settlements and Housing: A Conceptual Framework for Analysis and Policy-making.* London: Tavistock Publication.

———. 2009. 'Engendering Macroeconomic Modeling for Policy Analysis', in volume titled *Engendering Macroeconomics and Macroeconomic Policies*, UNDP and Zubaan (October)

———. 2010. Gender Integration in Macro Analysis for Better Policy, in *Gender Mainstreaming in the Asia Pacific Human Development*, Report by the RCC, UNDP Publication (March).

Sinha, Anushree. 2003. 'Informal Economy: Gender, Poverty and Households'. In *Informal Economy Centrestage*, edited by R. Jhabvala, R. M. Sudarshan, and J. Unni. Delhi: SAGE Publications.

The National Sample Survey 52nd Round. 1995–96. *Consumer Expenditure Health and Aged India*, July.

The National Sample Survey 60th Round. 2004. *Consumer Expenditure, Employment-Unemployment, Morbidity, Health Care & Condition of the Aged*, January–June 2004.

The National Sample Survey 64th Round. 2010. *Migration in India 2007-2008*, Ministry of Statistics and Programme Implementation, Government of India.

The National Sample Survey 65th Round. 2010. *Some Characteristics of Urban Slums 2008-09*, Ministry of Statistics and Programme Implementation, Government of India.

17

ANVITA ARORA
MATS JARNHAMMAR
FAIZAN JAWED SIDDIQI

The Green and Pro-poor Role of Informal Public Transportation in India

Urban transport has risen to the top of the agenda for many Asian cities in the last decades, as traffic jams and chronic congestions are becoming a part of everyday life. The cities' response to congestion has typically been construction of more roads, flyovers, urban highways, etc., which have led to an even greater increase in private vehicle owner-ship, creating a vicious cycle of cars and congestion. A well-functioning public transport system is essential to turning this trend and ensuring an environmentally sustainable and pro-poor urban transport system.

Cities are struggling to keep up with the ever-increasing need for public transport, and while some investments are made in public trans-port systems such as bus rapid transit and metro rail, these investments often do not sufficiently benefit the poor who remain 'transport mar-ginalized'. In this vacuum, Informal Public Transportation (IPT) has risen to fill the role as the 'people movers' for the poor in many Indian cities.

Despite this, the vital role that IPT plays in urban mobility is seldom acknowledged. Urban transport planning and policy response is often at best a quiet acceptance that these modes are here for the time being, but more commonly, policies focus on limiting and discouraging IPT. Very little is done to incorporate IPT in an inclusive public transport system.

In this chapter, we argue that IPT deserves to be acknowledged as an important aspect of sustainable urban mobility, especially for the poor. We discuss the merits and demerits of IPT from a pro-poor and environmental perspective and give policy recommendations for better integration of IPT in a comprehensive, pro-poor, and environment-friendly public transport system. The chapter is based on the Cities Development Initiative for Asia (CDIA) study, IPT in India, carried out by the authors in five Indian cities in 2010 and earlier research on the subject.

Urbanization and the Need for Mobility

Over the last two decades, cities have become the focus of development. As a result of destitution in the villages and economic opportunity in urban areas, India has seen a rise in migration from hinterland to the city. The economic growth of the cities has until now not had a signifi-cant effect on poverty reduction. As of today, poverty is rife in urban areas—75% dwellers in urban areas live on less than $2 a day (McKinsey 2010). The overall rich–poor divide in the country has increased in the last decades.

Transport facilitates development by providing access to resources and services. It helps students access education, workers access jobs, home-makers access shops, the ill access health care, and so on. Urban transport exists in many forms around the world—people can walk, use a bicycle or car, or ride communally in a large vehicle, such as a bus or van.

The availability of public modes of transport is one of the hallmarks of urbanity. In an urban society marred by high levels of poverty, it is all the more necessary that transport—the critical facilitator—be avail-able to all equitably, at an affordable price and an adequate service level. Care must be taken to make sure that transport needs of one group do not overshadow the needs of others. For instance, providing more road space for private cars, in a scenario where only a minority drives cars, while the rest are so poor that they find using public transport expen-sive, is appropriate from neither an environmental perspective nor an equity perspective.

As a result of increased incomes for some people in urban areas, there has been an increase in the number of private vehicles—both cars and motorized two-wheelers. This increase has led to congestion in many cities, which respond by increasing the availability of road space: widening road and building highways. However, this does not solve problem, as traffic congestion continues to increase.

Current Constraints in Urban Transport Planning and Investments

Cities, especially small- and medium-sized cities (SMCs), which are growing rapidly, are struggling to keep up with the increasing need for transport and mobility. With a low capacity for investment in public transport, there is a chronic backlog of investment in this sector.

Patterns of car-centric development adopted by most cities around the world in recent decades exclude the poor. And they are highly unsustainable from an environmental point of view. And yet, the response to congestion has been to construct more roads, flyovers, urban highways, etc. This has led to an increase in private vehicle ownership, creating a vicious cycle of cars and congestion. For the urban poor, car ownership, or even owning a motorized two-wheeler is beyond reach for most.

Sustainable, non-motorized modes of transport, such as walking and cycling, are indirectly discouraged in current transport planning. Little investment goes into building bicycle lanes, improving pedestrian accessibility, etc. In many Asian cities, walking and cycling means being subject to the mercy of motorized transport drivers.

A well-functioning public transport system is essential to turning the trend of increased private vehicle ownership. Improving public transport and discouraging the use of private vehicles should be a concern for most city governments. Present levels of investment in public transport modes are not sufficient and are often associated with high costs and subsidies. Financially, cities struggle with how to finance public transport investments within limited budgets and capacity. Importantly, even when formal public transport investments are being made, they tend to focus on highly resource-intensive projects such as BRT and MRT, which often do not sufficiently reach the poor. Reasons for this include poor coverage, flexibility, affordability, access, and capacity of public sector. Therefore, ironically, high subsidies often associated with major formal public transport investments tend to benefit middle-income groups rather than the poor.

Investments in public transport are especially problematic in SMCs, where people travel from 'everywhere to everywhere' and volumes tend to be too small for large-scale public transport solutions.

In the vacuum of the missing urban mobility options for the poor, IPT has risen to fill the role of people movers for the poor in Indian cities. IPT plays many roles: commuter modes for marginalized areas, feeder-modes for formal public transport, as door-to-door connectivity, etc.

IPT has been found to play a large role in the absence of formal public transport systems, especially in SMCs, where public transport has not yet developed or is insufficient. IPT has also been found to thrive despite significant formal public transport availability. In such cases, IPT often plays the role of a feeder and provides affordable mobility in areas that the public transport system does not reach.

IPT operates despite the state. It provides mobility for millions where formal transport systems are lacking, on a for-profit basis and without almost any support from the state. IPT, however, has received very little attention in the urban transport debate, where the focus has mostly been on finding ways to discourage it. However, this sector plays a critical role for the urban poor from two aspects—as a means of mobility and as a source of employment.

The Role of Informal Public Transport in Urban Mobility

Defining Informal Public Transport

Some authors use paratransit, intermediate paratransit, and informal public transport interchangeably (Cervero 2000; Golub 2003), while others use paratransit and intermediate paratransit to describe transit services that would still be described as IPT. Paratransit, also known as intermediate public transport, is defined as a mode that is intermediate between privately owned automobiles and conventional transit with fixed routes and schedules (Ahmed and Datta 2006). In this chapter, IPT is means of transport that is available to the public, but not sanctioned by the authorities (Cervero 2000; 2007). IPT has varying levels of informality. A transport vehicle that is available for communal use would count as IPT if it operates without a license and charges commuters a fare decided not by contract of carriage but whimsically by the vehicle driver or owner. Another transport mode that could count as IPT because of the informal manufacture of the vehicles— for instance, *jugaads*, which are vehicular contraptions manufactured informally by local mechanics. Cycle rickshaws could qualify as IPT when they operate without a permit; for instance, in cities where they are banned. A three-wheeled motorized autorickshaw could qualify as IPT when the driver charges a fixed fare on a per-head basis, charges more than fare stipulated by contract, or carries more passengers than legally allowed.

To discuss IPT systematically, it is necessary to break down the concept of informality in public transport. Table 17.1 helps illustrate different types of informality, such as nature of transport system and operations, informality of vehicle, and human aspects.

Because of its informal nature, IPT is often seen as something that should be discouraged. It is, therefore, important to understand how IPT operates, why people use it, wherein its informality lies, and in which ways it could be integrated into the public transport system as a whole.

What Role Does IPT Play?

IPT, along with cycling and walking, is the lifeline in most Indian cities. SMCs in India usually have short trip lengths and trips originating and ending all over the city. Moreover, 85% of urban poor live in SMCs (Mahadevia 2010), and their transport needs need to be met affordably. The economy and flexibility demanded by commuters in SMCs makes a formal public transport system economically and practically unfeasible without heavy subsidies.

In such cities, IPT systems form the self-styled, self-managed public transport system. Also, Indian towns often have narrow streets and alleys where public transport may be unable to enter, especially in slum areas. This is another winning point for IPT, not only in SMCs, but also more populous cities (Cervero 2000).

Due to fuzzy nature of IPT, the share of intermediate paratransit found in the modal split of cities may be an inaccurate reflection of the true share of IPT in Indian cities. In academic literature, IPT practices and

TABLE 17.1 Types of Informality

IPT Type		M3W	M4W - Matador	Cycle Rickshaw type 1	Cycle Rickshaw type 1	M4W - Minibus	Others
	Type of informality						
VEHICLE	Manufacture						
	Sale						
SYSTEM & OPERATIONS	Overcrowding						
	Fare						
	Routes						
	Driving permit						
	Stand/Terminal						
	Parking						
HUMAN	Ownership						
	Employment						
	Other criteria						
	Total						

their numbers are not well documented, and there is a great discrepancy between official statistics and what is visible on most Indian streets. A study in Amritsar in Punjab found that 94% of all passenger trips were catered to by paratransit modes (Luthra 2006).

IPT not only satisfies the transport needs of the urban poor, but it also forms an important mode of transport for people living on urban fringes. It also bridges the 'last mile' problem for relatively well-off. Shared autorickshaws operate aplenty around suburban train stations in Mumbai. Even the relatively well-off use them because they are quicker than formal public transport.

IPT in Present Transport Planning

Authorities in cities tend to overlook the 'illegal' nature of IPT because it fulfils the gap that public transport leaves. However, authorities have a disparaging attitude towards it. The scoffing at entire gamut of informal activities as symbols of backwardness is common in the developing world, and informal transport is no exception. There seems to be a cyclic logic to this. IPT is most prominent in developing parts of the world. It is this inverse relation between wealth and informal transport that prompts public authorities to ban them in hopes of conveying a modern, first-world image (Cervero 2007).

In general, it can be said that transport policy and planning take an active approach to some parts of the transport sector, such as private motorized transport, through the construction of roads, bridges, flyovers, tunnels, parking, etc. It also, to varying degrees, takes an active approach to certain public transport modes, such as light rail (through substantial investments) and bus and BRT systems, separate lanes, bus stops, terminals, parking, etc.

When it comes to other types of public transport, such as autorickshaws, cycle-rickshaws, minivans, informal water transport, the state typically plays a 'reactive' role. This can mean taking measures that discourage IPT.

Is IPT Green and Pro-Poor?

Having discussed the challenges of urban mobility, the constraints of current transport planning and role of informal public transport, the question must be asked what implications this should have for urban transport policy. Is IPT green and pro-poor, and can or should it be a part of a sustainable urban transport system? The question of whether IPT is pro-poor or not must be discussed from two perspectives: IPT as providing mobility for the urban poor, and IPT as a source of employment for the poor. The discussion on the environmental aspects focuses on environmental impacts of IPT and the potential for improvement.

Mobility for the Urban Poor

The poor confront everyday mobility problems. If the public transport services in the area are physically and financially beyond the reach of the poor, their poverty is reinforced. In many cases, IPT exists because there is no formal public transport system available to the poor. The largest chunk of IPT users consists of lower-income groups who cannot afford private transport. IPT arises because of many reasons, including a lack of formal public transport supply, different needs of people that cannot be fulfilled by formal public transport, everywhere-to-everywhere movement patterns in Indian cities, the high number of short trips, the lack of penetrability by formal public transport in dense city (slum) areas, and so on. Having grown out of a process where supply responds to demand, it is available and affordable (though definitely not always cheap) to the poor.

Policies regarding IPT modes, thus, have an effect on the poor as customers, as operators, and as employees. The issues involved may be complex. There has been a great deal of debate over what policies should be adopted towards various 'non-corporate' transport modes. Focusing on poverty issues, it is however widely agreed that reducing barriers to the informal supply of both passenger and goods transport will be a 'pro-poor' policy (UNDP 1998).

However, IPT also has a number of demerits which must be addressed. One has to do with affordability. While IPT is affordable to the extent that it is being used by low-income groups, it also represents a significant expense for them. A large proportion of monthly income is spent on transport. Therefore, compared to highly subsidized formal public transport, IPT is sometimes a quite expensive mode of transport. Other demerits have to do with health and safety. Exposure to toxic fumes from motorized transport poses a health threat to IPT users, and even more so to drivers). The poor traffic safety of many IPT vehicles in combination with threats from other high speed transport modes is a challenge.

IPT as a Source of Employment

IPT provides employment to many urban poor people. There is a range of IPT-associated services and industries. Though further research is needed on the significance of the IPT industry as a source of employment, studies suggest that 14% of the Bangladeshi population relies directly or indirectly on incomes from the rickshaw industry for their livelihoods (rickshaw-pullers, manufactures, garage owners, painters, repair men, etc). In Dhaka alone, some 20% of the population relies on pulling directly or indirectly. This amounts to 2.5 million people (Wipperman and Sowula 2007). This large workforce and its continued growth are attributable to two major factors: (a) unemployment in the rural agricultural areas and subsequent large urban drift and (b) easy access to jobs in rickshaw industry. As a result, non-motorized public transport is woven deeply into Bangladesh society through employment and cultural and socioeconomic contributions, especially amongst the poorest sections of society. In a city like Dhaka, the 'hard' transport planning issues cannot be fully separated from the 'soft' socioeconomic implications of non-motorized public transport policies (Rahman et al. 2009).

Is IPT Environment Friendly?

Whether IPT is environment 'friendly' or not is a complex question. First, there is a need to distinguish between different types of IPT, primarily between motorized and non-motorized modes. Non-motorized modes, such as the cycle rickshaw, naturally offer one of the most environmentally sustainable means of transport available from a pollution perspective. But it is accused of slowing down traffic and causing congestion (for cars). However, motorized modes, such as the two-stroke autorickshaw, are often criticized for being one of the worst polluters in the city. Though this needs further study, it is clear that compared to light rail and modern buses, autorickshaws still have a long way to go in ensuring environmental sustainability. Second, we need to ask the question, environmental friendly compared to what? As discussed, IPT fills the void left by formal public transport modes. Given the rapid pace of urbanization, it is safe to say that there will be an under-supply of formal public transport in the foreseeable future in many Indian cities. A well-functioning public transport system (whether formal, informal, or both) is a prerequisite for turning the tide of increasing private vehicle ownership. Therefore, when comparing the environmental effect of IPT, it must be kept in mind that the alternative is not that people would ride the bus. It is most likely that they would acquire private motorized transport modes, such as two-wheelers. From that perspective, IPT fills an important function to keep down even further environmental degradation as a result of continued growth of private motorized transport.

A third aspect is in seeing the potential for environmental improvements in the IPT sector. An interesting question to ask is why vehicles are so poorly maintained and why so little investment has gone into finding ways of improving their performance from an environmental perspective. The unsanctioned and uncertain situation for IPT in most cities results in a very short-term perspective on operating an IPT business, and consequently investment in vehicles. There is a potential for reducing greenhouse gas and other pollutants through relatively simple measures, such as improving engine performance, switching to biogas, and the introduction of electrical vehicles.

In summary, IPT has the potential for becoming a component in a pro-poor and environmentally sustainable public transport system. A policy that aims to integrate IPT in the transport planning in a sustainable way could have reduce poverty and improve the environment in urban India.

Integrating IPT in Public Transport Planning

While IPT fulfils critical mobility needs of millions, there are trade-offs. Policy should work to make sure that the trade-offs are not socially unjust or environmentally damaging. For instance, IPT is cheap enough to be affordable and appealing to urban poor; however, by operating at low profit margins and in the face of rising cost of living, drivers resort to loading passengers beyond capacity, thereby jeopardizing the well-being of everyone (inside and outside the vehicle). Environmental damage is especially important to take care of in case of motorized IPT. It is fairly common for vehicles to be poorly maintained and spew noxious gases aplenty. Motorized autorickshaws definitely do not do too well in per capita emissions compared to buses. Technology can definitely play an important role here. In the case of cycle rickshaws, pullers sell their labour cheap and often have long working hours and abject living conditions. Therefore, the good of IPT should be embraced—flexible working hours, flexible routing, and high frequency—while policy should create an IPT-like system by limiting IPT's follies.

An Enabling Environment for IPT

The present approach to urban planning in India (including for transport) shuns and disparages informal practices. The mainstream planning rhetoric is to do away with the informal because it is supposed to be malignant—a sign of underdevelopment. And the only alternative, according to this view, is the formal. However, as we see from studies in various cities, the formal public transport of today may not be what fulfils people's day-to-day mobility needs. It may not be what is appropriate in the actual socioeconomic–temporal makeup of a city. There seems to be a gap between the people, the planners, and the decisionmakers.

Stringently sticking to public transport solutions in their present form may not be economically prudent either. SMCs may not need large-scale formally organized public transport systems based on buses or rail. Since the trip lengths in such cities are usually short, a city may do very well with a very high-quality non-motorized transport network, aided by a quasi-formally organized low-carbon public transport system comprising compact vehicles (such a three-wheelers or minibuses) run by individual entrepreneurs. The city would then have a public transport system at a very small cost.

In megacities, the city could improve communal transport by augmenting public carrier capacity by using IPT-like services. This could lower the financial burden on the city exchequer and foster economic development, much like with SMCs.

Cooperatives and associations of IPT-like services should be encouraged to work in harmony with the city government, city-building professionals, and civil society actors. This close contact would help allay misgivings that one group may have about another. By emphasizing individual entrepreneur IPT service providers, there is a possibility of equitable local economic development.

All cities are unique. Even though they may have similar physiognomy, their detailed makeup is most often distinct. Therefore, cities' response and method of planning and managing transport systems need to be custom-made; the approach may be common but not necessarily the exact solutions. Therefore, city governments should engage in detailed cross-disciplinary study of the state of IPT or IPT-like services prevalent in their respective cities as a first step to understanding raisons d'être of these services' existence. Planners and decisionmakers should beware of understanding things facilely. For instance, IPT's follies are prominent—poorly maintained shoddy vehicles, pollution, overcrowding, etc. Looking at these, it is easy to conclude that IPT doesn't deserve merit and should be immediately done away with. However, in-depth investigation will show that there are underlying structural reasons for this.

Urban transport policy must take cognizance of the fact that IPT arises because there is a need for it, that it is an important part of the public transport system in a city and provides for critical mobility needs of people. Also, it must recognize the fact that IPT is not inherently malignant, even though it has shortcomings; and these are often result of structural imbalances. Policy should aim at helping IPT evolve into an IPT-like service that is basically a transport system based on the good of current IPT services (compact vehicles, high frequency, flexibility in routing, affordable, etc.). With this outlook in policy, cities should work on the following:

Physical Infrastructure

If IPT is to be upgraded into an IPT-like service, the physical infrastructure of the city must provide for it. Currently, very little exists by way of infrastructure for IPT in Indian cities. Most city infrastructure that IPT currently uses in cities is either sanctioned by authorities on a piecemeal basis and keeps shifting or IPT providers have simply taken over infrastructure not officially meant for them. Parking stands are needed by these services. IPT service providers raised lack of tenure over parking stands as one of their biggest concerns. They reported a lack of it overall, and specifically a lack of civic facilities provided at the existing stands. Due to a lack of tenure, harassment by authorities was reported. The problem of parking and stands is especially acute for cycle rickshaws, whose pullers say they are driven around the city like cattle. High-quality parking stands should be provided in the city wherever needed, and basic human necessities such as drinking water, shade, and benches, should be part of it at the minimum.

Other than parking, physical infrastructure should also include shelters for passengers on fixed-route services. They could be combined with bus stops in a way that does not create friction between buses and the IPT vehicles. Users naturally prefer being dropped off as close to their destination as possible. In current IPT practice, this results in the IPT vehicle stopping just anywhere to pick and drop passengers. While it may not be possible to allow such stopping everywhere, it may be possible to provide informal pick-up and drop-off locations other than the one already built for IPT-like services. This could mean providing simple shoulders at places or wherever not needed. Or even just an 'IPT vehicles stopping' sign.

In places, IPT vehicles should be given priority. A number of Indian cities are working on building priority lanes for buses. A similar thing could be done in places for IPT vehicles. In Paris, bicycles are allowed to ride in the bus lanes. If a bus driver wants to alert a cyclist, the driver uses a bicycle bell. Cycle rickshaws need priority lanes, either physically segregated or painted depending on the speed of other vehicles. Shelters and parking stands for cycle rickshaws would be helpful.

Regulatory Framework and Knowledge Exchange

Cities must find ways to regulate and control informal public transport with respect to environmental standards, traffic safety, and vehicle quality. However, the regulatory framework must be sensitive to the reality of IPT providers and users. Efforts will often be needed to assist the sector in complying.

Knowledge exchange sessions should be organized within the country and abroad, especially within the nations of the Global South, which often share similar problems. Pilot projects will be of much use in arriving at appropriate solutions.

Service Providers: The Socioeconomic Angle

IPT service providers, even though in the trade for profit, deliver a public benefit. This should be recognized and respected. IPT service providers across India work long hours (averaging 14 hours a day), hardly have any holidays, and have no social security. One of the underlying reasons for the numerous negatives of IPT, such as overcrowding and decrepit, polluting vehicles, is the economic feebleness of service providers. A majority of IPT providers do not own their vehicles and have to pay a daily rent. Those who own their own vehicles are not much better off because they are usually in debt and have to pay a hefty sum each month to repay the loan they took to buy the vehicle. The reality is that the people who deliver IPT services are economically unsound. In the face of the increasing cost of living in India, they find it hard to make ends meet. As a result, they are on the lookout for every opportunity to make a little more money. The easiest way to do it is to carry more passengers and spend as little as possible on maintenance.

Seeing the way IPT benefits a city, easy credit schemes should be set up for IPT service providers. There could be schemes for those beginning the trade different from those for those who have been around longer. City governments could help set up communal cycle-rickshaw or autorickshaw banks from which those wanting to offer IPT services could borrow vehicles for a fair rent. A 'group as collateral' approach could be followed for those who do not have cash or other collateral. In this approach, money or vehicles are lent to groups that are together responsible for it; in case of non-payment or damage to the product, the entire group is responsible. This method had considerable success in Bangladesh. Cycle rickshaw pulling could also be tied to the proposed National Urban Employment Guarantee Scheme.

* * *

IPT service providers need to be recognized and cared for as legitimate stakeholders in the public transport system. Social security schemes should be set up to provide a fall-back option for IPT service providers and their families in case of hapless incidents. The informal character of the trade may make it difficult to set up a traditional social security net. In IPT, there is no guarantee that a person is permanently an IPT service provider. And there is often no proof that a person is associated with the industry. Solutions can be found in informality itself. A good approach would be to discuss with the IPT service provider community itself which such measures could be initiated for them. A condition of economic benefits would be that the IPT providers would not break mutually agreed rules. There could be a point system in which IPT service performance could be evaluated. Following the rules would be encouraged by the immediate monetary loss that would otherwise result. A precondition for such solutions to work in reality is real-time engagement with the IPT service provider community and the building of mutual trust.

References

Ahmed, M. Ali and R.N. Datta. 2006. 'Utility of paratransit modes in cities of Assam, India', *Transportation research record*, 1971: 107–15.

McKinsey Global Institute. 2010. 'India's Urban Awakening: Building Inclusive Cities, Sustaining Economic Growth', p. 17, McKinsey Global Institute, April 2010.

Cervero, Robert. 2000. *Informal Transport in the Developing World*, UN Center for Human Settlements (Habitat).

———. 2007. 'Informal Transport: A Global Perspective', *Transport Policy* 14(6): 445–57.

Golub, Aaron D. 2003. 'Welfare Analysis of Informal Transit Services in Brazil and the Effects of Regulation', PhD Thesis, Dissertations, Institute of Transportation Studies, UC Berkeley, 09-01-2003, p. 7.

Luthra, Ashwani. 2006. 'Para Transit System in Medium Sized Cities Problem or Panacea', *ITPI Journal* 3(2): 55–61.

Tiwari, Geetam. 2002. 'Urban Transport Priorities – Meeting the Challenge of Socioeconomic Diversity in Cities', a Case Study of Delhi, India, Cities, 19(2): 95–103.

Mahadevia, Darshini. 2010. 'Transport & Social Sustainability', paper presented at Promoting Low Carbon Transport in India, Workshop, New Delhi. January 2010.

Rahman, Mamun Muntasir Glen D'Este, and Jonathan M. Bunker. 2009. 'Is There a Future for Non–Motorized Public Transport in Asia?'

UNDP. 1998. Summary data available at: undp.org.in/poverty_reduction/IUPR_Summary.pdf (retrieved 8 July 2010).

Wipperman, T. and T. Sowula. 2007. 'The rationalization of Non-Motorized Public Transport in Bangladesh', The Progressive Bangladesh.

Index

About the Editors and Contributors

Editors

Anushree Sinha is Senior Fellow at the National Council of Applied Economic Research (NCAER) in New Delhi, India. She has a PhD and a Master's degree from Jadavpur University, Kolkata and did her postresearch at the universities of Oxford and Pennsylvania. Sinha has published extensively on trade liberalization, gender, and informal labour markets among others, and is a member of various committees and scholarly networks, such as the Asia Pacific Gender and Macroeconomic Issues (GEM) network under the auspices of UNDP.

Armin Bauer is Principal Economist in the Asian Development Bank and has worked before for the German development agencies GIZ and KfW. He has a PhD in development economics and works mainly on poverty reduction and inclusive growth issues.

Paul Bullen has a PhD and an MA from the University of Chicago and a BA from the University of California at Berkeley, all in political science. Bullen is an interdisciplinary researcher, writer, and editor based in Chicago and Vancouver. He is the author most recently of 'The Role of Development Organizations in Pro-Poor Adaptation to Global Warming in the Pacific Islands', published in *The Environments of the Poor in Southeast Asia, East Asia and the Pacific*, edited by Aris Ananta, Armin Bauer, and Myo Thant (Singapore: Institute of Southeast Asian Studies/Manila: Asian Development Bank, 2013).

Contributors

B. Agastin is researcher at the Tamil Nadu Agricultural University, India.

G.M. Arif is Director and Chief of Research of the Pakistan Institute of Development Economics (PIDE).

Anvita Arora is the CEO of Innovative Transport Solutions (iTrans) Pvt. Ltd., an incubatee company of the Indian Institute of Technology, Delhi, India.

Shanila Athulathmudali is a researcher at the Center for Poverty Analysis (CEPA) in Colombo, Sri Lanka.

Amila Balasuriya is a researcher at the Center for Poverty Analysis (CEPA) in Colombo, Sri Lanka.

Banashree Banerjee is an urban planner and international consultant and teaches at the Delhi School of Planning and Architecture, India.

Dilruba Banu is working for the German Agency for International Cooperation (GIZ) in Bangladesh.

Shujaat Farooq is Research Fellow at the Pakistan Institute of Development Economics in Islamabad.

Karin Fernando is a researcher at the Center for Poverty Analysis (CEPA) in Colombo, Sri Lanka.

Santadas Ghosh is research fellow at the Visva-Bharati University in Calcutta, India.

N. Iqbal is Staff Economist at the Pakistan Institute of Development Economics in Islamabad.

Rajesh Jaiswal is an Associate Fellow at the National Council for Applied Economic Research (NCAER) in New Delhi, India.

Mats Jarnhammar is currently Managing Director at Living Cities, Sweden, specializing in social and cultural issues in urban development.

K.R. Kakumanu is researcher at the Tamil Nadu Agricultural University, India.

Mohd. Shahadt Hossain Mahmud is from the Comprehensive Disaster Management Programme, Government of Bangladesh.

K. Palanisami is researcher at the Tamil Nadu Agricultural University, India.

C.R. Ranganathan is a researcher at the Tamil Nadu Agricultural University, India.

Sunil Ray is professor at the Institute for Development Studies in Jaipur, Rajasthan, India.

G. Bhaskar Reddy is the director of the Odisha Watershed Development Mission of the Government of Odisha, India.

Binayak Sen is research director at the Bangladesh Institute for Development Studies.

Amita Shah is Director of the Gujarat Institute of Development Research, India.

Faizan Jawed Siddiqi is a Doctoral Candidate at the Department of Urban Studies and Planning, Massachusetts Institute of Technology.

Min Bikram Malla Thakuri is head of the non-governmental organization Practical Action in Nepal.

Shyam Upadhyaya is research fellow at the Institute for Integrated Development Studies in Kathmandu, Nepal.

Mohammed Yunus is from the Bangladesh Institute for Development Studies.